POE

A CRITICAL STUDY

POE

A CRITICAL STUDY

By Edward H. Davidson

THE BELKNAP PRESS OF
HARVARD UNIVERSITY PRESS
CAMBRIDGE, MASSACHUSETTS, AND LONDON, ENGLAND

Seventh printing, 1980

Library of Congress Catalog Card Number: 57-12965
ISBN 0-674-67450-2
Printed in the United States of America

Preface

In this essay I have undertaken what may be frankly admitted a philosophic inquiry into the mind and writings of Edgar Allan Poe. I know that professional philosophers (if they should ever peer into this book) would be shocked to discover what can happen when the categories of philosophical analysis are somehow displayed as literature; and I am quite certain that all of their objections would be valid. But when one deals with philosophy in literature, he does so in a full awareness that he is not considering "philosophy" as the philosophers have laid out their programs of thought; he is considering those concepts which somehow move from the abstractions of logic and epistemology into the murky deliquescence of literary ideas as those ideas are known and stated by literary artists in a period of literary history. Edgar Poe was a writer with a certain philosophic bent: his career, quite unplanned by Poe himself, was directed toward an understanding of certain principles of art, principles likewise of the mind and method of the artist, and even theories of the autonomous nature of art itself. From his very early poem "Tamerlane" to his last major expression in *Eureka,* Poe tried in his way to be a philosophic writer: he moved toward what, in terms of literary

Romanticism, is known as an organic or a unitary principle.

My approach to Poe's mind and writing has been primarily through the critical and metaphysical theories of Coleridge — through, in short, that basic investigation Coleridge made into what was Romantic consciousness and what the imagination was doing when it was making poems or any other works of art. Poe early read and absorbed Coleridge's principles, and even took the liberty of sneering at them; but behind Coleridge lay two centuries of philosophical and literary theorizing, all of which has, in recent years, been diligently investigated and sometimes brilliantly exposed. Yet what produced Coleridge or the Romantic mind was not precisely what produced the mind and art of Poe. Thus we may sometimes retrace a good deal of ground which is already familiar to students of the philosophic and artistic foreground of literature and thought in the nineteenth or, for that matter, the twentieth century.

We must also consider the special mind of Poe himself, not as that mind was biographically shaped in the first four decades of the nineteenth century but as it developed and matured within the special determinations of American thought and American art of that time. Poe did think and write in America; and whatever lack of the "American experience" may be charged against him, he nonetheless reflected certain of its social and religious ideas. I have not tried to make a case for Poe as a significantly American writer and as belonging in some vaguely conceived "main stream" of American literature. Quite the contrary: I may have increased the distance between Poe and his age or between Poe and his American experience. In so doing I have not sought to make any invidious comparisons; my purpose has been, primarily, to analyze the thought and the writings of Poe with respect to a total sensibility in a phase of Western history which we may agree, for the moment, to term the Romantic Imagination. I hasten to plead my right not to define or explore that large formulation at this time; I hope I have developed it with sufficient clarity and fullness at the proper stage of this inquiry into Poe.

My method is both thematic and chronological. That is, I begin where Poe began, with his earliest poetry, and follow him through his third volume of verses published in 1831. At that point I pause and analyze in the second chapter of this study a theory of poetry and of the imagination which, I trust, will go far to explain Poe's poetry and Poe's ideas concerning poetry within the special framework of Romantic symbolism. Thereafter, I have separate chapters on Poe's later poetry, on his early short stories, on the short stories of his mature years, and finally on the philosophic prose-poem which he entitled *Eureka,* a summary and climax of all that had gone before. Along the way I have allowed myself the freedom of intercalary chapters on topics which overlap poetry and prose.

Even with such permissions for latitude and self-indulgence, there must be, of necessity, emphases and gaps in this investigation. I have omitted most of Poe's critical writing; this is a serious omission, especially in view of the energy Poe expended on his critical writings and in terms of the interest which contemporary students and critics have shown in them. Poe's critical writing was largely journalistic and ephemeral; in his hard-pressed life he had time to write only a few carefully reasoned essays such as that on Hawthorne.

The principles contained in those excursions were, I would maintain, better demonstrated and more profoundly explored in the tales and poems than in the criticism itself. On the other hand, I have placed what may seem undue stress on a few poems and short stories — some of them are very thoroughly analyzed — and on that hitherto neglected novel, the *Narrative of Arthur Gordon Pym.*

Despite the wide extent which an aesthetic and philosophical inquiry would seem to permit, the range of this study is actually quite narrow. What I have attempted is an understanding of Poe according to two critical theorems: one is the general premises of what we shall, for the moment, call "Romantic idealism" from Wordsworth and Coleridge in England through Emerson and Poe himself in America; the other is a nineteenth- and twentieth-century philosophy of aesthetics and symbolism which, from Emerson, Horace Bushnell, Peirce, and William James, down through Whitehead, Cassirer, and their followers, however diverse they may be, has suggested that works of art are not at the mercy of psychology and "psychologism" but have meanings quite beyond anything material or temporal. So conceived, art is regarded as having a specific and autonomous function, both a part of and yet beyond the time and place in which it is formed; it is a way — for Poe the primal way — of man's knowing the world. The creative imagination does not move in an invented or made-up world but has its own mode of projection and therefore, in accordance with the idealist concept of expression, its own mode of reality. This "reality" is never finite nor positively located; it is a continual negotiation between the creative imagination which requires expression and the very necessities of art itself — those necessities which we know as the past, the history, the directions of the artistic world that may be, in terms of time, space, and location, far removed from the world of habit and daily existence.

My concern with Poe resolves itself, at the last, in my assumption that Poe was a "crisis" in the Romantic and the symbolic imagination. He came near the end (if such directions have "beginning" and "end") of the idealist or Romantic expression and mind. Occupying such a place in the history of art, Poe dramatized the whole problem of what the creative imagination does when it is seeking ways of communicating those ideas lying beyond the common denotative discourse of men.

I could not have written this book without the labors of the many critics and scholars who, for three quarters of a century, have made Poe the most thoroughly and intelligently investigated writer in American literature. They are a distinguished company who have set the biographical facts, the letters, the text of Poe's writings, and the sources and analogues far in excess of what I or any student can humbly acknowledge in footnotes or references. But since this study is not altogether a work of research and scholarship, it owes an equal or even a greater, debt to the whole critical sensibility of our time. I refer to the dual revolution in the criticism of the past several decades, the one semantic and epistemological, the other symbolistic and aesthetic. These make odd companions, to be sure, but in the general eclecticism which anyone achieves in coming to terms with his age and with the critical insights it has given him (and our age has offered us a bounty of such perceptions), one sees that, without any claim to thoroughness or originality, he ought to do the best he can to place a writer in a total perspective, both of the past in which that writer lived and wrote and of the more recent present in which he may be viewed somewhat differently. These, then, have been my limits and determinations. I have tried to use them not as preordained forms into which Poe and his art must fit but as a method of inquiry, an approach to avoid dogmatism, which may never reach a positive "conclusion" but which may find a number of ideas along the way.

E. H. D.

June 1957

Contents

POE

A CRITICAL STUDY

I

The Necessary Demon: The Poetry of Youth

Poe declared that for him poetry was "not a purpose, but a passion." [1] He was probably telling the truth. But, one may ask, what is "passion," and what was its direction and purpose? Poe doubtless meant that poetry was the expression of a kind of thought and idea which no other form of writing or art could convey. In his later years he went on to explore what poetry was, whether "passionate" or not, and what the poet was himself doing at the moment of poetic insight and creativity. Poe's poetry began as a presumably passionate expression of the mind and imagination of Edgar Poe; it ended as a commentary on and a "philosophy" of the whole Romantic concept of the creative imagination.

Modern critics frequently wonder why such bad poetry as Poe wrote could have existed with or even come from such a valid theory of poetry as Poe set forth. If the theory were sound, some argue, then the poetry should have been better than it is. Others, like T. S. Eliot, consider that Poe simply did not know enough and that he approached his moments of poetic activity with the brain power of an adolescent.[2] Or, Poe was really not poetic at all: he merely affected the manner of poetry, the incantatory method of the psalmist or magician, in order to produce "poems" which were not, after all, truly poetic. Then there was Baudelaire, who ascribed the "failure" of Poe the poet to the uncivilized barbarism of an America which had no place for poets and poetry; thus Poe was cruelly broken in an unimaginative, unpoetic world.[3]

We can, for the present, leave these questions aside and undertake an inquiry into Poe's earliest poems, which began where all youthful poets begin: with the self, with a set of stances or autobiographical incantations that appear to be disclosures of a young man's innermost being and yet may not be self-revelatory at all.[4] We may well initiate our investigation with those poems of youth and then see how there emerged from them a theory and a set of ideas which shaped the rest of Poe's career, whether in poetry, short story, novel, or an unsystematic philosophy.

2

Poe's first poem which survived may be one that is not in any of the editions or collections, except Whitty's. It was written when Poe was seventeen and entitled, "O, Tempora! O, Mores!"[5] A young clerk named Pitts was, in 1826, paying court to a fashionable young lady of Richmond, and Poe wrote this poem, in heroic couplets, in order to ridicule the forlorn lover in the eyes of other men who boarded in the same house. It may have been quite unlike the poetry Poe was doubtless already composing and would write in a year or two. The opening lines are as good, or bad, as any fledgling poet might compose at the age of seventeen:

> O, Times! O, Manners! It is my opinion
> That you are changing sadly your dominion —
> I mean the reign of manners hath long ceased,
> For men have none at all, or bad at least;
> And as for times, altho' 'tis said by many
> The "good old times" were far the worst of any,
> Of which sound doctrine I believe each tittle,
> Yet still I think these worse than them a little.

From this mournful condemnation of the present age, we pass into such quite clever satirical thrusts as these directed toward the person of the unfortunate Pitts:

> His very voice is musical delight,
> His form, once seen, becomes a part of sight;
> In short, his shirt collar, his look, his tone is
> The "beau ideal" fancied for Adonis.

This poem is so different from the kind of poetry which Poe afterward made famous that it has been with difficulty accorded a place in the Poe canon. Yet it suggests one element in the mind of even the youthful Poe: a sense of propriety, of ordonnance, of eighteenth-century discipline struggled for expression in Poe's poetic career at the same time that a very special, fictive Poe-self was conjuring and setting forth in the sometimes anguished and highly evocative poems which were to shape the poetic sensibility of an age. The farther Poe's career moved, the less this sense of restraint and balance was exercised in the subject and craft of poetry and the more it was granted an authority in his prose.

The earliest poem in the established Poe canon is "Tamerlane," first published in the volume of that name in 1827; and though afterward considerably revised, it nevertheless maintained a rather consistent form throughout its subsequent publications. Quite logically, the poem has been taken to be a hypertensive portrait of Poe himself, in the guise of the world conqueror Tamerlane (or Timour Beg), during those dismal months of 1827 when Poe had been forced to leave the University of Virginia, was working in the import house of his foster father, John Allan, and more especially, had been forced to give up his fiancée, Sarah Elmira Royster. In some respects Poe is Tamerlane and Miss Royster the Ada of the 1827 version or the unnamed maiden of subsequent printings of the poem; and in such a reading all of Poe's ignominy and failure of 1827 were properly readjusted in the dream legend he created as his revenge on a world which had treated and was still treating him with undue cruelty.[6]

Or again, the poem might be considered as forming that broader subject of Love vs. Ambition: the youthful Poe-Tamerlane sacrifices home and first passionate love for the sake of great achievement and then discovers that success without love is empty indeed. The subject becomes both pathetic and humorous, for we know that Poe had no chance of realizing his preposterous ambition of becoming the conqueror or of regaining his lost love; and the poem underwent necessary revision in order to diminish this theme of the arrogant, triumphant self because of the obvious disparity between the subject in the poem and the condition in Poe's own life. The more Poe saw this disparity, as no doubt he did, the more he reduced the Poe-as-Tamerlane identification and made a generalized hero, lover, conqueror, a Tamerlane who shares fewer and fewer similarities with his maker, Poe himself.

Still again, "Tamerlane" may well belong to those very frequent *Bildungsromanen* in romantic poetry, namely the poems which trace the enlarging consciousness of a highly sensitive and poetic intelligence. If this is the poem's theme, then it is indeed dimly conveyed, for, from the very opening lines, Poe sought a mask which would allow him to pretend that he was engaged in self-revelation but which would, at the same time, keep him outside and prevent him from truly revealing himself and the special conditions of his consciousness. "Tamerlane" is, therefore, confused autobiography: the hero is both there and not there as Poe chooses to make Tamerlane representative or wholly fictive.

This method of simultaneous concealment and revelation became, as we shall see, central to Poe's art: he was always "there" and "not there." And as his craft improved and his art matured, he was able to find and use ever more elaborate masquerades for obtaining both distance from and relevance to his poetic subject; the Poe symbol became almost the only subject Poe ever had, but a number of events had to occur and a variety of transformations had to take place before the self-as-symbol became sufficient. In his youthful verse Poe was unable to obtain the necessary distance: he was always in the subject and in the protagonist to such an extent that later critics have consistently made the mistake of identifying the subject only with Poe.

With these matters in mind, we might, however, look for the subject of "Tamerlane" elsewhere than in Poe's disappointed love affair, his eviction from the Allan household, or conjectures on his own emergent manhood and artistic sensibility. The poem is a masquerade of a side of a Poe-self who begins with a confession to a Catholic priest and ends with a very private monologue. The confession is only a device to get the reminiscence under way; almost at once Tamerlane disavows any real confession, for there is no God nor earthly minister who can shrive him of his "Unearthly pride" which has dared to challenge even God Himself. We are soon removed from a mere confession to a priest: we are projected into the soliloquy of a mind which is neither anguished nor penitent; it is a mind which is, quite simply, seeking some means of self-expression, of discovering how it came to be what it is at this moment of analysis and meditation. The masquerade is difficult or confusing, not because we must seek for other persons with whom to identify these fictive characters (Tamerlane, the maiden, the priest) but because Poe has sought ways of translating certain ideas into a set of rhetorical equivalents with which, as readers of romantic verse written at the opening of the nineteenth century, we are not quite familiar. We expect one thing and we get another.

What we expect is that Poe is writing poetic autobiography — and he is. We also expect that he will follow the norms which his contemporaries found adaptable to a variety of ideas and private impulses: we have become accustomed to the stricken deer, the lost self, the changing landscape, the dark night of the soul, the driven leaves (to name only a few) as consistently recurring elements in the romantic vision of man and his world. Some of these Poe employs in the logical discourse we expect from the romantic mind; others he uses in ways which are strange, almost newly invented. Or, to put the matter another way, Poe is treating a typical romantic or idealist subject, he employs many of the standard rhetorical devices and symbols — and he resolves the problem in an oddly different way.

"Tamerlane" is, in one respect, a refutation of the Wordsworthian premise that what the child or impressionable mind receives early in life remains the one determinant thereafter in maturity and age. Wordsworth treated this theme in various poems, notably in "Tintern Abbey" and the "Ode on Intimations of Immortality" (Poe could never have read *The Prelude,* which was published a year after his death). In these two poems, as everyone is aware, Wordsworth set forth the process of how the first vivid impressions are made on a receptive mind and then of how those impressions, which can never maintain their clarity indefinitely, pass into the ideas which a mature mind can contemplate apart from the natural objects which first brought them into being.[7]

"Tamerlane" begins with the growing child wrapped in the wonders of nature and highly susceptible to receiving inwardly the impressions made outwardly:

> The mists of Taglay have shed
> Nightly their dews upon my head . . .
> And tumult of the headlong air
> Have nestled in my very hair.

From these early and nebulous experiences we pass to more precise impacts which reality makes on a youthful mind; but the apparent quality of such a mind is that it in no way is receptive to these impulses, either in a "wise passiveness" or in the excitement of an illumination; this mind is wholly self-directional, and nature has no power to move it any way other than the one it is determined to take. Nature exists only to stimulate this youth; very soon it becomes the dramatization of whatever mood or whim Tamerlane feels at the moment.

The poem becomes a set of allegorical stances whereby the young Tamerlane bends all exterior reality to his own will: nature is only a mirror of his rapture or despair; the girl becomes his being and she exists only as he makes her in his own image ("I had no being but in thee"). Then we proceed more nearly along the Wordsworthian pilgrimage of the questing mind which seeks the rationale for its own being. In romantic experience this quest begins with the self *and* nature, turns to the single self as measure and key to the universe, and then makes some psychic adjustment between the world and the self. These transitions are the representative spiritual autobiography from Wordsworth through Carlyle and Newman. But with Poe the movement of the mind stops at the second stage.

Tamerlane is presumably a conqueror; but the conquest is so easily achieved that the poem must assume a quite different subject for the romantic hero-colossus. The real search is somehow to induce the "I" or self to give "A portion of his willing soul/ To God, and to the great whole — / To him, whose loving spirit will dwell/ With nature." The tragic threat is that his destiny cannot be fulfilled and that the "failing sight will grow dim." (Interestingly, in the first or 1827 version of the poem we are brought to the tragic finale, the death of all response: "There comes . . . A sullen hopelessness of heart.") At the end of the poem the protagonist returns, like Wordsworth and others who felt the resurgence of vitality in their original inspiration, to his homeland; he finds the maiden gone or dead. But what he chiefly discovers is that he can never regain what once he had possessed and lost, namely, the capacity to feel and respond; he does not even have the new and quiet sensibility of maturity when the mind is capable of living in itself and does not necessarily depend on the stimulus of natural surroundings: "rays of truth you cannot see/ Are floating through Eternity."

The Tamerlane (or Poe) method is to grant that the will has the power at every instant to make external reality into anything it wishes. The universe, by a process of fictive translation, becomes a total subjectivity:

> So late from Heaven — that dew — it fell
> ('Mid dreams of an unholy night)
> Upon me with the touch of Hell,
> While the red flashing of the light
> From clouds that hung, like banners, o'er,
> Appeared to my half-closing eye
> The pageantry of monarchy. . . .

The self may so compulsively grant existence to reality that the central "I" may deny that objective reality has any actuality whatsoever, and the only meaning to existence is what this protagonist reads into it. This act of translation — whereby reality becomes what the inner will ordains — reaches a point beyond which words have no meaning because, being tied to the actual sense-world, they cannot in any way convey what the inner self wills or thinks: "I have felt/ The letters — with their meaning — melt/ To fantasies — with none." Meaninglessness becomes a kind of entrance into a third realm of reality, beyond self and the world, a reality in which the poet-protagonist should, perhaps, know all:

> The world and all it did contain
> In the earth — the air — the sea —
>   Its joy — its little lot of pain
> That was new pleasure — the ideal,
>   Dim, vanities of dreams by night—
> And dimmer nothings which were real

became, Poe concludes, "a name — a name."

Poe began his poetic career on that far edge of romanticism wherein the chief danger is the assumption that whatever the mind knows and can give a name to *is*. Although rationalism and Kantian epistemology had defined reality as not simply the illusion of the single perceiving mind — things have existence both in the mind and apart from the mind — Poe early contrived some Humean, skeptical position that reality is meaningless; only a titanic "conqueror," like a Poe-Tamerlane, can give sense to appearance. But even that conquest ends in a fiction: the imagination as conqueror is never powerful enough to make the word or the "name" have duration beyond a moment's expression. Meaninglessness thereby becomes a value, for it is itself a meaning.[9]

There were ten poems in the *Tamerlane* volume of 1827. Each, in its way, simply restates some version of the title poem. Poe's voice could be lyrical as in the "Song" ("I saw thee on thy bridal day"), which was written on the occasion of Sarah Royster's marriage to Mr. Shelton. The pose is that of the wronged lover; the lady's "blush . . . was maiden shame" that she had weakly consented to marry the man she did not really love. A similar theme of the forlorn lover was undertaken in "The Happiest Day, the Happiest Hour"; in life at its moments of greatest sensitivity is the promise of ultimate destruction; or, to live at the top of feeling is to invite the sense of life's loss and death. In other poems Poe played with the question of factual and of poetic reality: the two seem in no way close. In "A wilder'd being from my birth," later "A Dream" ("In visions of the dark night") Poe sets forth the "dream" not as a refuge from the world's "chiding" but as the region of understanding and "Truth," of which this known world is a mere shadow. Already Poe was attempting to use poetry as a means of exploring that further range which lay beyond ostensible reality. Most of the poems were glimpses of autobiography. Some of them, like "Visit of the Dead" (later titled "Spirits of the Dead") and "Evening Star," were nonlocalized events which might or might not have occurred but which, in the act of poetic recall, became something different from the original moment in Poe's life. The earliest version of "A Dream Within a Dream" (in the 1827 volume called "Imitation") is a good example of how Poe began with a very private self as subject:

A dark unfathom'd tide
Of interminable pride—
A mystery, and a dream,
Should my early life seem . . .[10]

and steadily, in subsequent revisions and editions, extracted the confessional air and employed those standard generalizations which might concern Poe or any man.

What becomes apparent in this small budget of poems is not so much a conventional romantic anguish—the tones and expressions are commonplace enough—but that the poet is playing or assuming God in a rather unusual way. He has both made and known the universe; yet the universe has failed him, and he magisterially renounces it. In this rejection comes the cry of the prophet or the despairing psalmist. He calls upon his God; he cries aloud in his pain; he shrieks with joy as though receiving an illumination; he proceeds through a set of religious experiences (the lost self, the dark night of the soul, the dying, the rebirth) as though they have no meaning for anyone but himself. He is already his own vision-maker and law-giver; he becomes his own seer and writer of apocalypses because, as in "Tamerlane," he conceives the world not only as something outside of and apart from himself but as its maker's cruel joke and madness:

> Let none of earth inherit
> That vision on my spirit;
> Those thoughts I would controul,
> As a spell upon his soul:
> For that bright hope at last
> And that light time have past,
> And my worldly rest hath gone
> With a sigh as it passed on;
> I care not tho' it perish
> With a thought I then did cherish.[11]

In the Romantic period Shelley was a vivid example of this apocalyptic manner: he both renounced and made a religion. But what Shelley had done violently, Poe was already doing easily and passively: he assumes the religious guise of the wounded seer and prophet, for the world and its anguish are greater than he can bear. Therefore, he ends by renouncing the world and seeking a belief in some other world and in some other deity, even if he must become his own God, man, and Satan.

The mood of a poet who is his own God and prophet marks one salient feature of Poe and of nearly all his poetry: Poe feels himself the scapegoat, the innocent wronged one, the outcast. If there really is a God, He is on *their* side; therefore, the poet must be his own god or else find another one. A poet who envisions himself as Ishmael, however sincerely or impermanently, is likely to evoke the mood and create the apocalypses which measure the distance between himself and the rest of humanity. From the outside he creates his own heaven and hell as though from a special "angelic imagination," in Allen Tate's phrase.[12] He plays heaven and hell, God and Satan, and tends more and more to enter a private world from which reality and even meaning, normally considered, are excluded.

In Poe's next volume of poems, the *Al Aaraaf, Tamerlane, and Minor Poems,* published by Hatch and Dunning in Baltimore in 1829, this god-playing was to take on even more extended dimensions than it had in *Tamerlane.* In "Al Aaraaf" itself, the key poem to the volume, a curiously inverted myth-making reached fullest expression.

3

For a better comprehension of this longest, and most difficult, poem Poe ever wrote, we must begin with the then untitled "Sonnet — To Science" which served as a prelude to the 1829 and 1831 versions of "Al Aaraaf." Here is the sonnet in its less finished state of 1829:

Science! meet daughter of old Time thou art
  Who alterest all things with thy peering eyes!
Why prey'st thou thus upon the poet's heart,
  Vulture! whose wings are dull realities!
How should he love thee — or how deem thee wise
  Who would'st not leave him, in his wandering,
To seek for treasure in the jewell'd skies
  Albeit, he soar with an undaunted wing?
Hast thou not dragg'd Diana from her car,
  And driv'n the Hamadryad from the wood
To seek a shelter in some happier star?
  The gentle Naiad from her fountain-flood?
The elfin from the green grass? and from me
The summer dream beneath the shrubbery?[13]

The sonnet sounds like one more in the long line of romantic complaints against the destruction "science" has wrought in killing the myths once so meaningful to poets. The protest is, more seriously, against the eighteenth-century world view of an inanimate, mechanistic nature and a presumed animate, thinking man living in it. "Science" might be here synonymous with skepticism, the doubt on which Hume discoursed so effectively, that nature can exist at all if it is merely an extension of man's sense of causation: because man is, nature therefore exists — and exists just as man determines that it shall, whether it contain Diana and nymphs or laws of inverse squares or conservation of matter. The sonnet attacks the delusion of modern man that he can reduce the phenomenal universe to his own convenient, measurable detail; it is reaffirming, like Emerson's *Nature* and like *Moby-Dick,* that nature has wonders and comprehensible systems far beyond the trivially limiting perspective of "science" or man.[14]

If the sonnet is a negation of science or empirical knowledge, "Al Aaraaf" is the affirmation that the poetic vision is capable of re-creating what science and man's search for causality have destroyed. The imagination is god and envisions a universe of idea which far transcends the limitations of a mere space- and time-world such as Lockean rationalism had demanded. If "science" has played the "Vulture" and dissociated man's sensibility from the phenomenal world, Poe, in "Al Aaraaf," will attempt to put them back together again.

Poe tells us (and he is probably telling the truth) that he got the wandering star Al Aaraaf from the stellar body discovered by Tycho Brahe, a star which appeared on November 11, 1572, and continued to shine into December.[15] Tycho thought it a planet and put it into the eighth sphere. Poe made the star a wandering planet, he was correct in his astronomy, for it has the nature of a comet. The name "Al Aaraaf," furthermore, is not merely the name of the Mohammedan region located between heaven and hell but is the name Arab astronomers assigned the planet in Tycho's nova or constellation.

> O! Nothing earthly save the ray
> (Thrown back from flowers) of Beauty's eye,
> As in those gardens where the day
> Springs from the gems of Circassy—
> O! nothing earthly save the thrill
> Of melody in woodland rill—
> Or (music of the passion-hearted)
> Joy's voice so peacefully departed
> That like the murmur in the shell,
> Its echo dwelleth and will dwell—

With nothing of the dross of ours —
Yet all the beauty — all the flowers
That list our Love, and deck our bowers
Adorn yon world afar, afar —
The wandering star —

'Twas a sweet time for Nesace — for there
Her world lay lolling on the golden air,
Near four bright suns — a temporary rest —
A garden-spot in desert of the blest.
Away — away — 'mid seas of rays that roll
Empyrean splendor o'er th' unchained soul —
The soul that scarce (the billows are so dense)
Can struggle to its destin'd eminence —
To distant spheres, from time to time, she rode,
And late to ours, the favour'd one of God —
But, now, the ruler of an anchor'd realm,
She throws aside the sceptre — leaves the helm,
And, amid incense, and high spiritual hymns,
Laves in quadruple light her angel wings.

We have, then, the astronomical fact of a wandering comet, not a place between heaven and hell, but a kind of fourth estate: it is seen as a rectangle of four big stars near "four bright suns." This is a place neither good nor bad nor even earthly; it is the fact and actuality of the substantial idea which is not to be parcelled into "science" or skeptical realism but into the total idea which the separate parts of the universe contain.

Poe was also aware of Sir Isaac Newton's view that spirits guide comets; and here again he employed a pseudo-scientific concept to enforce his myth. For whatever other subjects the poem may have (religious or personal), the basic theme of the poem is in the group of lines quoted below. That subject is the power of the idea and the ideal to manifest themselves in reality, fact, and word. The poet is the world's major "realist"; for it is he who, as god, can make the word the prime agency of revelation; word-making is the reënaction of both the original and the ultimate creation. Thus the first twenty-nine lines rejected the "earthly" and took us at once to the outer edge of reality where there was no earthly sound, no earthly light, no earthly "dross." The poem is a postulation of a pure visionary ideality beyond the mean limits of our conscious existence:

> Now happiest, loveliest in yon lovely Earth,
> Whence sprang the "Idea of Beauty" into birth,
> (Falling in wreaths thro' many a startled star,
> Like woman's hair 'mid pearls, until, afar,
> It lit on hills Achaian, and there dwelt)
> She look'd into Infinity — and knelt.
> Rich clouds, for canopies, about her curled —
> Fit emblems of the model of her world —
> Seen but in beauty — not impeding sight
> Of other beauty glittering thro' the light —
> A wreath that twined each starry form around,
> And all the opal'd air in color bound.

The long succeeding section (lines 42–81) is an extended epic simile on this act of creation which, from primeval time, ordained that all things in heaven and earth should exist in the unity of beauty. The very flowers on earth had their origin in heaven and descended to earth in the forms of goddesses who loved the world so much that they were content to die on earth and be transformed into such lovely, ephemeral objects of flowers.[16]

Once the harmonious universe of order has been pictured, Poe can proceed with the action of his poem. Nesace, the titular ruler of Al Aaraaf, then sings her first song (lines

82–117), the very words of which have the power of bringing objects and intangible ideas into existence. She looks from her sphere in the mid-range of universal order far down through terrestrial space and sees the planetary systems which, in the far-past cosmological upheaval, were cast off from the central heaven and were made "drudges till the last" and "carriers of fire" with a monotony of "speed that may not tire." This further and lower range of change, speed, and suffering is, however, inhabited by certain "beings" who have "dream'd" an "Infinity" which is vaguely modeled on the pure idea of timeless thought and abstraction which Nesace herself can only partially know. This song Nesace sings ("Spirit! that dwellest where,/ In the deep sky,/ The terrible and fair,/ In beauty vie!") is really a prayer to God in the perfect heaven to have mercy on the inhabitants of the realms of chaos below: the "star" of earth has been patient in its long anguish, since first it was cast from God and ideal beauty; if it should be granted the hope of becoming not substance but "thought that can alone/ Ascend" God's empire, then perhaps the disparate and fractured parts of the total harmony can be put back together and man, so long denied the complete vision, be made knowing and sentient again.

"Abash'd" at her temerity in thus boldly addressing the Deity, Nesace hides her face; she hardly dare breathe, for in the realms of idea even a breath is a thought and "All nature speaks, and even ideal things/ Flap shadowy sounds from visionary wings":

> She stirr'd not — breath'd not — for a voice was there . . .
> Which dreamy poets name "the music of the sphere."
> Ours is a world of words: Quiet we call

"Silence" — which is the merest word of all.
All Nature speaks, and ev'n ideal things
Flap shadowy sounds from visionary wings —
But ah! not so when, thus, in realms on high
The eternal voice of God is passing by
And the red winds are withering in the sky! [17]

The Deity hears Nesace's prayer and (lines 133–150) speaks a series of reproaches against man's debasement of pure love and pure knowledge:

"What tho' in worlds which sightless cycles run,
Link'd to a little system, and one sun —
Where all my love is folly, and the crowd
Still think my terrors but the thunder cloud,
The storm, the earthquake, and the ocean-wrath —
(Ah! will they cross me in my angrier path?). . . ."

Yet He grants her permission to fly to the other spheres in the terrestrial system in order to prevent the universal perversion which degenerate man has already brought to earth. Mental darkness, like disease, can ulcerate the universal mind and destroy the purity of idea and beauty. Nesace (lines 151–158) prepares to fly from her midway sphere to restore the power of the ideal to the realms below. Here Poe closed the first part of his poem.

So far, the poem has developed a rather obvious religious theme, as it was intended to do if the maker of the poem were playing god. The theme itself was not especially original; it is, simply, the old notion of the decay of the world or the "paradise lost." The classic and memorable medieval statement is the *De Contemptu Mundi* of Pope Innocent III; but the Renaissance seized upon the idea with a special avidity because it had found a remoter historical and philosophic precedent than even the Middle Ages had known. Plato's view, probably derived from the East, was of the preëxistence of the soul in a natural and sublime state and of the soul's gradual descent through lower stages of being until it reached this dark material existence on earth. From this condition it will be rescued and returned to the primal beauty and purity it once possessed only after its long trial of purification. This doctrine fit well into the already accredited "contempt" literature based on the Christian view of man's long descent and falling away from God. The romantic mind of the latter eighteenth century gave the doctrine an additional force by emphasizing man's own power to elevate himself, not by reason and logic but by his intuition, his own godlike creative imagination which, if it cannot restore him bodily to the realms of pure serenity and knowledge, can push the perceiving intelligence or soul outward and upward into the regions of timelessness and abstraction. For Poe, neither the rational faculty nor "science," but only the imagination had this power. "Al Aaraaf" is, therefore, the romantic process of the soul's rediscovery of its original being. The midway region of that star where Nesace dwells is, in the present condition of things, about as far as man can expect to move upward in awareness; that upward movement would be enough to give man a full knowledge of the universe, were he not, like the Angels soon to be introduced into the poem, content with sensual enticement.

The second part of the poem opens with a description of the wandering planet, Al Aaraaf, which has obvious similarities to Milton's pictures of hell and paradise:[18]

High on a mountain of enamell'd head—
Such as the drowsy shepherd on his bed
Of giant pasturage lying at his ease,
Raising his heavy eyelid, starts and sees
With many a mutter'd "hope to be forgiven"
What time the moon is quadrated in Heaven—
Of rosy head, that towering far away
Into the sunlit ether, caught the ray
Of sunken suns at eve—at noon of night,
While the moon danc'd with the fair stranger light—
Uprear'd upon such height arose a pile
Of gorgeous columns on th' unburthen'd air,
Flashing from Parian marble that twin smile
Far down upon the wave that sparkled there,
And nursled the young mountain in its lair. . . .
A dome, by linked light from Heaven let down,
Sat gently on those columns as a crown—
A window of one circular diamond, there,
Look'd out above into the purple air,
And rays from God shot down that meteor chain
And hallow'd all the beauty twice again,
Save when, between th' Empyrean and that ring,
Some eager spirit flapp'd his dusky wing.

This is indeed the midway world wherein idea and sense awareness are blended in that partial condition, not quite the perfection of pure Idea in heaven but yet far more perfectly refined than the chaotic nature of idea and sense on the lower earth. After these descriptive passages (through line 47), the action gets underway with the return of Nesace from her intercessions with the Deity and her obtaining permission to journey far down through space to restore the wondrous harmony. We are led to believe that Nesace is not so much a presence as the very "sound" of an idea which can "revel" through space, just as light can be a physically sensed "murmur"

> That stealeth ever on the ear of him
> Who, musing, gazeth on the distance dim
> And sees the darkness coming as a cloud. . . .

Nesace bursts into the hall of her palace, ready to execute her divine commission; she must arouse the goddess Zanthe and other attendant spirits who, like the very order of beings far below, must similarly be awakened. She sings the song, " 'Neath blue-bell or streamer," as the call to wakefulness and full response and then the song of command, "Ligeia! Ligeia!/ My beautiful one!" to the goddess (for Ligeia is the deity of harmony) to go below and, with sounds and music, awaken the dead who have lain insensate throughout long ages on earth and who can be aroused only by hearing again the same pure music which they once knew in their original state of awareness. In the succeeding section (lines 156–174) the angelic beings of Al Aaraaf are on the wing to restore the eternal harmony to the cruelly deranged and fractured world of men below. They are, however, limited in their power and can restore only "harmony" or the sensorily perceived relatedness of things; they have no awareness of "Knowledge" or "Science" which would dim "the mirror of our joy"; nor do they have any moral being, for they do not know good from evil. This passage is indeed curious and warrants some special attention before we enter the final, dramatic action of the poem.

In the introductory "Sonnet — To Science," as we have seen, Poe was renouncing the rational concept of the disparateness of things, of form from idea, of fact from its symbol. He was struggling for the organic principle which he may never have achieved until many years later in *Eureka,* but which was so much a constant in romantic poetry that he could assume the principle without rationalizing its existence. However, in these lines on the divine "harmony" and the music both of the universal spheres and the lesser tones which resound in men's ears, Poe brushed aside nearly three hundred years of laws of attraction and repulsion between elements and particles of matter and returned to the cosmological scheme of the ancient world and the Middle Ages, the concept of the music and consistently maintained rhythm of all things in the universal harmony. It is not without both literary and imaginative significance that Poe opened this section with heavy borrowings from Milton; for it is Milton, in English poetry at least, who is the *locus classicus* for the idea that all things conform to the harmonious pattern which exists throughout all space and time. Music, therefore, was a means of both sensorily and spiritually partaking in the existence of God; to sing was an act of worship, for in the very rhythm of the song one came closest in his own being to comprehending fully the being of the Deity. The song, secular as well as religious, for the churchman as well as for the workman, was a personal alliance with the infinite.

Poe makes a curious and rather special application of this idea as a means of accounting for the existence of death on earth, that lowest and remotest place of existence. Death is the final acknowledgement of man's submission to his fractured and mundane condition; it is the ultimate insult to a being who, by an act of his own will, chose disorder and chaos. In other, higher regions to die is neither a terror nor a punishment; for with those superior beings "to die was rife/ With the last ecstasy of satiate life." Death is the sinking into the ultimate, promised condition of the self, just as the song is the engagement of the self in the unified experience of the universe. Angelic death is the return to the pure being which is in God; man's death is the punishment for his disharmony. Man might be able to break through or destroy death if he were able to restore himself to his lost, pristine nature.

Here (briefly to pursue this idea further) is one of Poe's earliest attempts at investigating the meaning and rationale of death, long before he would qualify his insights by pandering to the popular interest in the *outré* and the horrific. He brings the idea up to and leaves it in the high Platonic scale of abstraction: death is the well-deserved punishment man earned by somehow disturbing the music, the harmony of things; this idea is, of course, not too far from the Christian concept of the eternal fracture which St. Augustine and later Christian apologists turned into the doctrine of the "fortunate fall." Death on earth was the lowest stage man ever reached in the soul's downward pilgrimage from Platonic essence to brute form; yet death is the ultimate self-annihilation man must suffer and overcome if he is ever to return upward to spirit again. Only by the most arduous discipline and effort of mind can man restore the lost harmony and destroy death.

Then Poe dramatizes this disharmony among men on earth. Two guilty spirits (lines 174–264) undergo the human tragedy: Ianthe, one of Nesace's attendant spirits sent to restore the harmony, has fallen in love with Angelo, a being lifted from earth and granted the right of choosing to remain as mere sense or to proceed upward into purer being. We have enacted for us once again the original fall of man: out of sloth or some terrible fault implicit in their existence these two beings renounce any blessed condition and remain contentedly below. Their story lacks any pathos or real tragedy, of course; they are so willingly reduplicating the experience of the ages that their narrative is almost monotonously dull. Yet their fall — Ianthe's from the purer condition of Al Aaraaf and Angelo's from what has been briefly granted him as the removal from earth and the triumph over death — is not spiritual nor religious but wholly intellectual; they elected their passionate, sensory condition by an act of conscious intelligence; they were not put to the disadvantage which religion and especially Christianity impose, that they are the victims of a flaw such as original sin. Their love is not even a passion but the intellectual condition of choice, of full conscious knowledge and control over their destinies.[19]

Angelo triumphantly proclaims his fallen condition to Ianthe:

> "Ianthe, dearest, see! how dim that ray!
> How lovely 'tis to look so far away!
> She seem'd not thus upon that autumn eve
> I left her gorgeous halls — nor mourn'd to leave. . . .
> The last spot of Earth's orb I trod upon
> Was a proud temple call'd the Parthenon —
> More beauty clung around her column'd wall
> Than ev'n thy glowing bosom beats withal. . . .
> Ianthe, beauty crowded on me then,
> And half I wish'd to be again of men."

He was afraid of and therefore rejected the harmony man had long ago owned and lost. Ianthe, spirit of harmony on Al Aaraaf, has willed her own destruction and loss of godhead and attempts to reassure Angelo (lines 227–230) that "woman's loveliness — and passionate love — " are all-complete fulfillments of that glory and harmony man longs for; but Angelo, and the reader, know better. In Poe's allegory Ianthe is herself lost and will never possess the sentience she once had:

> Thus, in discourse, the lovers whiled away
> The night that waned and brought no day.
> They fell: for Heaven to them no hope imparts
> Who hear not for the beating of their hearts.

"Al Aaraaf" is Poe's early attempt to resolve, first of all, the haunting question of man's limited knowledge; it employs an elaborate machinery, and many literary overtones, to set forth the "paradise lost" toward which man yearns and struggles to return and to which, in time, he might very well approach as his perception widens and deepens; this return will not be through "science" or the causative dissection of the world; it will come, if ever, through the imagination, through the poetic vision, through the power to see the unqualified unity of idea and substance. Secondly, death is, like insentience and dullness, not a visitation or punishment of a god nor even a fault in the world's structure; death was an event in the history of man; man himself brought death into the world when he willed his descent through the stages of being and gave himself up, as did Ianthe and Angelo, to his lower nature. Death, like injustice and hate and evil, is a quality of mind and intelligence and can be overcome. Thirdly, history is the complex of the total nature of man, both fact and myth, date and legend; it is the fusion of the "then" and the "now" in a timeless continuum which man, even debased, can restore and imaginatively live in. Poe's poem, though truncated and incomplete, is one more document in that quest for the pastness of the present. "Al Aaraaf" bespoke a longing for knowledge beyond man's power to obtain; it was a religious fairy tale, in which Poe was able to masquerade both as God and as the handsome prince: God could make and know His world; Angelo, the handsome prince, lost his.

This religious quest for knowledge and sensitivity is most clearly expressed in Poe's poems on death. "Romance" (titled "Preface" in 1829 and "Introduction" in 1831), which was considerably expanded in its 1831 version and then restored to its earliest form in the 1845 volume, is perhaps the most significant expression of Poe's earliest ideas on a subject which was to attract much of his attention throughout his whole literary career.

The poem establishes two sets of opposites or dichotomies: the poet in youth and the poet advanced in years, and the poet of once-upon-a-time and the poet in the modern world. The term "Romance" (the first word in all versions of the poem) refers to what Poe termed the character of "presenting perceptible images with definite . . . sensations." Poetry, in contrast to Romance, presents "perceptible images . . . with indefinite *sensations,* to which end music is an *essential,* since the comprehension of sweet sound is our most indefinite conception."[20] Romance deals with the felt and known relationships between images and definite sensations, whereas poetry is a magical exercise and concerns those very same images but made into indefinite sensations and impressions.

Such a contrast is established in the first stanza, which pictures a young person's fresh response to the world; the riot and color of these impressions are confusing, perhaps because the very lines are to suggest the impact of this exciting world on an excitable mind:

> Romance, who loves to nod and sing,
> With drowsy head and folded wing,
> Among the green leaves as they shake
> Far down within some shadowy lake,
> To me a painted paroquet
> Hath been — a most familiar bird —
> Taught me my alphabet to say —
> To lisp my very earliest word
> While in the wild wood I did lie,
> A child — with a most knowing eye.

Why, one might ask, is Romance a figure that nods and sings, has a drowsy head and folded wing, stands among green leaves, and seems to be seen as reflected in some shadowy lake? The answer is that the poet as youth sees only a mirror-universe, not the world as fact; he is like a child existing in a happy illusion which he would like to but cannot keep forever. The jarring images are what a youthful, impressionable poet makes of the world; afterward, he will make something different of it.

In the second stanza the mood has changed. A number of years have gone by; Poe presents a set of contrasts to the highly wrought images he had drawn in the first stanza. Romance, which once nodded and sang, is now the "eternal Condor [or vulture] years" which, instead of softly responding to the wind, now themselves shake and disorganize "the very Heaven on high/ With tumult" which is quite different from the soft ripple on the "shadowy lake." What was once the easy relaxation and happiness in sensuous pleasure is now the denial that one can live with idle cares in a life overcast by an "unquiet sky." The poet, now in maturity, renounces any poetry which does not issue from the *"indefinite* sensations" which are outside the world of fact and reality. The stanza presents the world of the poet's maturity as all harsh, jarring fact:

> Of late, eternal Condor years
> So shake the very Heaven on high
> With tumult as they thunder by,
> I have no time for idle cares
> Through gazing on the unquiet sky.
> And when an hour with calmer wings
> Its down upon my spirit flings —
> That little time with lyre and rhyme
> To while away — forbidden things!
> My heart would feel to be a crime
> Unless it trembled with the strings.[21]

The poem may present, as Killis Campbell suggested, Poe's early Byronic attitude of renouncing mere beauty and undertaking the quest for truth. It may also consider a theme always haunting the romantic mind: the operation of the law of diminishing poetic returns. Coleridge's "genial spirits" failed; once the poet lost his youthful zest in sheer physical response, he could no longer be the kind of poet he had been.[22] Either he must find a new subject matter (as Wordsworth demonstrated in "Tintern Abbey") or he must abandon poetry altogether, as did Coleridge and as Poe virtually did after 1831. The poem is, therefore, one more in the long sequence of romantic studies in potential frustration — "potential" because the poet might never know when his "genial spirits" would be restored. Poe's "Romance" is not as cogently stated as Wordsworth's "Tintern Abbey" or

Keats's "Ode to a Nightingale," for the idea of poetic decline and collapse is merely entertained, not seriously considered.[23]

Only "Al Aaraaf" and "Romance" in the 1829 *Al Aaraaf, Tamerlane, and Minor Poems* warrant any considerable attention. The mood of the earlier volume — especially that of the forlorn, outcast lover — is maintained in the lyric "To ——— " ("The bowers whereat, in dreams, I see") : everything the lover has suffered from lips and eyes and words are compulsively made into that universal anguish which may "desolately fall,/ O, God! on my funereal mind/ Like starlight on a pall." The world buys its "baubles" with "that gold" which truth "can never buy." "To the River" doubtless poetizes an experience of merely seeing one's face reflected in water alongside that of his lady's; only in the shifting mirage of water and in his heart can her presence be truly felt. The same mood is shadowily set forth in another lyric titled "To ——— " ("I heed not that my earthly lot"); there the lover imagines himself dead-in-life and, presumably, insensitive; but the seemingly fortunate condition of being insensitive-in-life does not spare him the torments of love:

> Nor that the grass — O! may it thrive!
>   On my grave is growing or grown —
> But that, while I am dead yet alive
>   I cannot be, lady, alone.[24]

More suggestive of the direction Poe's later poetic muse would take him is "Fairy-Land." It attempts to do several things. One is that, like both "Tamerlane" and "Al Aaraaf," it is an apocalyptic vision of a region beyond this world. The "Fairy-Land" is ostensibly death and the world of the dead; but we are given what becomes so frequently apparent in Poe's treatments of horror and death, namely, an alter-ego, a kind of thought-ghost, who is sent through the experience and comes back to report on what it has seen: a fantastic valley wherein the moonlight falls on enormous, grotesque shapes. Then comes the morning and breaks the moonlit trance as if a myriad of butterflies had scattered. What is interesting in this early treatment of a "dead" world is that we have mere description struggling to be agony: nothing happens; no one really dies or lives; the moon and sun remain the same; only the protagonist who has "seen" these things is changed. And all the while the poet, and reader, have remained comfortably outside this scenic panorama of death-in-life. Nothing has been done to them. Poe was to learn that he had to do more than simply draw weird pictures; he had to dramatize his scenes and events of death.

These, then, were the major poems of the 1829 volume. They marked little change or advance over the earlier 1827 publication, except that "Al Aaraaf" had sought to incorporate some version of the difference between "ideal" and "real" worlds. The next volume, the 1831 *Poems, Second Edition,* as they were titled, marked a considerable change and an advance over the two preceding volumes. Poe's odd subtitling, "Second Edition," suggests that he wished to ignore either the 1829 or the 1827 editions; the designation is, however, peculiarly apt: both the earlier volumes are rather like single first editions of juvenilia; this new volume is the assumption of poetic maturity.

4

The *Poems* of 1831 contained only six new verses; most of its pages are filled with reprintings, and some considerable revisions, of poems which had already been in print in the two preceding editions. And all of them, reprinted in periodicals as Poe found opportunity throughout the succeeding years, underwent considerable revision before they found their place in the *Raven* volume of 1845.

Undoubtedly, the most noteworthy is "To Helen" ("Helen, thy beauty is to me"), which, except for "The Raven," has aroused more critical speculation and exegesis than any other of Poe's poems. Who, everyone asks, is Helen? Poe's own clues suggest that the poem might have had as its original (though hardly its ultimate) inspiration in Mrs. Jane Craig Stanard, a young matron of Richmond during Poe's boyhood and the mother of one of his school friends. She died in 1824 when Poe was fifteen.[25] That she may have been the original of Helen is worthy of some credence, except that enough evidence survives to suggest that Poe's own foster mother, Mrs. Frances Keeling Allan, could have been a prototype for Helen. Several critics and explicators have brought forward evidence to show that Poe might be here celebrating Mrs. Allan's coming with a lamp in her hand to kiss him goodnight, or that he caught in the poem a memory of Mrs. Allan framed in a window niche and reading a letter.[26] The evidence which exists is not conclusive either way, and really does not matter in any analysis of the poem's meaning. Nor is it of crucial importance that we be able to attach precise interpretations to such terms as "Nicean barks," "hyacinth hair," the "agate lamp," or "Holy Land." "Helen" is quite obviously Helen of Troy — and then a little more too. As the Grecian Helen she represents all the urgent longing which medieval and romantic poets sought to resolve as mystery, pure beauty, and the agony of never realizing in fact what the imagination continually sought as myth or fiction. In this term, "Helen" takes her place with Keats's Madeline in "The Eve of St. Agnes" or Ruth in the "Nightingale" ode, and with a whole line of ladies who found their way into the lyrics of Goethe and Schiller, the ballads, and into the post-romantic longing which lasted well into the nineteenth century.

The first stanza is an extended simile of going out and of coming back: thus Helen's "beauty" is like a number of things which bring the "weary wayworn traveller" back "To his own native shore." This stanza prepares for the completion of the action in the second, wherein the image of woman as pure beauty is a means of further establishing a relationship with the ancient world which is superbly realized in the two lines, "the glory that was Greece,/ And the grandeur that was Rome."

The poem is, therefore, not about *a* woman, Mrs. Stanard, Mrs. Allan, nor even Helen of Troy. Its subject is the way the mind can move toward the past and, in some such symbol as the indefinable beauty of woman, is able to comprehend a world and culture long vanished from this earth. The woman as tangible form actually passes out of existence: her "hyacinth hair," her "classic face," her "Naiad airs" are means and incentives for the poet to make the imaginative journey backward in time to an almost tactile, physical sense of the glory of Greece and the grandeur of Rome. The poem is, in short, the Idea of antiquity gained through a virtual sensing of physical forms, just as Roman Catholics obtain a "sense" of God in the worship of the Virgin Mary.

The third and final stanza fixes in immobility the shifting and backward movement of the other two. The "window-niche," the "statue-like" figure, and the "agate lamp" denote that the poet's mind is now in the past. Woman has ceased to be woman and is now "Psyche," or a titular spirit who is the connecting link with the time past. The one reference at the end to the "Holy Land" probably connotes the end of the quest in some mythic region which all men, ever since the Israelites in Egypt, have hoped to realize, if not in fact, at least in imagination.

"To Helen" is, therefore, an investigation of the poetic process whereby the imagination destroys or goes through ostensible reality and reaches some comprehension of a world of Idea that lies beyond. It is an act of revivification, of animating what Coleridge termed the "visionary deadness" of the mind and its responses to the world; poetry becomes a way whereby the whole range of mind and imagination can come alive. But that "way" must always begin with some determinable, sensory experience: here the action starts with the mind's comprehension of woman, but it can only start there; it must not be confined to an identification with some known woman in Poe's biography. It may begin with such a woman; it ends with the purest evocation of Woman as a timeless historical "way" of understanding, just as Henry Adams struggled to understand the Virgin in all her historical complexity.

The next poem in the 1831 *Poems* is a companion piece to the "Helen." "Israfel" is specifically about poetry and poets; it begins where "Al Aaraaf" ended; that is, "Israfel" takes for granted that such a mythic or hypothetical world of other, purer beings exists. The world of this poem, is, however, considered as entirely human, even subhuman: in "Al Aaraaf" Angelo, a man, was able to reach some midway stage of illumination; in "Israfel" not even the poet, the visionary, is capable of seeing beyond the lowest order of created things.

The poem begins (we shall follow the 1831 text) "In Heaven" where dwells "a spirit . . . Whose heart-strings are a lute." This is "the angel Israfel." The second stanza takes us one stage lower in the order of creation: far out in space "The enamoured moon/ Blushes with love" (or responds to the impulses of beauty emanating from the heavenly source) and "the red levin" (in subsequent editions they were accompanied in this response by "the rapid Pleiads") "pauses" in its pathways through space. The third stanza brings us more closely to poetry and poets, for we learn "That Israfeli's fire/ Is owing to that lyre . . ./ With those unusual strings." Poets and poetry should be concerned, therefore, only with the "unusual," or with the strange and other-worldly; by contrast, perhaps, prose can be the instrument of ordinary discourse. In the next or fourth stanza we are led to believe that another basic element in poetry is music; and here Poe's verse becomes highly suggestive of rather than directly conveying its meaning:

> But the Heavens that angel trod
> Where deep thoughts are a duty—
> Where Love is a grown god—
> Where Houri glances are . . .
> Imbued with all the beauty
> Which we worship in yon star.

The musical tonalities of the stanza itself convey the "thought" of music. Finally, we are informed, as a third determinant of poetry, that Israfel "despisest/ An unimpassion'd song"; the "Best bard" is he who composes the most exquisitely passionate or heart-felt poems — and in the sixth stanza Poe dramatizes, on the moment, the effect which such emotion can cause:

> The extacies above
> With thy burning measures suit —
> Thy grief — if any — thy love
> With the fervor of thy lute —
> Well may the stars be mute!

The final two stanzas return us, and poetry, to earth again where emotions and sensory experience are disjointed and ineffectual, and the poem closes on a note of apology that it is merely a poem and not that "stormier note" that "would swell . . . within the sky."

"Israfel" is, therefore, a poem on the theory and practice of poetry; it is a philosophy of poetry and attempts to set forth logically what "To Helen" had projected imaginatively: poetry is a way toward understanding both different from and superior to rational science, logic, religion, or any other learning processes of men. "Israfel," like the much later "Philosophy of Composition," sets forth the rationale of that way: poets and poetry must treat of subjects essentially poetic: poetry cannot be a mixed or bastard form — it is what it is and nothing else, and what it is is unmistakably poetic; again, poetry is a form of music: it should not be considered *as* music; it is simply one kind of music (for music is in its own way a form of understanding); lastly, poetry bespeaks passion, or emotion, but it must be, as Poe would enlarge his thesis, an emotion which is not just an emotion but which is an emotion which "becomes poetry." It starts as a passion or a human condition; it ends in a poem, an act of translating the original emotion into a form (the poem) and into a set of references (metaphors, images, similes, symbols). These together, the form and the references, lead or entice the imagination to go beyond that "visionary deadness" the mind might otherwise inhabit. Poetry is the unique way of breaking the enclosure of mere "world" and coming out, as it were, on "the other side" of comprehension.

"The City in the Sea" [27] significantly introduces us to Poe's incantatory manner; that is, the method of writing visions which exist both somewhere and now. Vision literature usually concerns what is past and gone; it is the cry of the despairing prophet who knows he can never see again what he once glimpsed. Poe seeks to make the vision a fact, with place, dimension, and time; thus there is "Far down within the dim west" a city buried forever beneath the still waters. A number of metaphors and analogies direct us to other lost or faraway cities, not only Gomorrah beneath the Dead Sea in Josephus' history of the Jews, but in the myths of the pagan Mediterranean world and the isles of the blessed far beyond the pillars of Hercules.

The poem is also, as we shall see later, a part of the interest in antiquity which was sweeping over the Western world as a result of archeological excavations. Poe is engaging in his own imaginative researches into the limitless past: "To Helen" was an imaginative thrust into the past by means of the extraordinarily evocative symbol of woman; "The City in the Sea" is the fact or actuality of the past which is there if one could but get to it. What Poe is evoking is not only the past as a fact but the interminable durability of the past.

His poem is an evocation of a time-sense — one that is in eternity or absolute time which is quite different from the transiency of time in man's world.

Yet even this permanence will have its end: "there is a ripple there . . ./ As if the towers had thrown aside,/ In slightly sinking, the dull tide." And hell, most durable of all regions, shall absorb even this vast empire of stillness and death. In the first or 1831 version the triumphant character of death is underlined in a pair of lines afterward dropped: "And Death to some more happy clime/ Shall give his undivided time."[28]

We might well conclude our treatment of the 1831 poems with "The Sleeper," in that early volume titled "Irene." (Other poems will be considered in due time and under another topic.) This poem is one of Poe's early statements on the belief that, while there is death, no one really dies. Death is a "sleep," or a transition from one stage of existence to another. Though this idea became muted in the revisions, it is quite apparent in these lines of the first version of the poem:

> The lady sleeps: the *dead* all sleep —
> At least so long as Love doth weep . . .
> But when a week or two go by,
> And the light laughter chokes the sigh,
> Indignant from the tomb doth take
> Its way to some remember'd lake,
> Where oft — in life — with friends — it went
> To bathe in the pure element. . . .[29]

In the revision these lines became:

> The lady sleeps! Oh, may her sleep,
> Which is enduring, so be deep! . . .

I pray to God that she may lie
Forever with unopened eye,
While the pale sheeted ghosts go by!
. . . Oh, may her sleep,
As it is lasting, so be deep!
Soft may the worms about her creep!

Poe's first intention seems to have been to illustrate the folly of human grief: it is grief that keeps the supposed dead in the tomb; when grief has abated, then the buried one is free to resume her new existence. The revision resulted not so much from a change in Poe's ideas or a doubt that life continues after this earthly existence is closed as from his growing avoidance of anything that might suggest the didactic. The original "Irene" had a message and moral; the later poem, "The Sleeper," was essentially pictorial and analytic; and if there is a meaning in the lines one may search where he may.

If Poe had written no more poetry after the publication of the collection of 1831, with its reprinting of nearly all the poems in the two earlier volumes, he might still be considered a minor poet of the nineteenth century. Yet his career as a poet was essentially finished: he said everything he had to say and, in truth, he would rarely say it any better. However much I shall have to say further concerning poetry and Poe's theory of poetry in subsequent chapters, I shall be doing so only because Poe made poetry into both criticism and philosophy; and the critical concepts and the philosophical stances he assumed had a direct bearing on the rest of his career in the short story and in the practice of criticism.[30]

The problem of poetic decline is virtually a constant in the history of romantic expression; yet it is different each time it occurs, whether in Wordsworth, Coleridge, Bryant, or Lowell. We might offer at this point suggestive reasons for the change or "decline" in Poe's poetry and then treat them more extensively in discussions still to come.

Of first importance is the realization which Poe may have tacitly admitted to himself that he was attempting to make poetry do more than it or any art form can accomplish. Poetry was, he thought, an act of discovery and penetration; from Coleridge he had obtained the view that man's perceptive powers can transcend this world of space and time and give him insights as profound and earth-disturbing as the great discoveries in the physical sciences.[31] Poe was not alone in this exalted view of poetry: in the same vein Shelley said that "poets are the unacknowledged legislators of the universe." From "Tamerlane" through "The Sleeper" we explore aspects of the inner self or profound mysteries concerning the exterior world. Yet we have not really discovered or come to know any more than what the poem, as a special instrument of expression, is capable of conveying. The idea has no existence outside the poem; the poem is not "real," any more than a presumed law of nature is "real": both are approximations, the poem is an act of deduction because it moves from causes to ideas and the scientific hypothesis an act of induction because it moves from facts to principles. The scientific principle or hypothesis is, we say, real or proved because it seems to describe a number of repetitious examples; the poem is real only once — the one time it became a poem.

Yet, perhaps because the poem had only its own unique existence and reality, it need not mean anything; it might be applicable to any number of situations. It should therefore present itself and its subject in whatever predetermining way the poetic imagination devised or brought forth and then let the reader make of it what he could. On such a basis Poe regularly practiced the subterfuge of concealing himself and his subject: "Tamerlane" was about Poe and his unfortunate situation of 1827 just as "Irene" was about the idea of life beyond the grave; but the poetic process required that the ostensible subject be somehow dramatized in a masquerade which would conceal the true meaning beneath the ostensible one. Nearly all of Poe's later revisions are directed toward this act of concealment or in making generalized some quite specific, even commonplace, theme.

Nevertheless, meaning could not, for Poe, be left in the luminous vacuity of impressionism of what any reader wished to make of the poem. Any theory of poetry which left the response entirely to the reader's capacity for understanding denied the special art of poetry any validity whatever. More and more Poe came to see that poetry was the product of a controlling mind, of the poet. The *Poems* of 1831 seem to have assumed that poetry can even be *about* poetry and that Poe was concerned with formulating a theory of poetry before he undertook to write very much poetry. He was, so early in his career, concerned not with what poetry says but with what poetry is. What "To Helen," "Israfel," and "The City in the Sea" tells us is that Poe was considering what the imagination does, when, all the while it is confined to the intransigence of words, it sets about treating a subject poetically.

As Poe scrutinized and wrote criticisms of other poems, especially after his coming to the editorship of the *Southern Literary Messenger* in 1835, he realized that logic, grammar, poetic form, even the necessities of syntax were matters for the poet to ordain and control and not for the reader to take for granted. Thus he was pulled in two directions: the one was toward the Ideal and the Idea, the comprehension of a meaning as anterior to the form it assumed in art or in nature, and the poem as merely a redaction in words of what existed apart from and even beyond words to convey; the other was toward simplicity, design, organization, and good sense; thus the poet was a maker and contriver who should at all times have full control over the idea since he virtually makes the idea when he makes the poem; and he should, if he is worthy of his craft, make certain that as many readers as possible know what the poem is about.

Out of this discrete opposition Poe formed his theory of poetry and his subsequent poetic practice; these matters we can more fully investigate in the next chapter.

II

Aspects of a Philosophy of Poetry

Poetry is a form of philosophy. It distills the major philosophic precepts of its time. One poet is not expressing his whole age and time: not even Shakespeare was the total record of the Elizabethan age; yet we rightly consider Shakespeare as the distinctly summarizing and even philosophic voice of his age.

Some poets are apparently aware that they are the "voices" of their age, and, like Tennyson and Longfellow of Poe's own time, are deeply conscious of their poetic place and destiny in their age. To be aware of such distinction is, however, not to have it. In order to explore the intellectual and philosophic poetic temper of the nineteenth century in America, one should not go to Longfellow, Lowell, or Bryant. He should go to Poe, Whitman, and Emily Dickinson, not one of whom was a "philosopher" (much as Whitman tried to be one), but all of whom form the record of the American poetic sensibility in the nineteenth century.

Different as at first consideration those three poets were, they were nonetheless very similar—certainly Poe and Whitman were—in their search for a unitary theory of the universe of man and God. Poe was different from them too; he was never touched by the profound reaches of the Puritan mind in quest of its own private center, as was Emily Dickinson; and, despite the influences of German transcendental thought and idealistic philosophy, Poe, unlike Whitman, always remained half-rationalist and half-organicist. In another term, he might be considered a return to the Middle Ages and to the schoolmen who fashioned the immense design of the "great chain of being." Yet he was also a citizen of his age, keenly aware of the fracture which Cartesian logic and Lockean psychology had made in man's conception of himself and of his world. In its way Poe's problem was very much like that of Henry Adams or of Wallace Stevens: that of seeing unity in diversity, of conceiving the design behind the apparent chaos, of marrying matter and mind. Poe was not, strictly speaking, a "philosopher" any more than Henry Adams and Wallace Stevens were to be. Yet he regarded his world and employed his art "philosophically"; that is, his poems, short stories, and certain critical pronouncements were projections of the mind and the imagination toward a metaphysical order and were attempts to phrase not the "why" but the "what" of man, his mind, and his world. The poem, the short story, the novel like *Pym* became the symbolic enactment of man's search for logic and meaning.

What we shall endeavor to do in this chapter, which is intercalary to the main adventure through Poe's career, is to watch Poe respond and give expression to some of the major currents of his age and then to see what trends in his artistic career these forces shaped. The best and easiest point at which to begin is with the youthful mind of Poe himself.

2

One of the most fascinating aspects of the Romantic mind was that it wore itself out or even destroyed its own imaginative powers. Romantic poets have so frequently exhausted their inspiration, made barren their special subject matter, or contented themselves with their own private meditations that the "Romantic agony" has become, with whatever justification, a commonplace of historical inquiry and criticism. In a very real sense, Romantic poets have been susceptible to the "agony" because, as poets, they began with a potential of private destructiveness, namely, with the self. Poe belonged to the company of Shelley, Coleridge, Pushkin, Verlaine, and others too numerous to mention; it is a very large and yet a very select company, each member a special case in himself and accountable only on his own unique imaginative experience.

The "agony" character of poetry need not primarily concern us here. It is that frustration and terror a poet realizes when he knows that he has nothing more to say or when he gropes through that murky region that lies between what the imagination envisions and what the poetic rhetoric fails to resolve. Poe was a victim of both these failures, these terrors; and their roots lie deep in his mind and in the age of which he was, however unaware, a part.

Every youthful mind, especially every poetically romantic mind, is solipsistic; it begins with an intuitive necessity to give credence only to itself and to its own intense experience. It sees everything from within, and it sees even the universe as a kind of opaque mirror of itself. Such a condition of being is natural and even healthy; in a writer it produces the endless autobiographical narrative of the accumulating richness of consciousness on the part of a growing mind: Dickens' *David Copperfield,* Poe's *Arthur Gordon Pym* and "The Raven," to *Swann's Way, Buddenbrooks,* and *The Portrait of the Artist as a Young Man.* In some respects Poe might be called the formulator of the theme: the subject of his poetry and of a great deal of his stories is the chronicle of the consciousness of a hypersensitive youth. One might also say that these "histrio" poses were means of his conducting his intellectual development in public.

Poe's development was limited to how far Poe could project or enlarge his own personality or his imaginative selfhood. His sense of self was, however, perilously close to an exclusive narcissism. The curiosity of this situation was not essentially its narcissism but its strangely hypertrophied emotional condition of always needing to be *in* another consciousness or being — as though he could continually invent imaginative protagonists of himself who would do what, imaginatively, needed doing in the poem or short story and all the while leave him safe and untouched. The drama always ended the same way: it was a double destruction, that of the Poe-self imaginatively and that of the invented self (woman, the visible world, God) substantively. Unless he could be "in" and wholly identify himself with that being or protagonist who was the doer of the poem, Poe had no subject at all; and the moment he achieved that state of identification — the moment when the self and its prototype were virtually indistinguishable — neither he nor that other being had any further imaginative existence. Poe's imagination reduced to complete disorder what it intended to use before any new shape or subject could arise; or, to put the matter another way, the imagination had to go through a process and come out on the "other side" before the original stimulus or insight had any usableness or meaning.

The rationale of this solipsistic act of annihilation is, admittedly, a matter for the most tentative speculation. Yet enough evidence survives to permit us to investigate further this question of an artistic mind delighting in its own destruction, the imagination destroying itself in the very act of creation, as a pervasive element in Poe's art.[1]

One of the major themes in Poe's whole corpus of writing is his longing for the mother, for a kind of female night-shape, who is never there and will never come. The pretty Elizabeth Arnold Poe died in Poe's infancy; and though Mrs. Frances Keeling Allan lavished on him an affection which was strong as it was deep, Poe never bore the name of this putative mother: for a boy growing up in Richmond, Virginia, not to bear the name of the mother and father was socially worse than having no parents at all. Thus Poe sought the "dream" mother who was forever young, forever soft, and yet forever unworldly; the foster mother who died when he was a young man could claim in death more of his devotion than when she was alive. In the last year of his life Poe celebrated in a sonnet this vision of the dream-mother who was a combination of Mrs. Allan, his mother-in-law Mrs. Maria Clemm, and all the visionary ladies he had ever seen:

Because I feel that, in the Heavens above,
  The angels, whispering to one another,
Can find, among their burning terms of love,
  None so devotional as that of "Mother,"
Therefore by that dear name I long have called you. . . .

This mother-image was, more importantly, one of the psychic projections of Poe's own inner world; the lost mother was a means of his acting out a number of themes which lay deep in his imaginative consciousness.

This longing for the mother was coupled with a fear of the dark and of the night. The child Marcel in Proust's *Swann's Way* suffered excruciatingly in the dark, but he could at least hear the voices below stairs, and eventually his mother did come to kiss him goodnight. Although we know nothing of the bedtime rituals in the Allan household,[2] we can understand that for the rest of his life Poe heard, over and over again, the voices of his imagination out of the dark and terrifying night of his childhood. In that strange blending of visions which were to possess him for a lifetime, Poe saw a mother-image cast in the dark night of fear and death. This night-shape was always young, a beautiful woman arrayed in the filmy dress of marriage or the funeral: the nightgown or wedding dress easily shifted into the grave clothes, and the innocent white of the bride was the pallor of death on the cheek. The early lyric, "I saw thee on thy bridal day," was, with very little change in metaphor, a version of Irene in "The Sleeper." In Poe the child became the man; and the mother who never came in the dark of the night grew into the demon lover, the poltergeist, who was to haunt him in all his poetry and in many of his short stories.

Such a mind is born or made an outcast. Poe later suffered a deepening of his feeling of displacement when, reared as a gentleman in a gentlemanly way of life, he found himself suddenly cast out when he returned to Richmond, in no very deep disgrace, from the University of Virginia at Christmas time of 1826. It was indeed one of the harshest blows life could deal him; biographers, for all their stress on facts, have not stressed it enough, for it split Poe's life in two.

Yet, like other outcasts or outcast minds, Poe enjoyed his special condition; he reveled not only in a "region of sighs" but in solitude. He developed early a capacity for introspection, and these private meditations, coupled with the power of self-expression, induced Poe to speculate on his own mind as outside of or as functioning apart from the world of men and reality. In that separation Poe sought, ultimately, the deepest meanings of his own existence — yet this speculation was going on all the while that Poe was setting up a number of barriers or defenses against final self-revelation.

The feeling of isolation or the sense of personal loneliness can actually become means of insight into the nature of the self and the world. They can become, not philosophies, but philosophic attitudes. Kierkegaard, whose mind was contemporary with and much like Poe's, put on his mask of the "either/or" whereby he could play the trifler in public and hold his mind in suspense and ready for speculation in the deepest privacy. Poe was similarly the histrio, the shaper of masks for the self and a teller of lies in order to conceal the cracks in a histrio's façade.[3]

Poe was also a citizen of the first half of the nineteenth century, a member of the generation which sought Waldens and brotherhoods of men whereby man might learn to express himself both in the privacy of his own mind and in the community of his fellowmen. He was of an age (it was an "age": Hawthorne and Melville were distinguished citizens of it) which tried to solve a question central to the modern world: if man is a mind, he cannot live in a mindless or mechanistic world. Either he must be mechanistic man existing in a mechanical universe, or he must see himself as a mind living in a world which also functions according to some intelligence. The solution Poe reached, as did Emerson, Thoreau, and Whitman, may not have been a permanent one (what solution could be?) but it had certain validity until the impact of evolutionary and Pragmatic thought.[4]

The romantic mind — and Poe is almost a touchstone for it — sought the answer to the epistemological dilemma — does man as mind live in a mindless universe? — by consistently undertaking the journey of mind. Whatever this questing self could find would be truth for itself and for its time; but the quest had to be undergone alone; if it reached its goal in privacy, it might then turn outward toward the world. But the social message could come only after a private regeneration: witness Carlyle's *Sartor Resartus,* Mill's *Autobiography* (and its famous description of the mind's rebirth in mid-life), Newman's *Apologia,* and Arnold's poetry. The private self was first mirror for the world and then the world could be seen as it truly was — a universe of mind which somehow was like the private self as a mind.

The first stage in this romantic quest was an act of destruction or renunciation: the real world was abandoned or reduced to the conditions imposed by the self as mind; then, and only then, could reality or world assume its being and actuality again. The writers I have just mentioned were ones who performed this double activity of intellectual making and reshaping. The curiosity of Edgar Poe is that he never came out of the first stage: the young mind's private indulgence in solitude and in terror and dream became the habit of a lifetime; his mind fulfilled itself — every time it wrote a poem or short story — by performing an act of destruction, a destruction of the sensible world as having any mind or reality whatsoever. What the child saw in its earliest impressions — the visions of the dying or dead girl-mother, then the youth's private longing for solitude, finally the literary capital which could be made from the terror of self-consciousness and the dark night of the seeking mind — these became the major imaginative enterprises of a lifetime.

Yet the "either/or," the split between the inner self and the outer world, was never complete in Poe: the mind which employed itself in the discursive journey of self-exploration was never quite the total enterprise. There was another side of his mind which, as it were, remained apart from the activity of the other. While one side — that of the undeveloped adolescent with its night fears and the dreams of the lost girl-mother — was engaged in an imaginative destruction of reality chiefly in the poetry and in a select group of tales, the other half of the mind was attempting to make sense of reality and to put logic back together: this side functioned in the tales of ratiocination, in the criticism, and in the philosophic prose-poem *Eureka.* The mind was split between, on the one hand, its delight in and horror at its own capacity for destruction and, on the other, its consciousness that the world was untouched all the time.

This fracture or dualism was, in Poe, only partly a question of his private mind or psychology; if it were wholly so, then all his writing would have been merely autobiographical, the outward expression of his own inner, private turmoil. The fracture was philosophical as well: it was part of the major stream of intellectual and artistic life from the seventeenth until well into the nineteenth, and even into the twentieth, century.

3

It was Cartesian dualism which left to future generations the problem of a split world. In science, the enlightenment derived from this division was enormous, but in art it willed to men's minds the question of the subject and its object, the artist and his material, the "I" and the universe. For the eighteenth century this division was a recognition of the highest convenience and potentiality: the world of reality left impressions on the mind, and those impressions, quite removed from the original stimulus in the world, were the subject of the artist's contemplation and composition. The artist thereby presented the general, the universal, the type, which existed in the human intelligence unquestioned by time and the variables of the world itself.

Romantic psychology and epistemology were, in great measure, an attempt to bridge this gap and to resolve this split. The artist's material could not be always conveniently "out there" as a matter for detached or even absent contemplation; the artist was an artist because, primarily, he underwent a continual process of reanimation by virtue of his very contact with the world. What the world contained, the mind knew; what reality stimulated, the artist could reduce to some order: but the knowledge and the order were not a set of determinants which philosophers, critics, and artists had agreed as existing (the leaf was not simply a generalized leaf, knowable from Aristotle to Pope) but were rediscovered, almost as if they had never existed before, every time an artist's mind and imagination sensed and knew them.

Philosophically, the question pertained to the relationship between the mind and the world. Do I know the world (to put the matter another way) because I have a mind which is capable of sensing and reflecting on the world apart from reality? Or is my mind an extension and still a part of what I might term "the world"? One question is rationalism or mechanism, the other idealism or organicism. And the answer which a writer or artist makes, instinctively or logically, determines the kind of art he will produce. On the one hand he may be Alexander Pope; on the other, Coleridge, Poe, or Wallace Stevens.[5]

The romantic artist has, generally speaking, subscribed to what Santayana termed "the higher superstition," which he further defined: "This views the world as an oracle or charade, concealing a dramatic unity, or formula, or maxim, which all experience exists to illustrate."[6] That is, the "unity" exists as an ideal which the artist or philosopher seeks to realize, but always he is haunted by the necessary recognition that the world *is* sense and mind, matter and soul, thing and idea which he can never quite bring into any permanent, ultimate coherence. He is forever tantalized by a split universe which is, he keeps insisting, really one.

Poe attempted one more solution to this dualism within a unity.[7] Subject and object, mind and matter, the artist and the world ought to exist in some functional and apprehensible design. If there is a split, then the artist's main business might be employed in demonstrating that there is one containing Reality within which are other modes and elements of being. Poe is an interesting example of one who acknowledged this fracture, the Cartesian dualism, and yet aimed to resolve some comprehensible and knowable design. Melville, as Mr. Charles Feidelson has shown, is an interesting example of another approach to the dilemma: Melville sensed that, if he permitted his own mind (as he almost did in *Pierre*) to shape the world in terms of his own private vision, the world of sensible reality was virtually annihilated; nothing would remain except the white foam from which Ishmael arose at the end of *Moby-Dick;* thus to render only the individual attitude toward the world would mean a retreat into introspection and loss of communication with the world. Melville's solution was only partial — and somewhat like Poe's: he allowed the Confidence Man his worldly masquerade and then assumed a private mask which he wore in his shorter poems, in *Clarel,* and in *Billy Budd*. The fracture was complete: the knowing mind was all; the world as perception was nothing or a chaos.[8]

Poe was more daring; he began where, as it were, Melville had left off. If Melville rejected the substantial world because it was a mass of unyielding, unknowable stuff, Poe early abandoned any organic conception which his basic monism told him ought to exist. Consequently, he had several methods of resolving the problem of a dualism within the One: he could, as Melville did eventually, abandon the world of substance and retire into the loneliness of the single perceiving self; or he could, as Emerson proposed and Whitman fulfilled, make the sensible world unite with or conform to the perceiving mind or self. Poe did neither. He was too much a rationalist, a child of the eighteenth century, to allow any condition but an epistemological separation between the mind and reality. But instead of retiring into the private imagination and making the world conform to the inner reason, or denying any existence to reality except what the imagination allows, Poe sent his imagination on a series of journeys which were means and acts of conquest of the mind over the material world.

Yet these were not always acts of "conquest." The action might be reversed and the conquered might overcome the conqueror. For somehow, in Poe's art, the imagination tended to lose itself in the process of going out or of making the material world conform to the imaginative premise. The material world was too often unyielding; instead of the mind's willing a comprehension, the mind lost itself and became the object (as in "The Raven" and "The Fall of the House of Usher"). By contrast, we might for the moment consider Whitman's "When Lilacs Last in the Dooryard Bloom'd" as an act of submergence and identification: the actors in this symbolic drama — the lilac, star, bird, the land, even the poet himself — all succumb to and go through death but, at the last, come out on the other side of death in a total transformation wherein the perceiving self has been able to reassert itself and its identity in the act of dying and being reborn.

Poe's usual method, from the time he abandoned the intensely autobiographical expression of his early poetry, was to send another self on the journey, an invented self which becomes or wills or understands; all the while the central "I" is detached, observing, and aware that what it knows or invents may be only an illusion, a fascinating masquerade which, for the moment, the imagination has been able to fashion from that reality which is ever diverse and separate from the knowing self.

In order further to explore and understand the implications of this "split," both philosophical and artistic, which determined much of romantic art and, more especially, Poe's verse and prose, we should consider two formulations. The first is, What is the nature and condition of any art that renounces the world of sense and the accredited language of discourse which men for centuries have assumed as "real" and meaningful? Or, what happens to poetry, or to art in general, when it denies the perceptual world and takes for granted that what the mind makes is the only reality? The second and one more pertinent for Poe is, What might happen if the imagination not only rejected the world of sense and meaning but attempted to enter a range of expression and experience where the artist could make any word or sign mean anything he wanted, either a nothing or a completely abstract symbol? These two questions are means not only of describing Poe and his poetry but also of linking him with Coleridge, his critical mentor, and one of the main streams of early nineteenth-century philosophical thought. Our present problem now turns on the nature and act of the creative process; in Romantic idealism, the mind is not a mere reflector of the world, a dark closet into which jets of knowable light are projected and made into ideas, but is itself a creator and knower.

4

Kant had shown, by his distinction between phenomena and noumena, that the mind does not operate upon brute matter and form ideas out of mere sense-impressions, as though it were putting together an elaborate jigsaw puzzle; if that were so, then the mind were forever a prey to outer circumstance and deprived of any ideas in continuity. The individual human mind knows because it is itself a part and product of a unifying thought manifested throughout the universe; there is both the individual mind and the all-ordering mind which "think into" each other.[9] For Kant the mind is both actor and creator; and in formulating this function of the mind in answer to Humean skepticism, he stipulated three elements of mental activity: Sensibility, by which we become aware of spatial and temporal objects; Imagination; and Understanding. The two latter functions are "transcendental," in that they take their origin in sense-data but go beyond the limitations of human knowledge which Lockean rationalism had sought to impose. They are truly creative, and they make known to the mind the only final perceptions which the mind ever achieves of the world.[10]

The line from Kant to Coleridge is straight and direct. In the *Biographia Literaria* Coleridge took over bodily these three functions of mental activity and then put his special emphasis on the second, the Imagination; for Coleridge was concerned less with what the mind knows and more with what that special faculty of the mind known as the imagination does when it is creating a poem or any work of art.[11]

The imagination is itself, for Coleridge, dual. The "primary Imagination" is the first stage of perceptual insight and illumination; it is the fullest, the most complete agency of perception, for it is the all-comprehensive, "esemplastic," or "building-up" faculty which takes the infinite diversity of experience and makes it into a whole; it does not leave experience a set of sporadic jets or flashes, as in Lockean thought, but instinctively combines experience into that continuity which men know exists. There is nothing special, Coleridge (and Wordsworth too) insisted, about this faculty; it is not given just to poets. It is the very basis of the most prosaic knowledge of the world; all men have it and use it. Poetry, though different as an expression of the mind, is only one way by which man has been able to make sense for himself of the sensible world; it is, in that respect, very close to science, philosophy, ethics, and religion.[12]

The primary imagination is, therefore, virtually an instinct in man: it is his faculty not only of deriving some sense of comprehensive unity in the world but also his capacity to "think back into" the world his own awareness of belonging in that whole. It is the highest reach of man's attempt to understand himself as participating in the design and as being shaped by the multiplicity which, nonetheless, he can know as a functioning one. Poetry is in this respect no different from other studies and knowledges: so to consider poetry as an expression of the primary imagination is to make it part of the same quest for understanding as can be derived from the science of the natural world or the philosophy of the mind itself. Here, then, romantic theory was sometimes content to leave poetry — in that nebulous range of expression and comprehension which might be all, or nothing.

Coleridge apparently saw the danger of such a program: of necessity poetry was different from other investigations, and its procedure was something distinct, if not unique. With the "secondary Imagination," which is Coleridge's own term, we enter the special domain of poetry; it was this concept which required of Coleridge his most searching analysis; for Poe the implications of this Coleridgean view are enormous. The secondary imagination was the destructive force; it was the operation of the mind antecedent to poetic creation, even to the imaginative stimulus which might eventually lead to poetic activity. This secondary faculty breaks through the range of everyday perception: that world which Coleridge termed "familiarity and selfish solicitude" must be destroyed. The primary imagination is the mind's first comprehension; it sees all things put together, but that apprehension cannot produce poetry.[13] The mind must pass through the world-as-all; "*that* world," in the words of D. G. James, "is dissolved and dissipated; and, out of the same materials, operated on however by a revivified imagination, a new world is made. The first is adequate to the demands of 'practical' life; but the creative re-ordering of the secondary imagination results in a world adequate to the demands of the 'contemplative' life which, if sufficiently developed, issues in artistic creation."[14]

This aspect of the life of the imagination may be regarded from another point of view. The primary imagination presents the world to the mind as substantively known and ordered. There may indeed be more for the mind to know, but such knowledge is merely the addition or further sense and intellectual data to the amount of knowledge already obtained. The secondary imagination is, contrariwise, a disordering or reordering of what is the known world and the mind's ideas. It consists, as it were, of a reverse process from the one by which the mind has reached its "primary" awareness. It brings to the attention of the mind, or imagination (the two are virtually synonymous in this respect), a constant skepticism and review of the world. The secondary imagination may very well end in dissolving what is "known" and end by creating a wholly new conceptual realm of idea quite on its own; and this new range of perception may become so "real" that the imagination or mind can live simultaneously in two dimensions or two worlds.

Poe's adherence to Coleridge's design was almost slavish; he never went beyond it or added to it but simply emphasized one element at the expense of several others. In nearly identical terms Poe made a tripartite division of the human faculties. The first is the Heart, the sensory or feeling organ (and is almost the same function as Coleridge's "sensibility"); its satisfaction is "Passion" or the "excitement of the heart." Its operation is within a *"homeliness"* or commonplaceness. The second is the Imagination, the perceiving or discovering power. The third is the Intellect or understanding; its satisfaction is "Truth"; its best realization is achieved in prose which "demands a precision."[15] These two latter functions, as in Coleridge's schema, are transcendental and therefore nonsensory; yet they alone can make the world fully known to the mind. Poe placed the imagination as the second or mediating faculty in order to denote its blending or esemplastic function between the other two; it is, however, a separate faculty whose principles and action form the domain of art.[16]

Poe's one significant departure from the Coleridgean design is in his assumption that these three distinctions are not so much components or parts of the human mind as they are separate actions of man's power of expression and communication. The imagination is, for Poe, the one truly creative or discovering faculty of the mind; the other two are either speculative, analytical, discursive, or descriptive.[17] They are not "lower"; they simply employ a different idiom and vocabulary of conveyance. Thus the mind lives not so much on different levels or ranges of experience: experience is all "there" from the first or is developed as life goes on; the mind lives in varying ranges of expression or means of making things known to itself and to others. The heart or sensory faculty is the everyday and may not be expressive at all but mutely knowing, as with habit. The intellect deals in scientific formulas, with precise instruments of measuring, and with the inductive method of verifying what the mind regards as true and permanent. The imagination, however, both orders and destroys; it goes through the world of reality or "selfish solicitude" and conceives some comprehensible reality which only the rhetoric (Poe thought of it as music or poetry) of the imagination may express and convey. The heart and the intellect are barred from such expressive understanding simply because they do not have the right language. The mathematical symbol for the square root of minus-one may be a marvelous tool of intellectual perception, but it cannot do what a bar of music or a poem can do to convey the something-other which lies beyond mathematics or the sciences.

As an outgrowth of this insistence on the comprehending or rhetorical power of the imagination, the romantic mind was led to consider the question of originality. Did the imagination know or shape the same known world in different modes of expression (as Wordsworth thought), or was it a faculty of making things known which had never been known before (as Coleridge, and Emerson too, considered)? If the imagination is a faculty for originating and discovering, then does it make known only what it knows within itself or does it have the capacity of really penetrating to something and a somewhere "beyond"?

The imagination is original; and it is not original. This paradox Poe could never resolve. Perhaps his most concise statement is in some of the "Marginalia" of 1844, wherein, discussing the *"pure Imagination,"* he noted that the work of the imagination is, first of all, to "combine things hitherto uncombined; the compound . . . partaking, in character, of beauty, or sublimity, in the ratio of the respective beauty or sublimity of the things combined"; these are, nonetheless, simply to be regarded as restatements of "previous combinations." Secondly, "the admixture of two elements results in a something that has nothing of the qualities of one of them, or even nothing of the qualities of either. . . . Thus, the range of Imagination is unlimited. Its materials extend throughout the universe." [18]

By a curious twist of his critical terminology, Poe discussed imaginative originality under the heading of the "mystic." This issue led him into some confusion: he had difficulty adjusting one view, as derived from Baron Bielfeld's *Elements of Universal Erudition,* that the mind can know nothing outside its own experience (therefore, the imagination is a chimera of the self) and that, contrariwise, the mind does receive impulses from the Ideal which it can reduce to shape and metaphor.[19] In other words, the mind, or imagination, cannot know the world outside itself, and it can. The imagination is supernatural, and it is mundane. Or: the world is itself insensible to its own dissociation and atomism, and so too are most men in it; the poet, however, is so keenly aware of this dislocation of parts within the whole that he attempts, imaginatively, to put the universe as an idea back together again. Poe considered this faculty and exercise of the poet or artist as "invention": the creative imagination makes the infinitely diverse knowables assume some conjunction and order. Poetry was, for Poe, the supreme act of inventive conjoining, and it was "mystic," as Schlegel had demonstrated beforehand, because it could convey only a suggestive or even ambiguous meaning.[20]

A poem, or for that matter any act of the imagination, is really two poems or acts: there is the primary expression or "story"—that the generality of readers can receive; and there is the "mystic or secondary expression" (conforming to the Coleridgean distinction of the secondary from the primary imagination) which Poe defined in his review of Moore's *Alciphron*: "With each note of the lyre is heard a ghostly, and not always a distinct, but an august and soul-exalting *echo*. In every glimpse of beauty presented, we catch, through long and wild vistas, dim bewildering visions of a far more ethereal beauty *beyond*."[21] The aim of poetry is to penetrate the barrier of resistant fact or the merely ostensible relationship of things and enter the range of the Unknowable—a range which, in another phrasing of the idea, Poe relegated to the limbo of illusion.

Yet this paradox and confusion were not major questions in romantic critical thinking. The solution was really made on the basis that what the mind perceived was something quite different from what the imagination made into art. Art was a different reality, a "something *from ourselves*." The imaginative insight and action was a "something from within" back upon the object which had given the imagination its first stimulus; "we imbue the object," Washington Allston wrote, "making it correspond to a *reality* within us."[22] In the subject-object relationship, the object achieves artistic reality only by a subject's perceiving it and making it known. What Poe further attempted to show (with the whole Coleridgean logic behind him) was that there is some mysterious, indefinable faculty, inherent in all men however varying in its intensity. Owing to this universal, innate principle all men can basically agree on what constitutes human or poetic truth. The ultimate finality and proof of this agreement are not in nature or in changeless ideal forms, but in men.

Poe's aesthetic principles simply put this faculty and principle farther inward. He removed it beyond history or science and allotted it only to an "Eden" which the artist or true lover of beauty can know. So far, in fact, did he remove it from the world of cause and effect that only in the destruction of that substantive world could the artist, or poet, find his center and thereby build his imaginative vision of reality. Only that special endowment of originality gave man the power to penetrate the actual world and create ever anew, each time the poem was written or the work of art was made, something-other than what the object or idea once was, not because the object or idea changes the mind nor because the imagination subjectively makes the thing into its own image, but because the imagination is able to make something wholly new: the poem, the painting, the sculpture, the musical composition never existed before.[23]

A poem is therefore the imagination's report on that exploration and comprehension; it becomes a symbolic construct of Unity, but it should not be taken as *being* that Unity. A poem is not "like" the Unity; it is an illusion or a "something about" that Unity. This is an important distinction which keeps the poem or language from ever becoming "real." The poem is a report by the imagination, but it is not what the imagination perceived. Words and language are man's reminder of his failure ever to make his own cognition real.

The logical end to this question regarding what poetry is and does is either failure or skepticism. The activity of the imagination is toward a powerful sense of the world's cohesion and unity as that world displays itself to the mind. Yet, contrariwise, as D. G. James has remarked, the "movement of the poetic mind . . . is towards a powerful sense of the world's limits; but it is compelled by an inward necessity to try to penetrate beyond those limits, and therefore to involve itself in inevitable defeat."[24] Skepticism is the realization that if words are not "real" in their conveyance of idea, then nothing is real; the poem and the imagination are illusory.

Poe could never escape the implications of this dilemma: either the imagination is real and reports reality in real words which have some durable meaning, or there is a world of fact that, though words are not "real," forever resists any means of bridging between itself and the mind of man. In the later "Philosophy of Composition" Poe tried to reduce one verbal reality (that of the imagination) to understandable terms of another (skepticism or human rationality); the analysis attempted to retrace rationally what had once occurred imaginatively by means of "The Raven." But, fully to appreciate the analysis, one must be where Poe was when he wrote the essay—on the other side of the imaginative journey on which the poem had taken him; yet one need not know the poem at all. "The interest of an analysis," Poe confessed in "The Philosophy of Composition," ". . . is quite independent of any real or fancied interest in the thing analyzed."[25] The analysis or reconstruction is not the poem; each is a separate exercise, one of the imagination, the other of the skeptical intellect.

If, therefore, poetry is finally beyond analysis, if it is not subject to the norms of inquiry and judgment, then what is its domain and what should it do? Poetry, as Coleridge stated before Poe, aimed at "awakening the mind's attention from the lethargy of custom, and directing it to the loveliness and the wonders of the world before us."[26] It was the action of the imagination outside itself and it reached toward endowing objects with existence and with relationship. Just as primitive man took for granted that his visible world was alive with voices and spirits, so the poet engages in a series of imaginative readings of earth. Ruskin's pathetic fallacy is not a "fallacy" at all but the demonstrative ascription of continuity and existence to sensible form around us. As Bacon long ago and Whitehead more recently have shown, there cannot be "just an apple" or "just a crocus" in a toneless, fragmented reality. Sensible objects are not fixed and dead.[27] They are brought to life and made known to us by acts of the poetic imagination. This act is a difficult and complex ritual which presumes to render the material world, not to the sense or rational faculties, but to itself. But the poem was not so much the act or ritual as it was two acts of perception: one was the poet's, the other was the reader's. The two joined in order to make the poem, for without completing that metaphoric and symbolic cycle the poem had no existence.

5

In the language of poetry might be the answer to the question of whether objects are real or whether they become real because a mind "thinks" reality into them. The romantic poet, or any artist for that matter, faced the Cartesian dilemma of the relationship between thinker and object, mind and matter. Locke had long ago failed to answer the question of whether the mind knows an object or whether the mind is confined only to its own consciousness and thus, as Hume demonstrated, is lodged totally within its own illusion.

This, then, was the rift of nearly two hundred years and extended from Lockean rationalism to Coleridgean idealism. The implications of this rift were, for Poe, enormous. With hardly a question he assumed that there was a split between the mind and reality and that separate functions of the mind made known one or the other: the understanding or the rational faculties supplied the mind with sense impulses and, eventually, with knowledge of the world; the imagination, that other faculty (with its two aspects which we have already seen) of perception beyond mere resistant fact, offered enticements to and then visions of the infinite, the ideal. The imagination may take its start from and even overlap the rational understanding; but the understanding can never encroach on the special domain of imaginative comprehension. In Locke's epistemology the charts and boundaries of the rational mind were so clearly defined that an Age of Good Sense was content to remain within them.

It was not Locke's separation of the faculties which was so much at fault; the special weakness of his ideas in which a century put its trust was the "tabula rasa" theory, the concept that the mind enters the world as a blank on which life wrote the lessons of "experience." Epistemology and psychology were thus happily joined — only to stimulate further confusion. At this point the German idealists and, more especially for Poe, Coleridge showed that the process or the "how" of knowing might be distinguished from the "what" of the mind's knowledge. The language question might be a means of solving this dilemma: for the rationalist words are not "real" because they are the links the mind establishes both sensorily and intellectually with the external world which, anteriorly, had impinged upon it; words are simply "made." For the romantic like Coleridge and Poe words are "real" because they are the inevitable, organic result of the mind's and the imagination's apprehension of itself and reality. Or, stated another way, the post-Lockean made words only fictions of things; the idealist, from Coleridge through Emerson to Poe, assumed that words are not only images of natural facts but signs of essences and absolutes. One may find the statements for this concept where he may — in Emerson's chapter on "Language" in *Nature* or in Horace Bushnell's Introductory Discourse on language in his *God in Christ;* whatever the location, in Poe as elsewhere, words were more than splendid fictions and signs; they could become the only reality man knew; all else was illusion.[28]

Poe, for his own ill or good, was part logician and part psychologist, part philosopher and part semanticist. He inherited and then elaborated a crux in the nature of cognition which he was never able to solve. The idealist or organicist, as we have seen, considered that language was "real" not only because it was the only way the mind could make things and its own ideas known to itself but because words were the inevitable necessity of the interaction of the mind on the world and of the world on mind. The word "stone" must, of all possibilities for naming that object, be in English the word "stone."

But the language-problem became acute when, however, the word "stone" need no longer have any relationship with the object stone; words could become stimuli for and avenues of meaning between mind and mind and might never again need referring to the object stone. One need never see a stone nor know what weeping is to be able to conceive of a "weeping stone." On this condition of divorcing language from the objects they denote, words can become anything the user of words wants them to be.

Thus any word had a double purpose and existence. On the one hand, a word had a very immediate, denotative meaning; it was a divisible thing of sounds and precise demonstration in dictionaries. On the other hand, the word was a "something-other," a suggestiveness, an abstraction, and a way into the farther range of perception beyond logic and beyond the normal discourse of man. By means of the poetic or incantatory process, the imaginative response of any reader could be enticed toward an ultimate symbolic meaning which defied the language of prose or rationality to define. Yet, all the while, this farther range of expression and thought was continually under the review of a critical, logic-making intelligence which was, of necessity, using the very same words, in whatever differing contexts, that had been employed in the poetic or imaginative discourse.

In addition to this view that language, even the same words, might have double functions, whether as precise meaning or as suggestive incitement to abstract, imaginative thought, Poe further complicated the language problem by conceiving that a poet could make words exist in a kind of third or separate dimension: a poet could make words, in the highly variable connotativeness of poetry, mean anything he might want. He could precondition what response the reader should have to the mood, texture, idea of a poem, and he could, even more, induce the same responses in all readers of his poem. If readers had differing ideas about or responses to a poem, then the fault was the poet's; the poem was not correctly made. Poe's savage attacks on his fellow poets were based, in most respects, on this assumption that poems are murky and confusing simply because poetasters have not properly exercised the techniques of their craft. Poems can even be original, quite unlike poems ever made before, by virtue of a poet's revitalizing the old or even inventing a new symbolism, a new use of language, out of which absolutely new poetic meaning could be obtained.

There was, nonetheless, a limit even to this imaginative freedom. Any word or symbolism, however revitalized or invented, had to be anchored in the world of sense perception; its beginning had to be in some objectification which men know as "real" in place and time. Thereafter, the creative imagination could proceed anywhere, so long as its symbolic order maintained some coherent and known relationship with the intelligible order of sense and reality. The stone is, in this context, not only a key to a sensible image (the object "stone") which should call up in every hearer or reader of the word a precise image of that object but is also capable of being joined to other words and ideas to set up in every hearer or reader a pathway and process toward some knowable, ultimate idea of which the stone-idea was only an impetus or a very small part. In poetry, where language becomes almost totally metaphoric and symbolic, this implicit connotativeness of words should mean that all readers of the same poem might, within certain indeterminate limits, obtain the same idea and response the words were meant to convey. Critics might carp and dispute, but the phrase, "the weeping stone," if set properly in the design and progress of the poem, should be universally the same in making an idea known through the communication of language.[29]

Here indeed was a paradox. Are words names for things or are they names for our *ideas* of things? If poetry were the symbolic expression only of our ideas of things, then the substantial world had been left behind or destroyed. The weeping stone is not an object; it is a metaphoric transference of the idea of weeping to a thing which has no power of itself to weep or feel any emotion. Is, then, the idea of a weeping stone existent only in the mind which is able to arrange words for the purpose of conveying the picture and the idea of a stone that weeps? The phrase and the attendant idea must lie either in the mind that can establish a set of congruences or in some extrasensory region neither of the mind nor of fact wherein the very words themselves have metaphoric existence.

Poetic language is therefore a denial of reality or the submergence of whatever seems real in the idea out of which the poem is made. Yet the destruction is only partial: it is the annihilation of the flat "given" world which threatens at all time to exercise its brute control over what the mind subsumes under meaning. Poetic language exists not in substance nor in the poetic mind which may have made the poem but in a neutral world, a kind of farther dimension wherein the mind or imagination functions as mediating between external reality and itself. Language, to rephrase our problem, is real and not real at the same time; in expressing an idea a poet is not expressing *his* view of that idea, for words are not inward nor even, as it were, mental. The neutral region of poetic language may, however, be so permitted to eschew any normal word patterns which designate the real that a poet might even be permitted to invent his own vocabulary—a vocabulary, it must be insisted, that could not be altogether his.

A century before these questions were fronting the Romantic mind Jonathan Edwards had raised the problem of the word as real, and he answered it in nearly the same terms. The word was, for Edwards, not itself "real," but it was a comprehensible relationship established, in a variable realm of knowledge, between man here and God there. The image of the spider held over the candle-flame in "Sinners in the Hands of an Angry God" was not the actual condition of man but was the knowable situation of man held by a mere filament over hell.[30] The only difference between the language theories, if so they may be termed, of Edwards and

Poe is that Edwards conceived the word as inevitably and necessarily *that* word, whether "spider," "candle," or "God's wrath"; and only through that one articulate word could man establish any knowable relationship with the infinite. For Poe, language was, however well man might agree on meanings, a world of itself, neither man's intelligible mind nor observed fact; the word or phrase did not possess a meaning; it obtained meaning the moment it was put in an arrangement with other words to form an apprehension. Prose conformed to a logic and habit of man's agreeing minds; poetry should obey only its own logic: whatever the poet made of language was ever a new creation.

In concluding these generalizations on poetic theory we might well consider one final point: if the poem exists in a neutral region, outside the world and mind of the poet and basically outside the private mind and substantial world of the reader, then what is going on when a poem is, as it were, releasing its meaning through the special, even the unique operations of language which the poet has somehow ordained? Poe reasoned, from such a question, that if he could find the norms of mental behavior in that special response men call "poetic" or imaginative, then he might be able to set forth valid distinctions between good poems and bad poems.

A poem, on any subject whatever, initiates a process which impels or drives the mind beyond even what the words themselves connote. The poet did not make that process; he may have been quite wholly unaware of precisely what he was doing when he was writing the poem — an unawareness of which Poe himself offers a superb example in his own "Philosophy of Composition." This process, for all that Poe tried to make a consistent logic of it, is not regular nor continuous. It may begin, initiate a train of thought or poetic response, and then skip any number of intermediaries or blocks and subsequently, even all unaware, reach a stage of comprehension beyond anything the words themselves can convey. Poetic language can operate so effectively in that midway or neutral phase of cognition that the ultimate and perhaps farthest range of poetry is a potential wordlessness; it was at this stage of music or the ideal fusion of word and sound that mere verbalized meaning would be of no consequence. "Meaning" would be in that pure neutrality of which poetic language is the only possible expression. Poetry would no longer be a thing or a sense experience but a unique drama in which the poetic imagination engaged itself differently each time a poem was written.

Poe attempted a blend of eighteenth-century rationalistic epistemology and nineteenth-century or Coleridgean ontology. Knowledge and being — these he sought to merge into a final construct which would be art or the expression of the imagination. He found most to his liking Coleridge's profound insight into the dual nature of the imagination and especially the activity of the imagination in the act of poetic or artistic creation. But he tried to go farther than Coleridge by setting up the imagination-in-process of the mind-journey along which the imagination could move from the illusion that is this sensible world to the fuller perception that is the truer reality beyond. Language was one of man's ways of making that journey; and though the language problem might never be solved, Poe continued his experiments, as we may now see, in his later poetry, in his short stories, in *Arthur Gordon Pym,* and in his philosophic criticism. They were all stages in a design which meant for Poe a struggle to reach a unitary vision, not necessarily of the absolute, but of some comprehensible system wherein everything, prose and verse, real and unreal, mind and substance, somehow cohered. The poetry of his later years, to which we may now turn, is one of the major expressions of that hope and that vision.

III

"The Raven" and Afterward: A Poetry beyond Meaning

The occasional poems Poe wrote between the 1831 volume and "The Raven" of 1845 are not of major importance. Most of them are variations on the poetic mind investigating itself or, to put the matter another way, they are studies of the disintegrating poetic imagination. We meet, for the first time in the mind of Poe, that condition in Romantic thought wherein the "I" cannot adequately inquire into or posit its own being but continually makes external reality, as it were, "stand for" it. In order, therefore, for the "I" to have anything to explore or write about, the imagination seeks to transform the world of external reality almost wholly into its own image. This hypostatized self can thereby do anything and go through any imaginative process and remain all the while untouched. These poems are versions of an externalized consciousness; but we never really know whose consciousness it is.

Two subordinate themes emerge in these poems of the middle years. One is a religious impulse which continually urges the will either to submerge itself entirely or somehow transcend its own mortal limitations. The other is the pictorial necessity: as his career developed (and especially as his short stories displaced poetry as an act of the symbolic imagination), Poe more and more sought physical embodiments for his abstract ideas; and once he had found such a representation, the object became a thing-in-itself and its attendant idea almost nothing. He was apparently seeking a way of entering the range of the visual arts wherein word and image might receive concrete exemplification. We may now take these two themes in order.

Poe was fond of quoting Joseph Glanville's aphorism (if it were ever by Glanville; it has so far escaped detection) that man need not yield himself to death "save only through the weakness of his feeble will." In the short story "Ligeia" Poe symbolized the power of the will to triumph over mere mortality.[1] The will is, in these poems of the middle years, not so much the religious concept of willing one's way to an understanding of God as it is of the artist's privilege to "will" anything he wants from reality. The will is a renunciation of visible reality and the recasting of the world wholly in terms of the most intimate visions of the self, even the power to make reality a direct embodiment of the self.

There emerged several ways by which the poetic will or imagination might embody this new demand of the "I" or the will. One was some new or different poetic rhetoric as a means of conveying this selfhood. Formerly, the monologues of "Tamerlane" or of "Al Aaraaf" or the songs in the early volumes had been adequate projections of this sentient self into the poems. Now Poe sought a further method of presenting a protagonist who might be, at the same time, both in and outside the poem.

Yet a protagonist could never fully serve Poe's purposes. He could not achieve that imaginative distance which even Byron in *Childe Harold* or Shelley in the "Stanzas Written in Dejection" had been able to obtain. He could invent only pseudo-real versions of himself which were merely aspects of his own titanic, and forlorn, will doing anything with reality it wanted. All the while, however, Poe was aware of the dangers of a didactic or autobiographical method; to avoid the mistakes for which he castigated Bryant or Longfellow, he more and more contrived a private vocabulary or an involved little language which, as we shall see in "Ulalume," served to conceal the self in such an elaborate masquerade that every act and idea had to be translated into an intricate anagram. The poetic will so longed to overcome the resistant world of fact that it more and more abandoned common rhetoric as a means of expression.

The other method of projecting the imagination as an all-powerful will was to move farther away from direct representation of the world and toward an extravagant pictorialism. Language itself did not seem to be able to project the mood or the impression; words were not of themselves sad or joyous or red or white. But if a dramatic and brilliant scene could be drawn, then the very picture itself would become an experience for the reader; as through a kaleidoscope, he might watch the vividly charged details and from them obtain the poetic idea which words of themselves were not sufficient to convey. We might now consider some of the poems written between 1831 and 1845 and see how they both prepared for and yet were curiously apart from "The Raven" of the latter year.

With "The Haunted Palace" (1839) Poe began virtually where he had left off with the 1831 volume. The poem is, as Poe stated, about "a mind haunted by phantoms — a disordered brain."[2] It is not about Poe's mind; it is about some mind or psyche seen from inside the mind itself and describing not only its present state of being but how that state came to exist. The "valley," or the world of the inner, subjective self, is "green"; it is inhabited only by "good angels"; and the "palace" is "fair" and "radiant." The world, in all its whiteness, is wholly good and innocent like the mind which inhabits it. "Thought" is monarch and can make the world conform at every point to its inner willing. Therefore, the union of "thought" and the world form a "fabric" that is, of course, very "fair." The second stanza elaborates this brilliant color scheme which the dominating self is able to see and to impose on the world: "Banners yellow, glorious golden,/ On its roof did float and flow." These colors of "Time long ago" signify the power of the imagination to create its total enchantment. Into this valley, as the third stanza changes the direction of the thought, came some "Wanderers" who looked "Through two luminous windows" (the eyes of the monarch Thought) and there saw all forms and "Spirits moving musically"; mind and body exist in harmony, and all exterior reality is so far under the control of Thought.

A sharp break occurs in the elusive fifth stanza. The one thing Thought or the self cannot control is time ("the old time entombed"); the mind loses all power over itself and over its world in the destruction wrought by "evil things" in black which destroy the valley, and the "I" has succumbed to the devastating assault of elements outside itself which, in the end, it could not control. The poem, therefore, demonstrates Poe's growing pictorial necessity: abstractions and ideas become translated into tableaux, a set of stylized and formalized pictures which enact the drama. The mind is a castle; the sovereign is Thought; the windows are the eyes; the attendant ideas are Echoes and graces, and the inimical world of reality outside, which for a time exists in complete subservience to the will of Thought, finally overwhelms and destroys the mind. The treatment is virtually a flat allegory; Poe would consider the same theme a number of times afterward, more notably in "The Fall of the House of Usher."

The "Sonnet — Silence" (1840), an experiment in a fifteen-line form which might anticipate the experimental sonnet-form Meredith used in his sequence "Modern Love," considers "the two ideas of the absolute and the personified Night," or, in another phrasing, the dual or twin nature of existence. Every idea or form exists both as an abstraction and as a body which is "incorporate." "Silence" is dual: "sea and shore," or water and land, and body and soul; everything is a representative or type of the twin nature of the universe. The silence of death as we know it is but a mere simulacrum of the absolute annihilation in death. The ultimate silence is a total nothingness beyond reality and God — and therefore, happily, beyond our knowing. With death or "Silence" we are actually concerned with versions of the Self — the self in mortal death and the self in absolute death or ultimate non-being. Poe posits a monistic dualism or a double unity: things and ideas are, and they are not. He establishes "A type of twin entity"; that is, an entity which can be itself and, simultaneously, something else. Or, to put the idea another way, everything has an essence, its unique distinguishing thing-in-itself; yet this essence contains another and still another essence until we approach the absolute essence of all essences. In the farthest range of speculation, far beyond mere appearances, would be a "silence" or death which would be the ultimate negation of life itself. Death as man knows it is merely a "type" of that unknown condition. Being and non-being are the necessary polarities of existence; we know so little about "silence" or non-being; do we know any more about life or being?

"The Conqueror Worm" (1843) was a dramatization of the abstract speculation contained in the "Sonnet — Silence." The poem considers God's likeness to man or, to state the proposition another way, God's willing His own death and annihilation. The universe consists of two parts, man and "not-man," or man and God (for God is not-man). Man, created by God, exists in these "lonesome latter years" when, as in the medieval views of the Apocalypse, the design of God is approaching its climax. The universe or the "theatre" contains only the endless clash of warring elements: the angels sit helpless and mute; God has so long abandoned any attempt at direction or intervention in His creation that His forces are "Mimes" or "Mere puppets." This is, therefore, the universe of chaos from which God has withdrawn His thought, and the only major purpose of the beings in it is to chase a "Phantom" known as "Invisible Wo." Into this senseless world appears a "crawling shape" which destroys human life. For a time the beings of God are stunned and inactive; then, shocked into action, the angels rouse themselves and end this tragedy of "Man."

"Dream-Land" (1844) considers the same theme from still another point of view. Where "The Conqueror Worm" presented the apocalypse of a dual universe, "Dream-Land" returns more nearly to the "Sonnet — Silence" in order to explore the idea of existence "out of SPACE — out of TIME." We begin with "an Eidolon, named NIGHT"; we have come to "an ultimate dim Thule," a place where everything that exists is in a state of disintegration, as though all matter and form were returning to its primordial condition of mere atomicity: "Mountains toppling evermore/ Into seas without a shore." The dead "pass the wanderer by — / White-robed forms of friends long given,/ In agony, to the Earth. . . ." Here the abstract idea of Night or non-being reigns forever; thus to have gone there and to have returned marks a journey into the very mystery of the universe before God had formed space and time.

The poem, like others of Poe's middle years when poetry was not his chief concern, was an attempt to write a psalm without any dominant religious impulse. Psalms, chants, and visions, whether joyous or despairing, posit some relationship, however tenuous, between a self and its God: the despairing psalmist cries out to his God, pleads for knowledge, or resignedly condemns himself to darkness. Poe employed all the devices of the psalm and the apocalyptic vision and omitted two essential elements: a worshipper and a God. Thus there is no struggle and no agony because the one who cried out really came back from "Silence" and from the "ultimate dim Thule"; and God is only the law of chaos and endless meaninglessness like the endless motion in the third circle of Dante's hell.

What began as an apocalypse ended in the picturesque, a series of formally arranged scenes which were intended to symbolize death and the condition of utter nothingness beyond our knowing. This habit of mind suggests Poe's strong poetic ties to the eighteenth century: the picturesque convention, whether in Salvator Rosa or Thomas Gray, was a means of ordering and methodizing nature into the associational patterns out of which "meaning" could be deduced. The sense-school of aesthetics and Burke's theories on the Sublime were means of stimulating the mind of the reader or viewer to go behind the picture to that Essence or totality of man's thought which all art contained. Poe's poems of this genre were what might be termed a "picturesque of consciousness", that is, he sought to investigate and to present conditions of mental awareness — life, death, being, non-being — by means of a series of topographical descriptions or apocalyptic visions which, as in the greatest moments of religious expression and ecstasy, would transcend the world of the commonplace and reach toward the infinite and the eternal. Unfortunately, Poe was confined to conventional religious and allegorical designs: the self is a castle, death is a valley, thought is an angelic creator, evil is a black monster, death is the blackness of night, and final annihilation is the "ultimate dim Thule." He had not yet discovered some potential variant on this conventional symbolism, as Melville did with the color white in *Moby-Dick,* or he could not find fresh ways of treating long-established symbolic referents, as Hawthorne did with the color red in *The Scarlet Letter.*

2

"The Raven" is the fulfillment of these poems written in the twelve or thirteen years since the publication of the *Poems* of 1831. In it are the uses of pictorialism to suggest the inner workings of a disturbed consciousness and also the religious necessity, the drive of a consciousness toward understanding. We need not concern ourselves with the debate over Poe's sources and borrowings, whether the talking bird came from Dickens' *Barnaby Rudge* or whether the verse form was borrowed from Mrs. Browning's "Lady Geraldine's Courtship" (a debt which Poe may have silently acknowledged in his dedication of *The Raven* volume of poems "To Miss Elizabeth Barrett Barrett, of England"). These matters have been sufficiently discussed or even settled to allow us to pursue questions of the meaning of the poem and its relevance to Poe's poetic thought and practice.

A year or so after the poem was published in January 1845, Poe published "The Philosophy of Composition," an exposition of the poem-in-process which, in its own time as in after years, cast a little light and much confusion on the poem. We have had occasion to consider that essay in terms of Poe's theories of poetry and of art; here we might briefly mention that the essay was more an attempt to outline Poe's view of what poetry should be and should do than it was a forthright demonstration of how "The Raven" came to be. Thus the poem is made, in its after history, to conform to a preconceived philosophy of poetic composition — as if poems were written out of a schema or philosophy! Nonetheless, there are inevitable clues in the essay to what the poem was meant to be and how it came to have the form in which it was afterward resolved. Poe could not help admitting us to the inner rationale of how the poem was made.

The major clue which the essay provides is contained in a long sentence buried almost unobtrusively in the argument Poe was developing that works of art are constructed with their ends or climaxes always well in the artist's mind from the very beginning. We read, in part:

> I saw that I could make the first query propounded by the lover — the first query to which the Raven should reply "Nevermore" — that I could make this first query a commonplace one — the second less so — the third still less, and so on — until at length the lover, startled from his original *nonchalance* by the melancholy character of the word itself . . . propounds them half in superstition and half in that species of despair which delights in self-torture — propounds them . . . because he experiences a frenzied pleasure in so modeling his questions as to receive from the *expected* "Nevermore" the most delicious because the most intolerable of sorrow.[3]

The clue leads us to an assumption that the student or protagonist moves from the real world of dimension and time to a chaotic, fictive world wherein nothing exists but the inner will and its morbid fantasies. Let us first follow the narrative action of the poem.

The opening of the poem presents us with an action which has long been under way. We are soon aware that much has occurred already: the young man has lost his loved Lenore, and the shock of that loss is not long past. Only by endurance or some act of will has he been able to maintain his balance or sanity. It is in such a perilously maintained balance, and in a room heavy with the remembrance of Lenore, that we met him on the December night, a night which of itself is not unusual in Virginia: a sleety storm and the gusty winds. There is nothing particularly unusual or *outré* about the student's room: as a titular goddess of wisdom, the bust of Pallas reposes on a ledge above the outer door. The student has sophisticated aesthetic tastes, for the windows are covered with heavy, lustrous drapes, and cushions are placed about the room in the style of the eighteen-forties. And the hour is midnight.

Into this special moment there is intruded a discordant rapping on the outer door. The student's first impulse is, in Poe's explanation, "adopting the half-fancy that it was the spirit of his mistress that knocked." He throws open the door and finds no one outside; at this moment, half of relief and half of disappointment, the young man assumes the mood logical in such a situation, the mood of jocularity that there should be any such disturbance at all, whether real or imaginary. He returns to his studies; then comes the rapping again. On this occasion the student goes to the window and throws open the outer lattice,

. . . when, with many a flirt and flutter,
In there stepped a stately Raven of the saintly days of yore;
Not the least obeisance made he; not a minute stopped or stayed he;
But, with mien of lord or lady, perched above my chamber door —
Perched upon a bust of Pallas just above my chamber door. . . .

At once, the jocular, humorous mood of the student is increased. Expecting, though not trusting, that the sound of knocking might have been the spirit of the dead Lenore, the sudden presence of an ungainly black bird is almost shattering. The lines quoted above are not how the Raven looked as he came into the room but the way the Raven appeared to the student in his amazement. The student feels such surprise to have a black embodiment of reality when he had hoped for a visitation of a ghost that his mood of jocularity increases, quite naturally, to one of hilarity. At once he takes the view that the Raven is a freak and a joke and he makes sport of it. He propounds the first in a series of three major questions: "Tell me what thy lordly name is on the Night's Plutonian shore!" The pompous and inflated rhetoric of this query is intended to underline the student's disbelief that the moment is real and, concurrently, his normal impulse to ridicule that which seems so very odd. The next stanza concludes this phase of the student's drama through what Poe termed "superstition," or the doubt that what is taking place should be taken at all seriously:

For we cannot help agreeing that no living human being
Ever yet was blessed with seeing bird above his chamber door—
Bird or beast upon the sculptured bust above his chamber door,
With such name as "Nevermore."

This stanza also concludes the first half of the poem and marks a sharp break in the action and the mood of the student.

Poe boasted in "The Philosophy of Composition" that his poem was only 108 lines long; he was also mindful that the action of the poem broke exactly at the end of line 54, wherein the mood of laughter and freakish humor turned into a quite different temper. The second half of the poem is action in disorder. The student quickly loses hold of himself and on reality: the bird's monotonous intoning of one senseless word drives him into reverie, into the deepest recesses of his being into which even the shattering impact of the death of Lenore had not plunged him. From this point onward, both the questions which the student asks and the one-word answer he receives are not "real" at all, that is, they are not voiced; they are elements in an interior psychic debate going forward in the young man's mind. What the Raven replies is merely what the student himself wants to hear, must hear as more and more he enters the dark, subliminal regions of his melancholy which leads toward madness. The Raven as an object above the chamber door has ceased to exist; the poem becomes, in the latter fifty-four lines, a dialogue of two voices or sides of the youthful protagonist who asks those latter two questions and receives only his own interpretive answer in the bird's one-word reply: "Is there . . . balm in Gilead?" (or, is there any further release from anguish?) and "Tell this soul with sorrow laden if . . ./ It shall clasp a radiant maiden whom the angels name Lenore?" (or, is there life after death?). These questions and their inevitable answers mark the student's shift from a perilously maintained balance of his faculties to their total disruption — a disruption which has taken place not because the Raven has done or said anything but because the protagonist has put into those questions and into the answers his most profound terror not only that Lenore is irrevocably lost in death but that he himself exists in a state of death-in-life: the line between human sanity and insanity, between life and death, is virtually imperceptible. The Raven, the night storm, the bust of Pallas were earlier conformable to the trusted routine of existence; they were facts to be depended upon to have place and continuity. But under the sudden impact of the strange and the terrible on the student's mind, these objects were turned into the symbols of his maddened mind; they have acted as part of the world which has driven the student from its early rationalistic consciousness, then into the terror of the hitherto concealed subconsciousness, and back again to consciousness, but now it is a consciousness that the student is utterly maddened by his melancholy, and the terror is that he knows he has been driven to madness. At the end, all of these signs and objects are frozen, just as the protagonist's mind is forever fixed in the inscrutable awareness that he will never again have control over his mind and that what we call sanity is only the veil that separates us from the total, and insane, mystery that lies all around us:

And the Raven, never flitting, still is sitting, *still* is sitting
On the pallid bust of Pallas just above my chamber door;
And the eyes have all the seeming of a demon's that is dreaming,
And the lamp-light o'er him streaming throws his shadow on the floor. . . .

The poem is, therefore, a set of stages in the process of self-knowledge or the power of human consciousness to be aware not only of its being but even of its non-being. Consciousness can be destroyed; but the destruction can itself become a deeper self-consciousness. At the beginning of the poem the young man is an innocent: even though he has lost Lenore and presumably knows death, he is ignorant and untried. Everything was outside; nothing had really happened to him. But as the drama proceeds and the terror increases, the question of the student's existence or Being itself dominates: he asks whether or not there is any sensitivity or perception in life which is beyond the barriers of ignorance we must endure in this existence. The replies, though in the croaking voice of the Raven, are really from the innermost consciousness and even the subconsciousness of the student: his life is like all life; there is a perpetual war between sentience within and insentient chaos in the outer world; there is not even the comfortable illusion of ultimate sentience in or beyond death. Being itself becomes an illusion, a something we posit and live by in this existence in order better to endure. Whatever order the world obtains is from within, is pure subjectivism, is, as it were, imposed from within the "room" of the student. When this order is disrupted, the mind loses all hold on itself and on reality.

Once the mind loses that sense of selfhood, however illusory that sense may be, it is destroyed; the poem is a symbolic destruction of the mind by the impact of reality upon it. The poem is also raising the central question in nineteenth-century or romantic symbolism: what is the relation between reality and the mind's ideas about reality? There is nature, and there is mind, two polarities which may be separate and yet interact in the endless program of symbolic consciousness. This consciousness is a way of making the world intelligible, not from the mind alone or from a positing of the merely sensible world which makes impressions on the mind called "ideas," but from the action of the adjudicating power known as the imagination. In romantic formulations, such as those we have already seen in Coleridge, the imagination, whether primary or secondary, was a third or medial range of understanding, neither entirely of the mind nor of the sensible world. So long as the response between reality and imagination, on the one hand, and that between the mind and imagination, on the other, could be maintained, the romantic artist found expressive means of rendering ideas and experience in vivid, determinable ways: Hawthorne's red letter and Melville's whiteness of the whale are representative cases in point. But, once a rift appeared or a breakdown occurred at any moment in the process of the mind's finding expressive terms in the symbols which, consciously or not, mediated between reality and itself, then the symbolism became meaningless or was destroyed altogether.

Poe's "Raven" was a historic crisis in romantic artistic creation. In hardly more than a moment, wherein the Raven symbolized for the imagination its reach toward a further understanding of the illusion of reality and the painful awareness of nothing on the "other side" of reality, the symbolic perspective opened — as wide as Ishmael ever saw from the crow's nest or as deep as Hester Prynne ever saw into the abysses of sin and revenge. Then, all suddenly, the moment was gone; and Poe ended the poem, not because he believed that a poem should not much exceed a hundred lines but because his own symbolic imagination could go no further nor say anything more. The bird, the bust of Pallas, the light remained fixed in immobility. Poe termed it the "soul," but it was the imagination which

> . . . from out that shadow that lies floating on the floor
> Shall be lifted — nevermore!

The symbol had, for a moment, been able to transform reality. Then the sensible world remained resistant; reality was very real, and the shaping spirit withdrew from the final admission that it would have to remain content with conjuring the whole world according to its inner dream or allowing the imagination merely to report what outwardly it saw. Between the jocular first question, "Tell me what thy lordly name is on the Night's Plutonian shore," and the last question, the poetic imagination had caught fire and expressed the terror of loss of self and even of non-being. But the factual world remained fact and chaos; and the shaping spirit had nothing more to do. Poe admitted in "The Philosophy of Composition" that he wrote the climactic stanza first; if he did, then his penetration and his symbolic adventure were doomed from the outset.

Thus we can see the split in Poe's imaginative world: there were elements of reality, and there were faculties of the mind or imagination. Between them there ought to be a union or a point of coherence. At their best, his symbols are such mediations—the image of woman in "To Helen," the dramatic bird and its voice in "The Raven," the castle in "The Fall of the House of Usher," or the shifting reality in *Arthur Gordon Pym*. All the while he was erecting a theory to this fusion of mind and reality, the poetic enterprise was destroying any semblance of that unity, first, in the failure of the hypostatized "I" in the early poems to transform the world according to the necessities of the governing ego, and then in the inability to make a substitute "I," such as the student in "The Raven," itself proceed through the reordering of mind and reality. "The Raven" is a virtual admission of universal disparity: the imagination is lost in the shadow that lies upon the floor, while the inanimate objects, bird and bust, stare out in triumphant rigidity.

3

In his poetry Poe was never again able to effect a mediation between reality and imagination; the controlling self or the imaginative "I" could not act the role of Tamerlane and make all reality submissive to its will; and the very spell-weaving, the incantatory process of transforming the sensible world to poetic use, could not endlessly re-create the actual into meaningful symbolic objects; or, rather, it served only to render differing objects as the same thing — hypostatized extensions of a Poe-self. This imagining self steadily withdrew into the method of pictorialism or the free employment of natural objects to mean anything it wanted. A good example of this pictorial method is in "Ulalume."[4]

The subject of "The Raven" was a difficult one, namely, the mind's loss of any hold on reality or the steps toward imaginative madness. The subject of "Ulalume" is very simple: the longing of a weary widower for a second wife after the loss of his first, yet all the while fearful that he might not find a great love in the second marriage. The poem was not written to or about any of the ladies to whom Poe paid his addresses, either in 1847, the year the poem was written and published, or in any other year of his short life. It was composed as the result of a mood of "never-ending remembrance," a very profound mood and one that has produced distinguished poems by other poets. But Poe's trouble was that he was ashamed either of himself or the feelings he had, and thus he set the poem in an elaborate, and confusing, pictorial masquerade wherein the action and the natural objects are means of intruding between the reader and the idea. The pictorialism actually becomes all that the poem contains; Poe let natural objects engage in his drama for him. He need do nothing; they would do all.

The action of "Ulalume" is a night walk through terrain which, though Poe did much to create mystery, is quite recognizably that between Fordham, where Poe was living in the latter months of 1847, and Mamaroneck, where his wife Virginia was buried. It was through such a region that Poe took walks to Virginia's grave. The place names in the poem, however much they have been accredited to mystery and fabrication, are easily determinable. "Weir" is a reference to Robert Walter Weir, the Hudson River landscape painter who was quite popular in Poe's day and whose work Poe could have seen in New York and in the annuals and periodicals. Weir's best-known subject was the Hudson River area presented in wild, misty, weird, and tortured shapes; Poe was verbally describing the same territory between the Hudson River and Long Island Sound in similar terms. "Auber" is still another evocative place-name. It pertains to the still well-known French composer of ballets, Jean François Auber, whose "Lac des Fées" was popular in the eighteen-forties. The association of "Auber" with a "dim lake" and a "dank tarn" would readily conform to Poe's frenetic landscape of darkness and mist. Thus "Weir" and "Auber" associate themselves easily with the rolling stretches, broken by ponds and small inland lakes, between the Sound and the Hudson or along the route Poe followed in his lonely night walks to the cemetery in Mamaroneck.

The name "Yaanek" is slightly different: it was employed as a metaphor for the anguished soul of the protagonist whose "heart was volcanic"

> As the lavas that restlessly roll
> Their sulphurous currents down Yaanek
> In the ultimate climes of the pole. . . .

"Yaanek" is Mount Erebus, the name assigned to a recently discovered volcanic mountain in Antarctica; it is suggestive of the hot emotional undercurrent of the poet's emotions amid the chill of exterior reality. These are the elements in the heavy pictorialism of Poe's poem and, indeed, of Poe's latter poetic career.

As the dialogue between Psyche and the "I" is developed, the poem becomes a debate wherein we have, not two speakers but the double voice of the protagonist who, as a double self, body and soul, walks through this strange landscape on All Souls' Eve when the dead may exercise power among the living. This double being is, therefore, directed by the brilliantly shining planet Venus with her crescent shape distinctly seen; she is, of course, the patroness of love, and, as in the much earlier poem "Evening Star," her influence is much to be preferred to that of the moon who presides over the dead. Venus has just come through Leo, a position astrologically unfavorable to her (one might mention in passing that the astrological lore is as exact and as faithfully developed as that in Chaucer's "Knight's Tale"). Though Psyche, or the soul, mistrusts these happy portents, the "I" proceeds unabashed and unheeding through the misty enchantment. The soul warns of the baleful influence of the moon; the protagonist, however, brushes these omens aside: "This is nothing but dreaming:/ Let us on by this tremulous light!"

The physical self or the "I" acts as though it were a free agent capable of directing itself; Psyche, or the imagination, knows differently and keeps holding back as the dawn approaches and as the light begins slowly to break. Suddenly the "I" is brought up short at the end of a long avenue where he finds the "legended tomb" and is reminded of "*this* very night of last year." Both time, as memory, and place are terrifyingly present; and the "I" stands as lost and imaginatively destroyed as did the young student at the end of "The Raven."

The poem is more than an autobiographical moment, concealed behind an elaborate and rather absurd masquerade; it is a nightmare journey of a self which has been deluded into thinking that external reality is not real but can be shaped into anything the imagination decrees. The astrological forces are at first interpreted as manifestations of the controlling self throughout the cosmos; the universe is merely the self enlarged; at the end the protagonist has come to a spot where death exists as a fact and where place and time are not elements to be manipulated according to the mind's desire. The poem has therefore investigated the incapacity of poetry or of the imagination to do anything with or go beyond whatever the chaotic world of sense presents. The symbolic activity can do nothing, for everything is external to the self; and so the drama of the poem is all in terms of an objectified reality of which Psyche or the imagination is fully aware but which the rational "I" refuses to acknowledge until the end.

For all of Poe's protests against didacticism, we are lodged in nearly pure allegory or the didactic; the same is true of the ever-popular "Bells," a set of four variations on the ages of man — youth, love, maturity, and old age. The sounds of the bells are not poetic evocations of the idea of death or of man's life on earth; they are concrete representations of those ideas and exist in an easy, accredited identity between the representation and the concept. The allegorical method, for Poe or any other poet, is not bad in itself (despite the disfavor which the very term "allegory" denotes in our time); allegory was essentially a refuge or retreat from poetic activity on Poe's part and became not so much a concrete embodiment of an idea as mere word-spinning.

Allegory, as a method, further endangered Poe's poetic career because the major subject for poems in the last years was the same subject of the earlier years, namely, a highly personal, autobiographical self and its longing, despair, joy, and frustration. Of itself, the self as subject does not endanger poetry nor jeopardize a single poet's career; but it did in the case of Poe, because the "I" never changed, it never developed or matured; it knew and saw no more at the end of its poetic journey than it knew at the beginning. The only variation was that the protagonist became world-weary and aware that nothing, least of all love, endures. The allegorical objects of these strivings and yearnings were almost the same as they had been twenty years earlier: the moon, the sunken grave, the beautiful girl laid out for burial, the beautiful ladies who still have life are, except for certain rhetorical flourishes, a "Helen" whether it is Mrs. Sarah Helen Whitman (in the later "To Helen") or a Helen of Richmond or a Helen of Troy. The allegorized representations of Poe's happiness or despair might have existed anywhere or any time, but they did not: they existed only as repetitions of Poe's fictive self which, all the while it dramatized its own inward quest for understanding, it was the purpose and business of poetry to explore and project. Poe in the last years, in "Annabel Lee" and in "The Bells," was where he was at the beginning: the subject had varied hardly at all; only the technical virtuosity had so improved that more seemed to be said than really was.

4

These were the perils of the secondary or destructive imagination. It was impelled continually to reshape the world inwardly, that is, according to its own powerful, subjective awareness of or feeling about life, death, time, space, unity, or diversity. Yet this urgent necessity of the self to reach out and go beyond the veil of intrusive reality was constantly opposed and even blocked by the rational, the critical, the objective faculty which was itself a function of and quest for self-awareness. The two might have canceled each other out, except that the rational, the critical assumed control and redirected Poe's imaginative insights into the short stories and into the critical formulations.

Yet the further danger that this rationalizing tendency brought to the life of poetry was, as Yvor Winters has shown, that poetry eventually became a mere handmaiden to a poetic theory.[5] Poetry had almost no reason for being except that it might explore and explain the murky deliquescence of rule and poetic law. The trouble was multiplied when, if the rules were suspect or failed of successful application, the poetry collapsed under the sheer weight of poetic theory or "philosophy." The laws of effect, mood, tone, music, length of poems reached their culmination in such a piece of expansion and overwriting as these lines from "Annabel Lee," wherein, by means of repetition, each stanza coiled back on and absorbed its predecessor before it could move on again:

But we loved with a love that was more than love —
 I and my Annabel Lee —

With a love that the winged seraphs of heaven
  Coveted her and me.

. . . . .

But our love it was stronger by far than the love
  Of those who were older than we —
  Of many far wiser than we —
And neither the angels in heaven above,
  Nor the demons down under the sea,
Can ever dissever my soul from the soul
  Of the beautiful Annabel Lee.

By such terms poems could be written about anything, or nothing, at all. The poet need merely shift the emphasis or the special tonality of a poem one way or another and he might well have a poem on love, life, death, the lost love, the pure love, or anything. The usable, expressive metaphors became so interchangeable and ritualized that a word or poetic image could be manipulated to mean anything Poe wanted.

It was, however, this act of manipulation, or a theory about it, that made Poe's poetic career a crucial event in the history of Romanticism. As a citizen of his age, Poe held steadily to the view that the supersensual and imaginative faculties of man might be guides to truth and understanding far superior to the formal, divisive logic of rationalists like Descartes and Locke, or Alexander Pope. The rational faculty of man was not so much lower as it was merely a fragment of the total perceptive activity of man; poetry was a farther projection of understanding because it made the sensible faculty cohere with and become a part of the all-seeing or esemplastic faculty. Yet, at the same moment that he envisioned such an ultimate comprehensive unity, Poe was constrained to regard mind and matter, imagination and reason, as separate and really at war with each other; there could be no "higher monism," only a painfully confessed duality or pluralism.

Poetry necessarily became an act of the destructive imagination — the secondary imagination which reduces everything to its will before it can create poems or any works of art. Having once reshaped the real world to its imaginative needs, a process best demonstrated in the shift from jocularity to terror in "The Raven," the poem then must abandon the rational intelligible world and undertake a journey toward ultimate meaning on, as it were, the "other side." But once "there" (as in "The Valley of Unrest" or the turgid meaninglessness of "Dream-Land"), then Poe felt continually impelled to redefine or reconstruct the meaning, not so much of that one poetic venture, as of poetry in general. Poetry was meaningful and meaningless both. Thus his last statements about poetry were not in poems but in critical determinations such as in "The Philosophy of Composition" and "The Poetic Principle."

This tendency to delimit or make a special magic of poetry was an expression of Poe's unwillingness to allow poetry to be "dream" or symbolic meaning often enough. His keenly critical, objective intelligence was continually applying a brake: art and poetry ought to have rules and a logic as clear and forthright as the rules of science. Yet the imaginative and critical faculties were not so much at variance as they were opposing expressions of the same penetrative activity: the human mind and will struggled toward understanding; yet it did not trust its own intuitive perceptions, or, if it did, it demanded explanations. Consequently, in Poe's career as a poet, the greater the exercise of critical intelligence, the less poetry there would be. Poetry more and more became an intellectual activity in which Poe not only made poems but enjoyed seeing himself in the act of making poems. The rules, or "philosophy," he developed both from his own practice of poetry and from his intensive criticism of other poets' poetry. Oddly enough, Bryant, Longfellow, Halleck, Mrs. Sigourney were not so much poets who came under his careful scrutiny as demonstrations of his own poetic theory; they provided texts in the problems of his own poetic quest; their poems were what he might have written had he not known better than they. They served to teach him to do better next time on his own. (This service brought the greater danger of Poe's plagiarism, a subject to which he was extremely sensitive because he was himself not averse to its sly practice.) But that instruction he received from other poets' practice marked the startling decline in his own poetic output after 1831: the more Poe thought about poetry, the less he was able to write it.

Poe's poetic world was one of continual dislodgment. It was never quite the same on any two occasions that a pair of poems began with words and ended with, presumably, an idea. Even the similes and metaphors of poems posited some private, very special discourse, the vocabulary of which had, as it were, long ago been established but the key to which had long been lost. Generally speaking, poetic metaphor is the tension that the poet necessarily leaves unfinished between fact and idea, substance and concept, reality and word. Wherever one begins in the explication of the metaphor (the basis for symbolic expression), he posits the fact and from it develops the idea, or he conceives the idea and watches its physical representation. Donne's "Anniversaries" are intensely symbolic and highly abstract; they begin, however, with the fact of Elizabeth Drury's death; from that recognizable fact Donne developed the whole concept of the decay of the world. Yet all the while death is sustained both as the fact (the dead body of the girl) and the idea (the inevitable running-down of the universe). The symbolism is the world of action, location, dimension, and normal perception.

The "dislodgment" of Poe's symbolic world, and thus of his symbolic imagination, is that the poem had to be a continual act of discovery. Since the actual world had been fairly well analyzed and charted already by the rational inquiries of science (Poe's early sonnet on "Science" is pertinent here), there was little left as the domain of poetry but the dream — the dream which, by means of magic, ritual, or incantation, could be raised to the vividness and coherence of reality itself. The farther Poe's poetic career proceeded, the more it left behind the personalized dreamer, such as the heroic Tamerlane, and entered the abstract, nebulous world of mere dream, as in "The City in the Sea" and "Dream-Land." The baffling character of Poe's dream-poetry is not so much that the symbols are strange and abstruse but that we are lodged in the dream without being informed how the dream came to be. We are given the last moments of the symbolic journey and never informed how it got under way nor even where it was going. Coleridge's Ancient Mariner at least seized the Wedding Guest and demanded to be heard; we are thereupon told why we must undertake a symbolic circumnavigation of the globe.

"The Raven" is almost a parable of Poe's poetic career. The poem is a dream, a rather special dream to be sure, wherein a protagonist began with the assumption that he was the maker and shaper of his life and his world: the bust of Pallas, the carpets, the night storm are emblems of this shaping spirit. As the action proceeds, the young man becomes more and more incapable of giving any direction to his existence or even knowing the meaning of life in any way. What gives the poem its dramatic intensity is that we see the student's mind in disintegration at the very moment that the young man is most keenly aware that he is losing all hold on external reality and on himself. He has the power of watching himself move toward meaninglessness, and even to enjoy the spectacle. We are left, with the student, on the very edge of nothingness; there is no life, no death, only the perilous illusion that he exists. By means of the questions put to the Raven and the interior monologue which he devises, the young man critically surveys what he is helpless to control.

When Poe divorced poetic language from fact and when he denied the word anything but its assumptive or purely imaginative meaning, he was left with the only conclusion available to him: the language of poetry creates its own unique reality which has nothing to do with sensible reality or even with the denotative reality the word itself can otherwise convey. The word "red" in a poem is, by this logic, a universe away from the word "red" in a prose sentence. The first can be manipulated in whatever way and into whatever meaning the poet designs — or it may have no meaning at all but exist as a sound and rhythm which, however, impel the reader or hearer into the farthest mysteries of idea and dream. All the while Poe's symbolic imagination was poetically destroying reality and creating a substitute reality and dream. Each new destruction was an act of symbolic self-destruction: and unless he could somehow return to the dimensioned world of reality and, as it were, begin all over again, Poe had nothing more to say in poems. In substance, he had very little to say after 1832; he merely intensified the dream. And when he could no longer incite or induce a dream, as he only occasionally could in "The Raven" and in "Ulalume," he contented himself by writing prosy verses to his lady friends. But Poe's artistic development was not paralyzed by the waning of his poetic imagination or the fallacy of his language theory: the short story, itself in his hands a prose-poem, was the next stage in Poe's expressive symbolism.

IV

Death, Eros, and Horror

I have called this chapter "Death, Eros, and Horror," because I should like to move, for a time, from the higher range of speculation and analysis in order to consider those matters which pertain to Poe rather directly throughout the time in which he lived and wrote but which are rather remote from our own time and sensibility. These matters might be called "fashions"—literary and cultural fashions which, more than a century ago, impinged themselves on art just as do the anti-intellectualism, the extravagant brutality, the disgust toward women (to name only a few) in our own time.

It is not enough to say that Poe, in poetry and short story, cleverly capitalized on a popular commodity of his day and outdistanced all rivals in the dramaturgy of death and the dead. Certainly, all the way from the Gothic romances to the very popular gift annals and periodicals of the day, the corpse, the tomb, the mourning survivor were so frequent as to be almost overwhelming. The first half of the nineteenth century, at the popular level at least, shuddered to its heart's content; and the delight in fictive death did not abate until death became a real matter of common life in the Civil War. Only an age that had only recently freed itself, through the advances of medicine and innoculation, from the immediate terror of death and from the brutal shock of killing in war could afford the complacent pleasure of seeing so many reproductions and reading about so many examples of death, past and present, as did the age of Poe.

Yet attitudes toward death are not only fashionable but also sociological; in fact, one might well go on the premise that he could interpret any age of history if he knew enough about its burial rites and its folklore of death. The often unspoken and unwritten codes of death and the dead can become an index to a society. Poe, perhaps better than any other writer of his time, defined the idea of death as that idea was held most sacredly by Americans in the third and fourth decades of the nineteenth century. However strange and exotic his treatment may be to us, it offered no bafflement to his contemporaries; he was for his age a historian whose reports of death might well be regarded as generally recognized and applicable to his time and as rather suggestive of his own special artistic aims and limitations.

First of all, Poe came fortunately on the world's scene just as the ritual and mystery of death were being transferred from the aristocrats and specially favored to the middle class. The industrial revolution freed many ordinary people not only from the necessity of living out their earthly lives in only one spot but also from the universally held belief that they must die into anonymity in the churchyard whose earth is disturbed at least every generation or in the common, mass grave. Death in the middle class was rapidly becoming a very important item in the whole productive and consumptive economy of man: man lived in this world according to the necessary, and precarious, prescriptions of his station and fortune, but he must also die and be buried in proper accord with his station. What he left behind him was the final touchstone to his earthly existence — a will, testaments, a gravestone with mystic symbols, or even a mighty mausoleum to hallow his bones and bear witness to his dignity. In the history of western Europe this demand of common man for palls, processions, and the ceremony of bell, book, and candle stemmed from the aftermath of the terrible visitations of the Black Death in the seventeenth century; and, with the aid of Protestantism, ordinary man even assured himself that, if he were not quite equal to his betters in this world, he might, like Lazarus in Abraham's bosom, outshine Dives in hell. Out of such a demand there arose the undertaker, himself to become the priest and administrator of easeful death.[1]

Indeed, death became more than a demand for equal rights of the middle class in this world and in the world to come; it also became an act of snobbery. One's position in society could be demonstrated to the very last in the gracious act of holy burial. No longer, even on the frontier of the United States, did the pine box and the hole in the ground suffice; one must be buried in success. Death was truly swallowed up in victory, not so much of the soul's passage into infinity but of the body itself in all its local, economic prestige; every American could aspire to what that otherwise ordinary man, Benjamin Franklin, had achieved when he designed his tomb and composed his epitaph. The grave and the mortuary emblems were the ultimate proof of the democratic success-story in many a city, village, and crossroads.[2]

Especially in the South and in an old city like Richmond, which had such a strong effect on Poe, had there grown up a set of strongly enforced pieties regarding death and burial. One died and was buried as a lady or gentleman and received from one's survivors the fitting tributes. Long before Mark Twain ridiculed the southern tradition in the poetry of Emmeline Grangerford, the burial service was a kind of canonically rigid office recited in the stylized landscape of death. There was very little deviation in any direction until at last the body was finally put away and the mortuary emblems sealed. Poe's poem "The Sleeper," modeled rather closely on the burial ritual in the Book of Common Prayer, proceeds through a set of formal stages: an invocation or call to the mourners, then a litany to the dead, beginning "Oh, lady bright! can it be right — / This window open to the night?" afterward a series of questions or appeals to which there is no answer; finally, the consignment to the grave: "My love, she sleeps! Oh, may her sleep,/ As it is lasting, so be deep!"

In poem and short story, Poe provided his age with a handbook on how the upper middle class should take care of its dead. Yet, by reason of the rigidity and monotony of the ceremony, Poe seems to have been reminding his age that the symbols of death were frozen and meaningless. Christianity professed to teach the life after death. Christian ceremonial, grown stale with time and repetition, had gradually lost its force and, far from asserting that the grave is merely the entrance to another life, had become content to let the catafalque, the gravestone, or the mausoleum be the indestructible symbols of its belief in immortality.

If death were specially dignified in the middle-class culture of the early nineteenth century and reached in Poe one of its most significant, and contemporary, expressions, so too was death then as always very close to sexual love. The metaphysicals in the age of Donne were not the first to discover that one could love into death and die into love or that, in each act of love's consummation, one came closer to death. In a later economic property structure one may well "die into love" at the very moment of union: at marriage the woman "dies" by changing her name and identity for the sake of receiving her husband's name and identity; therefore, in the nature of a "union of the two" comes a denial of the separateness of the one. Long after Poe had set down his versions of this theme, death and love reached their ultimate romantic fulfillment in the musical apotheosis in the *Liebestod* of Wagner's *Tristan und Isolde*.[3]

The governing symbol in most of these nineteenth-century versions of love unto death and dying into love was, of course, the dead young woman — the Ulalumes, Morellas, Ligeias, Lenores of Poe's tales and poems. In a period of a hundred years this symbolic young woman had undergone a slow and certain change. She had begun, in the latter seventeenth and the early eighteenth century, as the seduction motif in the dramas of Wycherley or in the novels of Richardson: a creature of infinite fertility whose inevitable drama concluded when, willingly or not, she was brought to bed with a man. But the seduction theme had only a limited appeal and expression: by the time Fielding wrote his *Shamela* and John Cleland his *Fanny Hill,* the obvious flaws in the tale of seduction had been revealed: the young lady was "seduced" only at her own will and desire.

By the opening of the nineteenth century Eros had undergone a considerable change. Seduction, either as tragedy or as jest, was no longer acceptable as a subject: Scott's Effie Deans is a striking exception to this generalization; but Scott was interested not in Effie's seduction but in Jeanie's strong-willed pilgrimage to save her sister from death.[4] Middle-class morality had become so dominant that any supposition of a young woman's yielding to the bestial passions of man was unacceptable. Moralists and sentimentalists had done their work well: woman before marriage was a commodity, a means of continuing the human race and providing hands to work in future generations. If she were flawed or unfaithful, then she could not fulfill her holy, and economic, mission. Once an economic valuation had been put on woman's chastity (in theory, if not always in fact), then the seduction theme was neither amusing nor informative. One might conclude this point by mentioning that the seduction theme never had any place in early American literature: the first novel written by an American set forth the awful penalty that poor Charlotte Temple paid when she trusted her seducer; throughout the many editions and reprints of that novel, she became an everlasting warning to girls who might be tempted to follow their instincts rather than their sense of social and economic discretion. In some respects Royall Tyler's *Contrast,* the first American play, was more to the point: the pretended seducer was a fop and a fool and, what was worse, anti-American; the ladies had no trouble resisting his blandishments.

It is easy enough to find humor in these matters; what is

more to the point is that an age which eschews one representation of Eros will find a substitute Eros. If a middle-class and commercial morality prevented the exposition of seduction in life, it found an equally titillating theme in "death as seduction." Or, to state the idea in other terms, if woman could not be presented seductively in life, she could be displayed in erotic postures and in seductive disguises in death. Death became a means of enticement: death was the great seducer, and the "ruined" girl was laid out for burial in the landscape of ruin and decay.

In another odd direction which this theme assumed, woman in death became equated with woman at marriage: the corpse was the bride, and the grave clothes were the bridal dress. Woman as a sacrificial emblem in the allurements and pieties of marriage reached the ultimate sacrifice in dying. In an age when many women did die young after their many miscarriages and child-bearing, death indeed became a kind of second dying to which marriage had been the first. The wedding and the burial service became a nearly duplicate ritual: the wedding gown was the shroud; the hand, tremulous and cold at the wedding ceremony, was the hand cold in death; and the burial office reënacted the wedding ceremony. As in love and life, the woman could be appealed to and wooed all over again in death. Poe's poems and tales are ritual incantations to the erotically desirable young woman who is forever white, aloof, reserved, virginal, bridal, whether she lies on the wedding bed or the funeral bier. This commingling of the living and the dead woman as infinitely desirable is nowhere better suggested than in a passage in "Morella": "And in the contour of the high forehead, and in the ringlets of the silken hair, and in the wan fingers which buried themselves therein, and in the sad musical tones of her speech, and above all . . . in the phrases and expressions of the dead on the lips of the loved and the living, I found food for consuming thought and horror. . . ."[5]

Death was, therefore, hardly "death" at all. It was a means whereby an age, while morally disapproving of the earthy frankness and seductions of a preceeding age, nonetheless enjoyed what it officially banned. No age is without what W. H. Auden has called its "sexy airs"; and if popular expressions of eroticism are prevented in one way, they will break out in another. Thus the age delighted in fashionably exquisite, nubile young women in erotic poses of death such as this one from Henry Chorley's *Conti,* which Poe quoted with approval in a review in the *Messenger* for February 1836:

> Madame Zerlini was there — flung down upon a sofa. . . . Her head was cast back over one of the pillows, so far, that her long hair, which had been imperfectly fastened, had disengaged itself by its own weight, and was now sweeping heavily downward, with a crushed wreath of passion flowers and myrtles half buried among it. Everything about her told how fiercely the spirit had passed. Her robe of scarlet muslin was entirely torn off on one shoulder, and disclosed its exquisitely rounded proportions. Her glittering *négligé* was unclasped, and one end of it clenched firmly in the small left hand, which there was now hardly any possibility of unclosing. Her glazed eyes were wide open — her mouth set in an unnatural, yet fascinating smile; her cheek still flushed with a more delicate, yet intense red than belongs to health. . . .[6]

Behind these popular designs of woman in death was gathered the force of a reading public which had only recently been released into a world of imagination and was demanding that these themes and tantalizing rituals, hitherto consigned to bawdry and the word-of-mouth story, be expressed in both popular and moral appeals. We say, now long afterward, that death was "sentimentalized"; what we mean is that the terror of death was concealed behind a set of masks and mimes which were part of that substitute reality any reading public enjoys. Poe was the cleverest man of his time in setting up these disguises for horror and not the horror itself. Death became not an event or an action nor a condition of total non-being but a series of seductive postures. Children may not have died, nor did men, but women did, by the thousands in the popular poetry and song of the era; and in the beautiful young woman, the flush of life still on her cheek, her eyes just closed in her last sleep, the chamber arrayed for her final rites, the age found its satisfactory counterpart for the overripe, bosomy, hoydenish, or simpering, creatures who had been similarly gratifying creatures of substitute passion in an age just past — or in one soon to come.

If Poe succeeded in giving form to other amorphous shapes of death in the popular American mind, he more than succeeded in becoming the laureate of death and love as part of democratic individualism and the economic success story. What gave the American belief of life after death its special poignancy was the generally held faith that there could be no true *physical* death; for, unlike other religions or phases of Christianity, American Protestantism could not solve the problem of its own insistent eschatology except to affirm, all the way from Wigglesworth's *Day of Doom* in 1666 to the dramatic "last" day of William Miller in 1843 and 1844, that there would be a physical resurrection either at the moment of death to this world or at the sound of the great trumpet for the opening of the next world. The nineteenth century was strewn with the forlorn hopes that this very body one carries with him through life must be the very shape he will assume in that hereafter which begins sometime tomorrow. From William Miller through Twain's ribald Captain Stormfield is the line which cut through the century's impatience with any concern with "soul" or "oversoul" and demanded that this body which lived and, by God's beneficence, succeeded in this world must of necessity have a life and a reward for that success in the next.[7] In the very nature of democratic individualism and an individualistic economy there was a passionate sense of identity and of the single self as having gained the success, the victory. Death might seem a denial of this success: Croesus can go a progress through the guts of a beggar as well as can a Jukes or a Kallikak. But the American success story would not permit the ending of the saga at the grave: the dead one might be "gone," but he still survived in his accredited possessions which were translated into the symbolisms of an after life. His land was his grave, his house became his tomb, and his coffin his bed to sleep in; and to the end of mortal time he would have the hushed and protective care of those adornments which were the proofs of his life beyond death.

Death was, therefore, a sociology, an economic self-insistence, and, finally, a pictorial device, a landscape. Perhaps Poe's versions of death and the dead are more scenic and pictorial than anything else: from the beginning to the end of his career he was happy to stop any action which might be proceeding and linger over the grave, the twilight spectral moon, the emblems of mortality and annihilation. To state the premise another way, Poe became a verbal landscapist of death in much the same way that a whole school and movement in painting had discovered in death one of their most vital subjects. This topic is much too broad and important to receive more than a summary treatment here. Suffice to say, the romance of dying and death as a dramatic scene were brilliantly and starkly set forth to the eighteenth and nineteenth centuries in such very popular seventeenth-century painters as Salvator Rosa and Nicolas Poussin; one might also include minor but no less popular painters like Desiderio, Guardi, and Hubert Robert.[8] In a very real sense these painters, owing to the first really vivid reproductions which nineteenth-century line drawings and reproductive plates made possible, helped form the melancholy sensibility of the age. Magazines, postcards, framed reproductions, with a proliferation almost as complete as photographic reproductions in the twentieth century, brought the terrible landscape of death to thousands of homes and minds in America. In substance, each man or woman — and women were the chief objects of this traffic — could have his own private gallery collected from these popular masterworks by the Italian and French landscapists and by certain Americans who were not far behind in technical proficiency.

The major ingredients of this taste were Ruins and Catastrophe.[9] The two fused in the pictorialist of decay and in the seer of catastrophic apocalypse. Poe was very close to the painters of his own and of the recently past age.

The history of ruin as a subject for art is long and tangled. When the painters of the Italian Renaissance discovered ruins, they were moved to emulate the wonders of the ancient world which lay all around them in such haunting shards and fragments. Thus art entered upon its noteworthy "classical revival." In the seventeenth century, however, a reaction set in, and the painter began to look with a differently scrutinizing eye at the remnants of the past which he saw around him. Chiefly in Rome he began to study intensively the shapes and structures that were laid out in such brilliance and decay. He began to cherish ruin for its own sake. "The imagination thus let loose," William Gaunt has written, "did not merely copy ruins. It built them into a kind of philosophic sport. It was a lunar spirit which led to the construction of dead cities and disquieting arcades of fancy. In this strange form of creation it seemed as if ruin fed upon ruin and propagated after its own nature, filling a world of dream with spongy products of unreason." [10] Rome, the crepuscular half-light which bathed the silent monoliths fallen in decay, and the "philosophy" of ruin and death as the major subject for painters and writers all fuse in a twilit sensibility that affected more artists than only Edgar Poe.

Death was not only landscape; it was human posture too. The new anatomical freedom which artists obtained early in the nineteenth century marked not only a change in the presentation of human forms but in the precise or symbolic rendering of death itself. In preparation for his terrifying "Raft of the *Medusa*" (1819) Gericault kept corpses in his studio and made himself a pathologist in recording the horror of death. Anatomically, he made a complete break with the classic past with his study of the human body not in the repose but in the convulsive spasms of death. The same new freedom occurs in Delacroix's "Barque of Don Juan," where the dead and the dying lie in grotesque poses over the sides of the becalmed lifeboat. These painters, and others, had seen the terrifying reality of death in the several revolutions in France and were moved to give it plastic shape and form.

The philosophy of ruin was further aided by a half-century's excitement over the discovery of Pompeii and Herculaneum. A few tourists saw those frozen glories of a world buried for nearly seventeen centuries; thousands of people avidly read and stared fascinatedly at the numerous reproductions which appeared in American periodicals throughout the nineteenth century. There, in the glimpses of those two unearthed tombs, men obtained a real hold on the past which could finally come alive for them — a past which had been most fortuitously buried in 79 A.D. when Rome was at the peak of her power. In the South this vision of Rome and things Roman coalesced with the long tradition of classical studies for young men of the law and of society, with the pseudo-Roman architecture which Jefferson had introduced after studying the Maison Carreé at Nîmes, and with a generalized American hero-worship which tended more and more to recast its leaders in the guise of the Caesars until Horatio Greenough cast Washington as a Roman senator wearing a waist-high toga.

Yet, however much gloss and romantic discoloration may have been cast over a reborn sense of the past as ruin and decay, an age of archeology which had known a Winckelmann was coming to a sense of the past not only as a dream but as a fact. Time itself became not a linear continuum, a parceling of history into ages and periods, but a vast amorphous idea in which the objects from the past assumed a timeless reality. Death was, archeologically speaking, almost denied; for the monuments and tombs of men could come alive and speak to men just as did the unmoving shapes in Poe's poem, "The City in the Sea." What the newly discovered world of ruin and the imaginative idea of death revealed to the romantic sensibility was the very important aesthetic conception that works of art exist not just as things made by artists in place and time, subject to the historical accidents that make the lives of men what they are, but as symbolic presentations that exist in a time-dimension beyond their mere making. In fact, art would be man's triumph over time and death and decay: the uncovered statue, the lost poem, the frieze across a temple's top — these and a thousand other artifacts were designations and proofs that, though a mind and hand had shaped the creation, the power of creativity and the sense of beauty had long antedated and would long postdate the fallible body which had wrought the thing. Thus, as we shall see in another connection, the Romantic critical intelligence sought a rationale of art and experience beyond mere temporal location: the Romantic mind was one of the first crucially to investigate the theory that an artist works more deeply than he can ever know and that aesthetics may exist in a dimension which is not local to Greece or Italy or timed to Phidias or Michelangelo. To an extent, the Romantic interest in ruin and decay was to find that all physical substances become lost but that all intellectual constructions have the potential boon of immortality simply because they exist in the life of the mind and the imagination. A rediscovered past, especially the past of Rome, merely confirmed the impression of how contemporary all art and thought can be.

In America, however, the romantic version of ruin and

decay met head-on the parvenu industrialism and its off-spring, the doctrine of progress.[11] In the art of Poe especially, and perhaps less dramatically in some of his contemporaries like Washington Irving, the clash between a vision of antiquity and the new world of brawling destructiveness to anything that was past was of considerable consequence and warrants some tentative exposition.

The gospel of progress, especially as it received its fullest expression in the nineteenth century, is wholly inimical to any idea of ruin or the past. A ruin is a denial of progress, and the past was constantly, as it is still to this day, to lie like a dead weight about the dynamic present. Progress is a denial of the past and of death in each day's fresh, productive assertion of life. But at the very time this assertion was being made and became so well engrained in the very experience of millions of people, a whole generation of artists in America were making ruin and death an exploration and a philosophy; and not content with simply affirming the glories of some nebulous past, whether of Greece or of the innocent native in the New World, these writers and painters recoiled in horror from the new industrial world now coming into full maturity: Blake was not alone in cursing England's black Satanic mills while seeing visions of Heaven and Hell.

What prophet and poet saw alike was the modern world of ruin, a world which raised up and then ruthlessly demolished its structures within a year or at most a lifetime. The change from virgin timber to smoke-blackened walls was everywhere apparent from Birmingham, England, to the Connecticut Valley and Lowell, Massachusetts. Ruin became almost an obsession; for it was a dual philosophy of ruin —

that of antiquity, glorious and colorful and deeply limned with meanings for the present, and that of the contemporary world, with its inglorious grime and the disgraced landscapes. Antiquity was what man had lost in stupid destructiveness which Gibbon's corrosive irony had underlined; the ruinous present drove sensitive minds to recoil in horror all the way from Coleridge's High Churchism to Carlyle's angry Gospel of Mammon. Poe's sonnet "To Science" is, in its way, a fusion of both attitudes.

Thus the vision of death became ever clearer in the first half of the nineteenth century as the artistic sensibility struggled both to conform to a doctrine of ruin and decay as popularized by the painters and to turn away from a modern passion for destructiveness which, as with Irving, produced a contempt for the present and a longing for peace and stability. Yet, whatever turn the artistic imagination or critical faculty might take, the central attraction was the theme of death which, until the mid-century point had been passed, was conveniently not an action nor even a symbol but a landscape. Death as a place, conventionally or exquisitely furnished with the house or castle, the room, the coffin, the gravestone or mausoleum, was, after all, a painless scene. It passed readily into an affirmation of one's financial station; and, in the tableau, it merged with a substitute sexuality, a landscape of emergent consummation. The central object in that stylized tableau was the Irene-figure, freshly adorned for burial: the whole scene was only an enlargement of the bridal chamber, as if the walls might open on infinity; the room was not a room but the place of the dead woman, and the coffin easily became the bridal bed. The gown, the long hair, the immobile virginity of those young women were all sublimated versions of love-into-death in which both love and death had ceased to have any motive or drama.

For Poe the theme of death steadily weakened because he could allow the subject only a limited presentation. Partly because of a new economic version of death and partly because of the growing cult of "woman in death," Poe could not go beyond the more ordinary ranges of expression in his age. The woman must die and be buried as though she were still the unravished bride; the man must remain to mourn. Part of a culture, and a good deal of Poe's explorations, were written in that summary statement.

2

Death and horror would seem to be associated, and indeed they must be in any investigation of the mind and art of Poe. But we must now consider the theme of horror as something apart and as available for inquiry for its own sake.[12] We must also consider this theme, as we have the topic of death, as contained in both the poetry and the short stories, though our emphasis will of necessity fall on the poetry. Yet it was such a theme as that of death or horror which binds Poe's story-writing career to his poetic experience and writing; by only slightly shifting the emphasis and the rhetorical devices he could write "tales of horror" just as ably as he had written poems of horror, and then come back, in his later life, to write poems of death and horror again. One might easily draw a line from the very early "Tamerlane" through "The Fall of the House of Usher" to "The Raven": all of them were studies of stages in consciousness when the real world slipped away or disintegrated and the mind found itself fronting the "horror" of its own loneliness and loss.

First of all, we might define the Poesque version of horror as that region or mysterious middle ground where the normal, rational faculties of thinking and choice have, for reasons beyond knowing, been suspended; ethical and religious beliefs are still the portion of men, but are powerless to function. All power of choice and all sense of direction have been lost; in fact, they have been so long lost that the nightmare world of presumed reality obeys no laws of reason or stability. It is a highly complex metaphysical condition wherein the constants of heaven and hell are fixed at their opposite polarity, but between them is the vast region wherein the human will is situated and is powerless to effect any variation of its own existence. It is a realm where the will cannot exist, not because it never had an existence but because it somehow lost its power to function. It is a world like that in "The City in the Sea": moral man once lived in that long-ago world, but now everything is shadowy and atrophied. In such a horror world men are moral mutes or paralytics; they are like Roderick Usher, the "Last of the Visigoths," at the very end of a long line of ethically directed ancestors. Horror is, then, the urgent need for moral knowledge and direction — and its total lack. The characters in such a situation can only dream of a condition which once existed but which they would never be able to follow, even if they were able to recapture it. They are like the creatures in Poe's most complete allegorical presentations, those in the apocalyptic visions like "The Conversation of Eiros and Charmion" (1839) and "The Colloquy of Monos and Una"

(1841): they are the victims of an Apocalypse which has had no perceptible reason for being.

Yet even the lack or the negation of a moral principle had to be based on some system of good and evil. A Christian view, such as Hawthorne propounded, conceived that sin entered the world with man and remains with man forever, while nature exists outside either in a dualism with man or in an implacable state of indifference to him. The naturalism of a Melville or Mark Twain, to draw a brief contrast, found the basis for evil not in man but in the primal order of nature and at the center of the universe itself: man is thereby lodged in a universe of evil, and his tragedy is that he alone of all forms of life can both know and strive to meliorate his condition. This naturalism, as it was with Twain, can be driven far enough to exonerate man of all blame or consequence for the rigidly deterministic order.

With Poe we are hardly concerned with "evil" at all, insofar as evil might be considered inherent in man or in the phenomenal order; in a sense, his one prescription for evil is its absence: never to know evil nor to have been engaged in any moral struggle is the condition of horror in which the Poe protagonist must exist. In such a nightmare world all the prescriptions for evil and good are matters for nostalgia and regret; they were part of some other state of being from which man has moved or which has long passed from the earth. Only when these protagonists are, like Michaelangelo in "Al Aaraaf" or the strange creatures in "Silence" or "The Colloquy of Monos and Una," on, as it were, the "other side" can they at last realize what it was they never knew.

One might make a case for Poe as a religious writer: he

employs the form and the action of the religious experience. But man is not the only "apocalypse"; Nature is too, itself a chaos wherein nothing exists according to any law or order that man can know. The "god" has gone away, not as in eighteenth-century rationalism because he has organized and set going a mechanically perfect world — such a physical reality would argue that the god had at least left his thought behind — but as though in some pre-Darwinian organic design from which even the god's thought has been removed. Thus life, death, and moral judgment have long lost their reason for being.[13]

So far, then, we have set forth two conditions of horror: one is the fading of any moral law into an apocalypse of man's last "distempered" things in which anything may happen; the other is the total freedom of the will to function, at the same time that there is nothing to will "for" or will "against." Its judgments are in a vacuum because it pretends to act in a world where no discoverable controls are operative. Such a doctrine, to which Poe gave numerous expositions, was afterward arresting to Baudelaire and to others in the nineteenth century who had broken the hold of any theory of original sin and who yet could not quite bring themselves to the sociological view that society, not man, must somehow be at fault. It easily becomes a mechanistic theory in order to account for inexplicable, nonmechanistic forces and events.

3

Horror was, however, not only a philosophy or a method of explaining the mystery of the universe; it was also "psychology" or a method of inquiring into special states of mind. It was a means to externalize, in vivid physical objects, inner states of being and a method of portraying the mind's awareness of itself. These "objects" of horror were not themselves necessarily horrible; they were what they were because a mind saw them and was even destroyed by them. In one way this was Poe's contribution to the dark subliminal literature of a later time: he demonstrated that states of consciousness are not simply isolated conditions of madness but are somehow intimately and intricately related to the physical world around it. Poe's fault (to hasten ahead of our exposition for a moment) was that, once he had found a vivid externalization for a condition of inner consciousness — a crack in the wall, a black cat, a portrait, an insistent heartbeat — the physical exemplification assumed command; and in the succeeding narrative, whether in poem or in short story, the objectification was out of all proportion to the inner condition. One might say that the symbol ran away with the idea; Poe was content to let the convulsive dance of objectified forms enact the drama. Thus rhetoric and landscape conveyed the agony.

Taken altogether, these conditions of consciousness which Poe exposed did not suggest that Poe was revealing himself or aspects of his own inner being but was actually detailing certain stages and varieties of what might be termed the "Romantic consciousness." Horror was therefore Poe's insight into Romantic self-consciousness — into the tendency of the Romantic mind to consider that its own psychic response to life and to the world was a sufficient subject for life. The tendency need not have ended in "horror"; it did end in the capacity of the Romantic mind both to create and to be almost simultaneously scrutinizing itself at the moment of creative activity. We might explore some of these conditions of consciousness as they are contained in certain of Poe's poems and short stories.

One obvious quality of the protagonist or "I" in these discourses was its inhuman arrogance and self-exaltation. This was the frame within which the Romantic ego functioned: it had to expunge its weaker, grosser self, to descend into a private hell, to suffer self-loss, and to rise again; it was Goethe's Werther, Carlyle's Teufelsdrockh, Byron's Manfred, and Shelley's Prometheus, all of them primal explorations of the self becoming aware of and making peace with its unique self and experience. Poe's "I" is different from them all in one significant way: while he may be endowed with extraordinary learning and may have the power to accomplish vast aims, he can never weep like Werther, curse like Teufelsdrockh, rage like Manfred, or suffer like Prometheus. He is not the Romantic hero-god; he is only a little man. He is the Romantic hero reduced to the limited vision of commonplace men, and yet he is required, certainly according to all the literary and philosophic antecedents of which Poe was aware, to live and die in a hell or heaven which is totally beyond his comprehension. Only on rare occasions are this hero's sufferings magically alleviated by his knowledge of vortices in the Scandanavian maelstrom or by the timely arrival of the rescuing army to release him from the swinging knife of the inquisition.

What marks Poe's studies of a man caught in some inner or outer horror is that, for all the sufferings the protagonist must undergo, the fictive "I" never learns anything. The anguish is wasted because the sufferer comes out of the action precisely the same as he went into it. Nothing has really occurred "inside"; there was no inner consciousness to begin with, and the pilgrimage of the questing self had been wrought entirely in terms of the scene, the natural objects in easy accord and attendance, and the incantatory spell-weaving which somehow reduced the tangible world to a mere logarithm. The symbolic projection took precedence and triumphed over what it was originally designed to prefigure and represent. Therefore, nothing could happen to the mind caught in the terror of an event; everything must happen to the outside world which is made to envision the agony. All the while the mind remains unmoved.

One may seek to account for this curious ambivalence as one will. One might say that the symbolic interaction of the mind and the universe, the subject of Wordsworth's "Tintern Abbey" and of Emerson's *Nature,* had begun to disintegrate under the monotony of the attachment to nature which the Romantic inquiry continually sought. Coleridge complained that his "genial spirits" failed, and so they did; Poe never complained that he was losing the power for fresh insight, but the evidence is plentiful that he did early lose it — or perhaps he never really had it. He went through all the complex motions of Byron's adjudicating between self and reality, Shelley's intense search for the meaning of the One behind the mask of reality, and even Keats's quest for the meaning of poetry and the intensely felt poetic moment. Poe's world of the mind was limited to the world of primary sensation and to the terrors which afflict children. It was the boy's erotic world without any sense or knowledge of Eros: women become the victims of horror; they are married, they suffer (only Morella ever bore a child, and it was a monster), they die or are killed; and they were all the while the sacrificial victims to a mere man, not the Romantic hero-god.

We might account for this externalization of inner states of being not only on the score that Poe's mind did not deeply search the infinitely variable symbolisms between itself and exterior reality by which reality itself is transformed as Melville transformed the universe from the crow's nest, but also on the supposition of the rhetorical or language problem. Poe was enormously successful in his own day, as he still is in ours, because he somehow arranged a set of well-known counters that would inevitably give his readers the shudders. But he did so at his own cost.

While in his poetry he was dedicated to giving new meanings to the poetic imagination, in his prose tales Poe was content to employ a set of invariable metaphors which would be, for him, immediately clear. Thus the names for exterior objects became an instantaneous direction for the mind to follow between the idea and its externalization. Every state of mind had, therefore, a readily known representation. The language of prose (we must be careful to insist that this was not Poe's theory of the language of poetry) consisted of a set of metaphors by which anything could be presented: a lion is a strong man, a fox a cunning man, a grave the terror and anguish of death, the underground cavern the secret past, a plague the terror of the invisible world, and so on. Throughout Poe's tale-writing career these metaphors remained almost invariable; they had no power of yielding to the unique circumstance. Perhaps to his own age these devices were vivid because they had not been too long in the literary domain; in a later time they command little interest not so much because they may be worn out as because they bring only a moment's connotation.

We are, at this moment of our inquiry, where this study of Poe began, with Poe's language sense. Yet we have said, and will further say, enough concerning Poe's symbolic imagination — whether words were signs of natural facts or whether they were magic keys to regions of thought beyond man's knowing — to leave the subject in abeyance here. If poetry moved toward unintelligibility or abstraction, prose more and more shifted toward immediate clarity. No fault can be found with such a procedure — except that in his prose tales Poe was still trying to engage in the symbolic enterprise which was essentially the province of poetry: he was seeking not only terms for meaning but even the "way" or the symbolic journey along which one goes toward meaning. An idea is not simply, suddenly known; it is itself a process; it too has its own life and mind, and the knower must himself come into some congruence with it. Poe tried, by means of virtually unyielding and invariable metaphors in his horror tales, to project something like what he had projected in his poems of horror, such as "The Sleeper," "The Raven," and "Ulalume." He finished with a number of rigid counters, like movable pieces on a playing board, which meant only what they said they mean.

We might return to the topic which opened this chapter and consider, finally, death as horror as well as economics or Eros; for presumably the ultimate horror would be death and the annihilation of the sentient being who was the center of these inquiries into the dark regions of inner being.

One of the curiosities of Poe's treatment of death was that

death became a very elaborate ritual: just as the New England Puritan from Samuel Sewall to Emily Dickinson wanted to know every step of the way by which a friend or relative had left this world and gone to the next,[14] so Poe was the laureate in the manner of proper, gentlemanly dying. But one element marks all these deaths, however horrifying they may be: they are all apocalypses; that is, they all concern the time before and the time after death; they do not portray that moment of anguish and loss of being which has formed so much of the imaginative experience in American literature from Edward Taylor to Hemingway. With Poe, the fact of death is very much like the Crucifixion narrative which ends with the Cross and resumes when the stone is found rolled away from the tomb. The god or man did not really die; he merely shifted his location. One stage stops at the final glimpse of death; the other begins already on the other side, and, imaginatively, we have never really gone through.

Such a view and treatment lend themselves very readily to the apocalyptic method. That is, the death of one person is magnified into a universal catastrophe, just as at the death of Christ the graves opened, the veil of the temple was rent, and the sky darkened. Three of these apocalyptic visions are Poe's striving to present the ultimate symbolism of death.

The earliest of the three is "Silence, A Fable" (1838). The tale begins where "Al Aaraaf" left off, that is, with Ezekiel's Old Testament view of last things. The "waters of the river" do not flow to the sea but have "a tumultuous and convulsive motion"; for miles on either side of the river are vast regions of "gigantic water-lilies." Beyond as far as the horizon is a "horrible" and endless forest. Situated somewhere in his vast desert of whiteness and convulsed waters is "a huge gray rock" upon which the moon shines and reveals the mystic word "Desolation." The protagonist of the narrative has a demon's power to call up spirits from dead bodies. He summons the hippopotami who come to the foot of "Desolation" rock and roar "loudly and fearfully beneath the moon." Then, at the end, the protagonist curses the silence; all the elements obey: the sun stands still; the thunder dies away; the lightning dims, and all matter reverts to its primal condition of utter and endless deadness. At the last the crepuscular light shines on the mystic rock and reveals the word "Silence."

The tale is hardly more than a sketch and crudely approximates the vision-literature such as in Ezekiel ("And the lynx which dwelleth forever in the tomb, came out therefrom, and lay down at the feet of the Demon, and looked at him steadily in the face"). It is a curious mixture of the spell-binding Protestant evangelism of the 1830's with the sensationalist rhetoric in the magazines. What the tale does, however, is to make the universe engage in the catastrophe; it is a projection of a kind of "cosmic unconscious" which drives the assumed order of nature back to its primordial condition. What Poe is fumbling to express is the idea he worked out with such care in *Eureka*: the history of the universe is an expression of a law; and that law states that all matter had a single locus, a primal Oneness, from which it was dispersed throughout all space. In time the dispersive force will be withdrawn, and all matter will return to its primal unity, its Ur-condition again. What Poe was trying to express by the mystic word "Desolation" was the presently observed state of total disunity and by the term "Silence" the inevitable coalescence of all substance.

"The Conversation of Eiros and Charmion" (1839), titled on its appearance in 1843 "The Destruction of the World," is a continuation of this apocalyptic vision of what might happen to the physical and intellectual universe when it exists beyond horror, that is, when discontinuity and incoherence are constants rather than aberrations. As the story opens we are situated beyond life and death; indeed, we have passed through and have reached the state from which we can view death from the comfortable vantage of hindsight. Then we retrace our way and consider the steps leading to the death of the world: a passing comet extracted all the nitrogen from the atmosphere surrounding the earth and left the highly flammable air ready for a spark to set off a terrible cosmic explosion. In the debacle, however, only the earth was destroyed; thus there came about "the entire fulfillment, in all their minute and terrible details, of the fiery and horror-inspiring denunciations of the prophecies of the Holy Book."

What Poe has here attempted to do is to establish a historical and symbolic relationship between myth, or prophecy, and the scientifically known constitution of the universe: the assumption is that what physics and chemistry have latterly revealed, Jewish scripture and Oriental legend have long anticipated. There is, consequently, a demonstration of the universal law of both matter and being which functions from Unity to dispersal and back to Unity again; this principle is so basic to the whole universe that not only the physical constitution but the very elements of thought itself are symbolic exemplifications of its eternal operation.

"The Colloquy of Monos and Una" (1841) was the last and most complete of these rationalized apocalypses. It is the after-story of men who have suffered in their mortal life from Cartesian dualism, the separation of the mind from physical reality, or the hypertrophy of the intellect at the expense of the emotions and the moral sense. In the last days of the world, "taste," that mediating faculty which can lead "to Beauty, to Nature, and to Life" and which holds "a middle position between the pure intellect and the moral sense," had become moribund. Man had to pay the penalty by being reborn to beauty and to unity; death, the great ignominy to man, had become the great illumination.

Poe's apparent purpose in the tale was to offer a rational account of the passage of the human consciousness from life through death to the life-beyond-death on the other side where occurs a final "merging" into "Love" or the harmonious principle uniting all things in the mind of God or the One. Individual existence is not so much purified as it is returned to the primal order, the absolute focus from which the dispersive function had originally begun in the origin of time itself and of all matter.

These tales were Poe's rationalizations of horror; that is, the principle of horror itself seems to imply that the horrific is that which suddenly interrupts or shatters the rational order of the universe; however completely that order is restored, the human mind forced to endure that "apocalypse" or shock will be forever dislocated or maddened. The young man in "The Raven" will never recover his "soul" or his acceptance of the coherence of things after his terrible insight, not only into his own madness, but into the madness of the universe itself. The young man in "The Pit and the Pendulum" was able to maintain his sanity by the power of his will to escape the swinging knife-blade just long enough to be fortuitously rescued from a private psychic world which every moment threatened him with insanity and annihilation. These and other inquiries into the dark world of the mind suggest that Poe, however much his horror was a rather simple externalization of inner states of being, was demonstrating that horror itself or various phases of loss of self might be ways into farther and deeper understanding. Horror, madness, and death are man's avenues into the ultimate rationale of existence of which our own mortal existence is but a crude fragment. Man in his earthly habit lives on the virtually unquestioned assumption that he can predict and understand nearly every event that occurs in his own life and in the diurnal motions of the planets; Poe, however much his rhetoric may have been apocalyptic and frenzied and his narrative struggling to be *outré,* was nevertheless writing a series of quite moral poems and tales concerning the evidence everywhere before man's eyes of the total disunity and incoherence of his own life which is an infinitesimal part of the universal "plot of God." Man must, however, be terrified or driven to comprehend that what seems to be fractured is actually a segment of the universal design and what appears to be madness may be "divinest sense."

Occasionally Poe treated this theme in such a tale as "The Fall of the House of Usher," a masterpiece of horror which we shall investigate under another proposition, or in his further studies of the crack-up of a human mind. In *Eureka,* published in the next to the last year of his life, Poe made a final and thorough investigation of the principles of unity to diffusion and back to unity again, principles which underlay the theory and practice of the horror poem and tale in his earlier years.

V

The Short Story as Grotesque

Poetry may have been a "passion" for Poe. It could never be a means of subsistence; when, by 1833, he had published three volumes of verse, the world, critical or popular, had paid no heed. He thereupon turned to writing short stories. Almost as though in willful humor, he submitted a sheaf of tales for the fifty-dollar prize offered by the *Baltimore Saturday Visiter* and won it. From that time forward he was to be both poet and short-story writer and, even more, a critic.

So far, Poe's career as a writer had been all of a piece: he had dedicated himself to poetry; yet he was forced, even before he had reached full poetic maturity, to abandon poetry or else not to take it with the comprehensive seriousness which had been his initial impulse. His career became varied: he was by turns poet, critic, short-story writer, editor, and sometimes plain hack because Poe's creative energies were subserved to making money.[1] Romantic apologists, considering Poe as a demonstration of the artist's condition, regard this necessitous change as a tragedy for art. Baudelaire was among the first to blame America for the penury and death of Edgar Poe, the poet and artist. It might more wisely be said that the times may have killed Poe the poet, but they made Poe the short-story writer and critic.

For whatever reasons one may assign or surmise, Poe became, about 1833, a writer of prose tales.[2] Those first short stories, written between 1833 and 1837 — their number can never be known with any certainty — were all together to be known by Poe's own designation, "Tales of the Folio Club." When no publisher would undertake to issue them as a book, Poe printed them variously in the *Southern Literary Messenger.*[3]

Poe wrote these early tales with the primary intention of burlesquing the popular and best-selling tales in the magazines of the day, tales of passion, of horror, of the remote and *outré,* of death and the dead — in short, of that staple of popular reading consumption which so delights an unintelligent audience and which is so easily forgotten except by the student who is willing to labor long in regions of little surprise or merit. But Poe's burlesques, or "grotesques" as he afterward termed them, served him far better than bringing him twenty-five or thirty dollars for each submission or the pleasure of ridiculing what so many readers took with gasping seriousness: Poe played the sedulous ape in reverse. By imitating the tricks and devices of the popular tales in *Blackwoods*[4] and other English and American magazines of the day, Poe learned how to write a short story. He became extremely adept in all the mannerisms, and even some of the competent craftsmanship, which even the most inferior stories sometimes expose. "Most of them," Poe wrote, "were *intended* for half banter, half satire—although I might not have fully acknowledged this to be their aim even to myself."[5] With some variations in stress, technique, and character Poe turned fooling into art: from the very early "Metzengerstein" and "The Assignation" it is not very far to "The Fall of the House of Usher," only five or six years later. What Poe began by burlesquing and ridiculing he afterward discovered could be made a masterly inquiry into the diseased and sin-ridden soul of man.

The fictional prose burlesque had a long and distinguished history in its own right of which Poe was quite well aware—the fantasies and hoaxes all the way from Chaucer through Rabelais, Cyrano de Bergerac, Swift, and Thomas Love Peacock. In the hands of such noteworthy practitioners it had achieved a form, a style, and even a moral earnestness such as marked *Gulliver's Travels,* Johnson's *Rasselas,* Voltaire's *Candide,* Jane Austen's *Northanger Abbey,* and Peacock's *Headlong Hall* and *Nightmare Abbey.* Though these writings are not "sources" for Poe's burlesques, especially those which rested heavily on the Gothic tradition, they suggest that there was indeed a long literary tradition for the form and that the longer the form had existed in the English-speaking world, the more markedly sophisticated and consciously literary it had become. Poe's youthful apings of the form were almost painfully literary and affecting the grand manner, replete with offhand allusions to esoteric learning, with quotations, and half-farcical citations—with, in short, that acceptance of erudition which the hoax and lampoon easily invited.

Yet to trace the literary antecedence to Poe's burlesques gathered in the Folio Club Tales would tell us very little except what we already know: that Poe was a very clever young man. We might summarize the long tradition of the literary hoax and narrative burlesque by stating that it was essentially a coterie expression; it was written for and directed toward only those few who were aware of the joke and who could at once appreciate the author's casual references and his "little language." No such coterie of sophisticated readers existed in America; a country had to be older and better settled than was the United States in the 1830's to produce anything more than Freneau's squibs and lampoons or Trumbull's *M'Fingal.* Yet there was in America a very lively encouragement to and actual practice of the lampoon, the hoax, the elaborate jest because of one very salient feature of the American character — the fondness for verbalisms and verbal humor, the skill for developing elaborate verbal tricks and grotesqueries as a means of reducing men to a common democratic denominator or of deflating frauds and phonies.

In a note to "Hans Pfaall" Baudelaire remarked that Americans "like so much to be fooled" and considered that this fooling of people was Poe's main "dada" or fetish which betrayed Poe's Americanism more than did any other facet of his writing; the rest of Poe's mind, Baudelaire concluded, was "profoundly Germanic and sometimes so deeply Oriental." [6] Baudelaire could be brilliantly wrongheaded, but he was right more than he realized: Poe's grotesques were indeed American and deeply rooted in the American pioneer tradition that feigned a seriousness which masked the absurdity just beneath the surface of the joke.

Much of this American humor, which reached one of its major expressions both in Poe's early tales and in Mark

Twain's major writings, was based on the situation of an essentially classless society that nonetheless needed to contrive artificial distinctions of caste and class: since there could be no peasant nor aristocrat, not even in the presumably aristocratic South, there could be only the "ins" and the "outs," the wise and the stupid, the normal and the abnormal. The grotesque in Poe's hands assumed that those who belonged were ridiculing those who were "outside." His only variation in the form was to allow only a very small minority to "belong," and thereby nearly the whole of society became the butt of his ridicule.

Still another element of American ridicule and humor in the early nineteenth century was its basic cruelty;[7] it was the cruelty of those who in a classless society were convinced that they "belonged" and were as fully resentful of any challenges from those who might threaten to unseat them. Because their social and economic position was precarious in the extreme, their humor was a necessary support to their pride of place and family and heritage. The joke in America has been so long directed variously at Negroes, the Irish, the Swedes, the Jews, and all other so-called minority groups that it has been regularly used as a means of defining social position and privilege. Baudelaire to the contrary, Poe well recognized the force of absurdity directed with mordant cruelty against those who were somehow outside.

Yet Poe's hoaxes were not cruel or savage in the way Mark Twain's would become, with their attacks on miscegenation in *Pudd'nhead Wilson* or the assault on human degradation in *Huckleberry Finn*. Poe's are, generally speaking, undirected and objectless; his are what might be called "verbal cruelties" and depend on rhetorical violence rather than on vivid and forceful presentations of human situations. To a great extent Poe was in this respect a member of a dominant southern literary tradition all the way to William Faulkner: the rhetoric is frequently more highly charged than the action it is intended to convey. By this means one can justify the violence of shooting off the nose in "Lionizing," absurd as the situation is. Other matters of violence were similarly made into involved verbal manipulations and jokes: beheadings and burials alive, in sum, a whole budget of whimsies which Poe, by only a slight variation of rhetoric and style, made the compelling subjects of his "arabesques," the narrative representations of his fully developed powers in his mature years.

Cruelty was a standard component of native American humor; another was the tendency to be irreverent in the presence of profoundly maintained beliefs or ideals. From the very beginning American jests have been directed at the government, at love and marriage, at the manifold beliefs which are otherwise accepted with religious intensity; yet, curiously enough, American humorists have seldom been regarded as dangerous or inimical to the national ideal. One of Poe's typical subjects was to ridicule learning: the biggest fool is, of course, the presumptious wise man who, like Hans Pfaall, confessed that his "ignorance . . . so far from rendering me diffident . . . merely served as a further stimulus to imagination; and I was vain enough, or perhaps reasonable enough, to doubt whether those crude ideas which, arising in ill-regulated minds, have all the appearance, may not often in effect possess all the force, the reality, and other inherent properties of instinct or intuition." American humor has frequently made stupidity a kind of national virtue and intelligence a vice. In "Hans Pfaall" Americans "soon began to feel the effects of liberty and long speeches, and radicalism, and all that sort of thing. . . . They had as much as they could do to read about the revolutions, and keep up with the march of intellect and the spirit of the age."

These, then, were some of the determinations of native American humor which shaped Poe's early experiments in short-story writing. Many of them would remain with him throughout his whole career, for, by a curious reverse process, what he early lampooned he subsequently made into the subject matter of his memorable tales. Only a slight shift of emphasis would remold "Metzengerstein," with its theme of the compulsive past working out in the present, into "The Fall of the House of Usher"; or "The Assignation," with its rather absurd narrative of the powerful metaphysical connection between a man and a woman, into "Ligeia."

These tales of Poe's apprenticeship also early made apparent a shift in Poe's mind from the tale as mere sensation and effect to the "arabesque" or the tale of moral insight and symbolism. Specters, images of death and the dead, the terror of the unknown — these and others became means not just for excitement but for the quest of the imagination toward a further understanding. When poetry failed or was abandoned in Poe's mid-career, the prose tale became a substitute means of working toward that intuitively apprehended realm where fact and idea, substance and concept might meet. In a "prose poem" *Eureka* the two elements were joined; along the way, however, a number of artistic and symbolic pathways had to be explored, sometimes in much the same way as the poetry had sought them out, before full exploitation of the narrative form could be realized.

2

One might readily assume that a young writer's first venture into an unfamiliar literary form, especially if at first he did not take his venture with any true seriousness, would be not only strongly imitative but also markedly literary. That is, these early Folio Club Tales did not come from an inventive mind, like for example Mark Twain's in his own experimental buffooneries, recasting its observations on the world about him; rather, Poe's sprang from a very clever imitative intelligence which was recasting experience at several removes from any original observation. The ghosts of Cyrano de Bergerac, Rabelais, Swift, and Locke (not the philosopher but the author of a well-known voyage to the moon) hover over nearly every sentence. Only in later ventures into the grotesque did Poe approach any subject of the real world around him; otherwise, his short-story writing from the very beginning exhibits that lifelong tendency, even when dealing with New England Transcendentalists or the inflated literary reputations of the day, to recast everything in terms of the remote, the recherché, and to demand, as though there actually did exist a coterie of readers who were initiated into these mysteries, that the reader be himself sufficiently learned to comprehend or to laugh at the presumptuous erudition which the tales affect with such mock seriousness.

Even more than a young writer's imitativeness and literary mannerisms, these tales of the grotesque reflected certain sides of Poe himself. In an odd way they form a segment of inverted autobiography; for Poe, all the while he was ridiculing sacred ideas of government or learning, lampooned some of his own most solemnly maintained convictions and illusions.[8] "Mystification," in its earliest form as "Von Jung" (1837), turned inside out the painful memory of his student days: "I have seen an ox-cart, with oxen, on the summit of the Rotunda" of the University of Virginia. The portrait of Hermann, deleted from subsequent printings of the story, had interesting autobiographical overtones:

> His head was of colossal dimensions, and overshadowed by a dense mass of straight raven hair, two huge locks of which, stiffly plastered with pomatum, extended with a lachrymose air down the temples, and partially over the cheek bones — a fashion which of late days has wormed itself . . . into the good graces of the denizens of the United States. . . . The forehead was massive and broad, the organs of ideality over the temples, as well as those of causality, comparison, and eventuality, which betray themselves above the *os frontis,* being so astonishingly developed as to attract the instant notice of every person who saw him. The eyes were full, brilliant, beaming with what might be mistaken for intelligence, and well relieved by the short, straight, picturesque-looking eyebrow, which is perhaps one of the surest indications of general ability. The aquiline nose, too, was superb; certainly nothing more magnificent was ever beheld, nothing more delicate nor more exquisitely modelled.[9]

In other ways Poe made sport of himself. "How to Write a Blackwood Article" and its companion piece, "A Predicament," ridiculed what were later to be his most reasoned ideas of art. These grotesques and others were Poe's permission to make fun of himself; the more he got away from himself and from his youthful autobiographical impulse, the less he engaged in this graceless self-portraiture, itself a form of ill-concealed sentimentalism.

Still another interesting facet of Poe's mind becomes apparent in these early tales. It was what might be called "verbal violence" — the employment of profane or forbidden words in contexts which would ostensibly belie any profanity or lewdness but which would nonetheless allow the writer, for those who would be knowledgeable in such matters, to be explosive and irreverent. In American humor this element was very strong in speech, as it always must be in the popular dirty joke; what has survived in tall tale and horselaugh has been fairly well cleaned up and made presentable; the original was doubtless far more raw and gamy than what folklorists spend so much time collecting. Again, this tendency toward the strong and the violent in language which all the while masquerades as respectability occurs in periods of culture and literary history when codes of expression, however amorphous and unwritten, insist on a decency beyond which writers do not generally dare go. In our own time, so fully committed to the four-letter word and the foul expression, this rigorous adherence to a supposedly "Victorian" inhibition is difficult to understand; in the age of Poe it was so solemnly observed as to pass almost without question.

But when the injunction of decency in language could be broken, as it necessarily was, the wreckage was almost catastrophic: it might sometimes seem as if a writer were attempting to see how far he could go without incurring the outraged wrath of his reading public. In nineteenth-century America the spectacular, though privately circulated, example of this verbal breaking-out was Mark Twain's not very funny "1601; or Conversation as It Was by the Social Fireside in the Time of the Tudors." Poe was in no way as capable or inventive as was Twain: most of his expressions are like those of a boy who is trying to show off, and all of them were excised or made innocuous in subsequent publications of the tales in which they first appeared. Yet these tales were safety valves of a profane impulse which exists variously in everyone and which somehow needs or gains expression. Briefly to trace Poe's infractions of the code of decency is to see how far he dared go in affecting innocence but indulging in profanity and even in obscenity.

"Some Passages in the Life of a Lion," or "Lionizing" as it was named in its earlier versions (the tale was first published in the *Messenger* for May 1835), however much it may have aimed at satirizing monstrously inflated literary reputations, was probably not about the "nose," the ostensible mark of superiority which the hero-narrator bears, but about the penis. For one reason, there are a number of striking similarities between Poe's preposterous fable and Sterne's story of "Noses" in *Tristram Shandy*: the same pretense at innocence, the slight twists of words and phrasing necessary to unmask the trivial lewdity, the piling up of insistent repetitions to lead one to suspect that "noses" might be intended to mean something else.[10] This story was afterward so revised that hardly a sentence of the original remained in the version of his tales which Poe published in 1840.[11] The involved word-play and the sly innuendoes could hardly leave any doubt of what was the real subject of the narrative, but the concealments apparently were sufficiently clever in Poe's time to pass muster without giving offense.

In "Never Bet the Devil Your Head" (1841) the salacious wink and the profanity were more feebly contrived. The hero's name is "Toby Dammit"; the point of such a sentence as the following is in the absence or inclusion of the comma: " 'Dammit,' said I, 'What are you about?' " or " 'Dammit, . . . the gentleman says *ahem!*' "[12] There is the doubling of profanity with a certain raw crudity: the Transcendentalists (the point of the ridicule is leveled at the New England cultists and followers of German idealism) refused to pay for Toby Dammit's funeral; "so I had Mr. Dammit dug up at once, and sold him for dog's meat." The lusty plain-speaking of the frontier ill suits this mannered story.

In the early *Saturday Courier* and *Messenger* versions of "A Tale of Jerusalem," a rather graceless story which smacks of popular, low-intelligence anti-Semitism, the name of the Jewish high priest is not, as it later became, "Abel-Phittim" but "Abel-Shittim."[13] The name is, for a Jew, quite probable; but Poe was apparently seeing how much he could be offensive without giving offense. Furthermore, at the end of the earlier versions (Poe afterward cleaned up the whole story) were these words: " 'Let me no longer,' said the Pharisee wrapping his cloak around him and departing within the city — 'let me no longer be called Simeon, which signifieth "he who listens" — but rather Boanerges, "the son of Thunder." ' "[14] The connotation is obvious: the Jews within the beleaguered city of Jerusalem have been affronted by receiving from their enemies a pig for the sacrifice; now Simeon the Pharisee is saying (and the meaning is especially apparent after all the word-play on "Abel-Shittim"), "Let me be called 'the son of wind-breaking.' "

These are the major verbal contrivances which Poe employed in his tales of the grotesque. That he afterward excised most if not all of them need not argue that his sensibility became refined or that pressures to conform were imposed upon him, but that, as soon as he began to take seriously a narrative form he had earlier lampooned and regarded as beneath literary contempt, he quite rightly deleted these word-plays which might detract from the artistic design of the tale or mislead his readers into regarding the tales as not very clever jests. Yet something private and almost compulsive lay behind the obscenity and profanity: crude diction or elaborate devices to convey and yet at the same time to conceal a scabrous intention suggest a potential aim on Poe's part to ridicule or get even with a society which could find amusement in and yet be fooled by these seemingly innocent expressions. The very outrageousness of Poe's verbal twists as well as their utter inapplicability are indications not only that Poe was unaccustomed to profanity and obscenity but that he had some insulting or violent intention which demanded expression but which he could voice only in these quite ludicrous puns. Afterward he revised the stories and never again affected the manner. The change was not moral but aesthetic: he realized that in the whimsy, the satire, the grotesque, or the hoax mere word-play would count for little but that the totality of effect would depend on the inevitable suitability of all parts, verbal or artistic, to the whole design. Furthermore, Poe must have found his early bad-boy pose unattractive: for a brief period it had found relief; subsequently it was to find its outlet in forms of violence which were not merely verbal—in the horrific, the macabre, in brutality as revealed in such a masterwork as *Pym*.

3

Poe's production of these tales of the grotesque steadily declined after 1838, with "How to Write a Blackwood Article" and "A Predicament," and 1839, with "The Devil in the Belfry." He published "Why the Little Frenchman Wears His Hand in a Sling" in 1840, "Never Bet the Devil Your Head" and "Three Sundays in a Week" in 1841, "Diddling" in 1843, and "The Balloon Hoax" in 1844. For one thing, these tales were as close to social criticism of the times as Poe ever came; they contain just about all he had to say about New England Transcendentalists, slavery, the business world and the acquisitive mind, and other topics pertinent to his age. They are, in part, failures because Poe was not in any way a social critic, nor was he even interested in an imaginative projection of the issues of his time.[15] Thoreau transformed the dimensions of his age by relocating the issues in terms of personal history, either at Walden or in the protest of "Civil Disobedience"; Melville embarked on a naturalistic cruise wherein the ocean, sky, ships, and men were mythic projections of man's eternal desire to satisfy his longing: the fictive world of argument and circumstance was replaced by brute objects whose shapes became the lineaments of man's desire and confusion.

Poe's social ideas failed of expression not because he was indifferent to issues: if feeling were a measure of his intention, then he would have annihilated the New York literati or the "Frogpondians" of Concord. A forceful social criticism derives not from a writer's passionate espousal of causes or his flaming determination to correct abuses but from his basic coming to terms with reality itself. Social consciousness and criticism are bound up with the artist's making reality "real." Whitman, from the 1855 Preface to *Democratic Vistas,* could continually envision democratic vitality, or corruption, in terms of "adhesiveness," a metaphor of sensual physical love which was a means of reducing to a vivid personal expression a concept that otherwise would have remained an abstraction. Social criticism in writing might be considered as a method of personalizing a set of abstractions; these abstractions are salient lines between a writer's creative imagination and the world outside so long as he not only believes in them but can use them. Whitman's brotherly arm around the shoulder, Mark Twain's journey into and out of society from *Huckleberry Finn* through *What Is Man?* or Faulkner's naturalistic redefining the southern present in terms of a variable time-scheme out of the past are cases in point. These are means of making reality not so much "real" as a private symbolic spectrum whereby man and society reform themselves into an inner dream. A hoax or grotesque such as Poe wrote was hardly more than a crude compromise with reality; it always remained outside.[16]

Thus these early experiments represented Poe's compromise with the factual world around him — with law, commerce, finance, politics, and slavery. They were compromises only, hardly more than verbal contortions and puns for the sake of the joke or the surprise. In that compromise something needed to yield, either art or reality; neither did, for the reason that Poe had, from the beginning, construed art and the imagination as a totally refracting and transforming agency: one "went through" reality in order to reach the vision, the truth, on the other side. He had learned too well his lesson from Coleridge; and he had never aimed, like Wordsworth and Thoreau, to redefine social experience and present history in terms of a private autobiography in which the journeying self became the measure of man. Poe could only play verbally with appearances around him; in "The Business Man" the satire on the instinct for money-making was blunted against a cheap gargoyle with no relevance at all to the theme of the story. In "Never Bet the Devil Your Head" Poe was, for a time, effectively satirizing German idealists until the word-play took over, and all that remained were the ineffectual puns on "style" and "stile" or on a contemporary reader's ability to hurdle Carlyle's "style" without breaking his neck or his head.

Yet, by writing these tales of the grotesque, Poe discovered not only that he could, in fooling, outdistance his tale-writing contemporaries whose prose cluttered the popular magazines but that he could learn to handle such necessary matters as plot, dialogue, description, and even some degree of simple character exposition and analysis. But the chief gain from these early experiments was his learning how to handle what might be called the "moral fantasy," a narrative which is so obviously a fable that it could not be regarded as a realistic presentation of life but a tale whose implications reach very far into man's illusions of himself when placed in the withering light of what he really is.

One of the hitherto unexplored tales in Poe's early canon is "Four Beasts in One, or The Homo-Camelopard," first published in the *Messenger* for March 1836, just before the beginning of the *Narrative of Arthur Gordon Pym.* The tale, presumably based on any one of a number of historical analogies, is of the Seleucid king, Antiochus Epiphanes, whose chief pleasures were murderous and bestial: he enjoyed putting Jews to death, and he delighted the populace of Antioch in disguising himself as an animal and running through the streets of the metropolis and requiring the adulatory kisses of the populace. One day he dressed himself as a camelopard or giraffe and rushed through the crowded streets announced by a ragged, hysterical urchin and preceded by a chorus chanting a vulgar Latin hymn. This time, however, Antiochus did not complete his absurd gambit: the animals locked in their cages for the entertainment in the hippodrome were so insulted by this man-beast that they broke out and raged through the city. Only after they had been finally caught and returned to their cages were the ultimate honors of winning the foot race bestowed on the drunken, bloated person of Antiochus Epiphanes.

This story is like others of Poe's best expressions in fantasy — like, for example, "The Masque of the Red Death" and "Hop-Frog." Its aim is to reduce man from his assumed humanity to his bestial counterpart and, as in the fables of La Fontaine, Rabelais, Voltaire, and Swift, to reveal that disgusting underside of man's existence. Yet the tale has all the farce and grotesquerie of Poe's other fables: the tricks on words and puns, the distortions for effect, the affectation of vast erudition, the clumsy jocosities; but what gives "Four Beasts in One" its brilliance and distinction is that, as the story unfolds, the farcical action establishes the bestial nature of man which lies just beneath the surface of civilization; man is the destructive beast, whereas the animals are humane. The apparent absurdity of such a fantasy is, like Swift's assault on the human race in the fourth book of *Gulliver's Travels,* the very means of establishing this seemingly far-fetched relevance of men as beasts and the beasts as superior men. Such a commentary becomes especially mordant because no one is encouraged to take it seriously; but all the while that one is so beguiled into enjoying the joke, the fantasy moves toward disgust. Only in fantasy should one be so innocently betrayed into self-recognition.

One might well regret that Poe did not more frequently employ his genius in such an exercise. So long as he need not have been deluded into considering himself a clever satirist of local absurdities he might have followed the range of bitter satirical fantasy which could have reached a level equal to that of Lucian, Heine, and Byron. Poe's last venture into the form was "Hop-Frog," a savage indictment of those who wield power for their own amusement and pleasure; the hunchback dwarf got his revenge by inventing a game so ludicrous that it entrapped only those who were evil enough not to take it seriously.

These grotesques were, therefore, Poe's apprenticeship. By cleverly modeling his own tales on the standard devices of Bulwer-Lytton and the horde of scribblers whose stories of horror, love, death, titanic hate and revenge, and all the other popular staples of a middle-class reading public, Poe found that he could not only equal but even surpass these contemporaries at their own contemptible literary game. Therefore, Poe did not have to move far from the ludicrous sentimentalism of "The Assignation" to the terrifying inquiry into a woman's hold on a man even after death as in "Eleanora" and "Ligeia." But Poe learned from these exercises which, at first, he refused to take seriously, more than a mere budget of tricks and narrative methods. He learned a method of employing scene and physical surroundings as such an integral part of the action that sometimes man and nature co-exist in some vast, terrifying continuum, beyond time and beyond understanding but reaching toward a new world of mystery where even meaning cannot penetrate. This comprehension reached its fullest expression in "The Fall of the House of Usher," wherein no physical object exists except as some haunting figuration of the profound inner drama of Roderick Usher and his sister Madeline. Poe also learned from these early experiments in the short-story form that even the farcical and absurd need design and order; later he thought sufficiently well of the tales to reprint them all, either in the collected volume of 1840 or in the *Broadway Journal* in the 1840's. What these later versions demonstrate is that Poe was aware not so much that a tale had to have a moral point but that every word should somehow cohere in the main design and every texture blend. Weak as some of these narratives were, they yet were given their share of review and revision. From the looseness and verbosity of "Metzengerstein," it is not very far to the salient compression of "The Masque of the Red Death," in which very little fact and information are given but in which the tone and movement are all.

Finally, Poe was further encouraged in these tales to leave behind the accepted naturalistic world around him and to explore the indeterminate regions which poetry had suggested. These tales are indeed "poems," and Poe always remained a poet even when he was contributing some of his most uninspired narratives to the periodicals: "Why the Little Frenchman Wears His Hand in a Sling" and "Three Sundays in a Week" are hapless cases in point. Eventually the tales investigated some of the same themes which had been the province of the poems: the extent to which man can give idea and meaning to the farther range of experience beyond mere sense; the method of making known the variables of meaning itself — these symbolic tangents which the word and the image can establish in the human mind; and the tragic dislocation of man in a world which, however well that world assumes an order in the mind, nevertheless forbids any ultimate participation or sense of kinship. Poe was one of the first modern symbolists to inquire into the rationale of the single self, the special organism, and know that the primary recognition of that self is its own lonely identity. The more Poe explored that theme the clearer became the view that, while art, whether short story, poem, or novel, was a means of penetrating what Yeats considered long afterward the masks of identity, art was similarly self-destructive: it sought the infinitely variable ways of established knowable relations between mind and world, self and being, time and the universe, and yet it was finally bound to the one minute apprehension which only that tale, or that poem, could on the instant suggest. The question became, after all, a matter of individual apprehension and the penetration of the masks of identity which for Melville were white and deceptive but which were for Poe, however illusory they might finally show themselves, the only reason why art existed at all. Otherwise, man might just as well be content with a brute, unyielding naturalism of things-as-they-are. In the *Narrative of Arthur Gordon Pym,* Poe's fullest inquiry into this theme during his middle years, the world as substantive and "real" slowly dissolved as a voyage to the mystery of identity unfolded.

VI

Arthur Gordon Pym

Only twice did Poe try his hand at a sustained narrative, first in *The Narrative of A. Gordon Pym* (in two installments in the *Southern Literary Messenger* for January and February 1837 and separately as a "finished" book in 1838) and, second, in *The Journal of Julius Rodman,* published serially in *Burton's Gentleman's Magazine* from January through June 1840; of the latter work Poe thought so little that he never attempted to print it separately or gather it among his tales. In a way, one narrative is commentary on the other; both begin at the same place in the creative imagination — with the facts of a voyage or a journey to unexplored lands. One remains earthbound and text-confined to its sources, which Poe quite ruthlessly copied, extracted, or revised; the other, *Pym,* takes off from its sources, comes back to them for supporting details, and then transforms and makes them into art.

In their ways both are hoaxes; they presume to recount adventures with a complete, an almost deadly seriousness and base the separate incidents on undoubted facts which science and exploration could confirm. For *Rodman* Poe relied almost entirely on Washington Irving's *Astoria,*[1] itself a derivation from other narratives, and on the journals of Lewis and Clark. For *Pym* Poe undertook, in part, to recast the narratives of J. N. Reynolds, Captain Cook, Benjamin Morrell, and John Cleve Symmes's *Symzonia* (or "holes at the Poles"), all of which were detailed accounts of voyages to and scientific findings at the South Pole in the years before the Wilkes expedition, fitted out by the United States Navy in the 1840's, went to plot the ice caps and uncharted regions of Antarctica. These two pieces were, indeed, intended to be hardly more than hackwork which a hard-pressed editor of the *Messenger* and *Burton's* needed in order to fill the issues of his magazine.

Pym has been generally ignored or scanted by Poe scholars and critics (both Woodberry and Quinn were revolted by its "brutality" and hurriedly passed it by). Because it is the most complete and sustained work of his career, it may reveal far more of Poe's imagination and especially its truly symbolizing activity than do the short stories, excellent though they are, or the poems and criticisms.

In *Pym* are brought together and given full statement some of the basic concepts which have been hitherto unresolved in Poe's poetry and tales. I therefore place the work at what I call "center"; it stands, as it were, between the poetry and the fully mastered prose in the short stories; it partakes of something of both poetry and prose (one as imaginative journey and the other as investigating sides of the self), and, while it appears to be unfinished, it forms the most complete statement Poe ever made of his artistic practice. Afterward were to be the explanations and rationalizations — in a "Philosophy of Composition" and in a "Rationale of Verse." These were the precepts which were laid down after the practice had been insured; and that practice is most truly, and perhaps all unwittingly, detailed in *Pym*.

As a "work of art" the book is obviously uneven: much of the learning is borrowed (the sources have been carefully explored) and not much artistry, such as marked Melville's fusing of the imported fact with the imagined action, has gone into shaping these crude elements into the full design.[2] We have seemingly unrelated digressions on penguins and albatrosses, the geography of Antarctica, the history of South Polar exploration, and the curing of "biche de mer." These are obvious blemishes which prevent the book's achieving stature among the memorable "voyages" by Americans — Cooper, Melville, Twain, and others, who have sent young heroes off on strange adventures. Again, the narrative breaks into segments — five of them, by an artificial count; characters loom importantly at the beginning and then disappear. Lastly, the end of the book is either absurd, monstrous, or mysterious; for all that happens is a voyage in an oversize canoe into a blinding white light near the South Pole — as if Poe had no more to say and thus stopped his narrative short; he even increased the implied insult by adding an appendix in small type in which he essayed to clarify certain confusions — and clarified nothing. Howsoever these charges may be applied, the book is large and disheveled; one might make out a case for its apparent looseness of form and then attempt to make a case for its meaningful "organic structure." It does have structure, whether organic (therefore "growing from a seed" and equalling a totality of design) or not is hard to say; it does have a beginning and an end. Somewhere in the amplitude of its growth there is a middle, and that may rest on infinity.[3]

Poe's primary intention is easy to discover: he wished to capitalize on the popular interest in Antarctica during the 1830's; the Arctic regions had been fairly well explored, but the South Polar regions were the last *terra incognita* on the globe. Already Holland, France, Russia, Germany, and England had explored and pushed into that strange place; and there arose a kind of national test of prowess and supremacy among the nations to see which might gain the glory of really charting that vast region. Not until the renowned Wilkes expedition of 1840–1842 was this region really to be known; Poe, when he wrote his farfetched tale, had at hand only the accounts of Captain Cook, Benjamin Morrell, J. N. Reynolds, and a few others. That the area was land or water had not been established (Poe supported the "land" theory, which was correct); and popular interest, if not sound judgment, was inflamed by John Cleve Symmes's theory of "holes at the Poles": by sailing over the edge of the South or North Polar region, men of earth would discover a vast interior region of other men and other civilizations which had flourished for thousands of years unknown to each other. To retail the popular background to Poe's *Pym* is to narrate the whole course of South Polar exploration and interest throughout the thirties. Poe had at hand a few books; they were enough to supply him with the facts. With or around them he spun his fable.

Yet, as one reads *Pym,* he is attracted by an appearance of something that betokens more than a mere hoax or the literary employment of a popular craze. The narrative gets out of hand; it does not stick to a voyage to the South Pole — in fact, the narrative does not reach the white waters of Antarctica until very late in the book. In sum, the reader is reminded that *Pym* is very like Melville's chartless voyage in *Mardi* — somewhat confused, heavily allegorical, irresolute in its symbolism, in short attempting to articulate some design which never quite comes into view. One extremely perceptive critic of Poe has pointed out the suggestive parallels between *Pym* and *Moby-Dick,* almost as though Melville were aware of what Poe had done before him and had consciously imitated some of Poe's method and design.[4] Nothing of these matters can, with present evidence, be proved; what does emerge, however, is that Poe was, like every American writer of distinction, probing for some "deep axis of reality" (the phrase is, of course, Melville's applied to Hawthorne) and employing an invented fable as his frame of investigation.

In such terms, irresolute as the book is, it is a study of emerging consciousness, a very special intelligence and awareness which is Arthur Gordon Pym's (and, to an extent, Poe's); unlike Melville's "consciousness" in *Mardi,* Poe's is narrowly confined: whereas Melville assumed diverse points of view in order to encompass his political, religious, and ethnic vision, Poe steadily defines and sharpens the point of perception until all else fades before the intensity with which a Pym-self regards the world and itself. This self-as-imagination begins with the real, substantial world, follows the poetic direction of penetrating and destroying that world, and then goes even farther in order to set up on "the other side" certain symbols and keys to the mind's perception of reality. The book is indeed finished: that Poe himself published it as a volume under the auspices of Harper and Brothers (interestingly enough, the publishers of *Moby-Dick* a few years later) is not sufficient attestation to the book's completeness. It was "finished" in the sense that Schubert's B-Minor Symphony, known as the "Unfinished," was completed: in both the artistic intention is complete within the range that the writer or composer set for himself. However ill-organized it may be, *Pym* is a study of the emergence and growth of the knowing and thinking self. Though Poe wrote other inquiries into this subject, he never made quite so complete an investigation as he did in this sustained narrative whose theme might be those phrases from Plato's *Symposium* which Poe used as the epigraph to "Morella": "Itself, by itself, solely, ONE everlastingly, and single."[5]

2

The plot of *Pym* is quite simple. Arthur Gordon Pym, at sixteen, has a passion to go to sea. His friend, Augustus Bernard, is the son of a whaling captain of Nantucket. One night they engage in a boyish prank of drinking as much wine as they can hold; on a mutual dare that same night they take a sail in Augustus' boat, the "Ariel." When a stiff breeze blows them out to sea, Pym, who knows nothing of sailing, discovers that Augustus is hopelessly drunk. Only by the sheerest luck when they are run down in the darkness by a homebound whaler and picked up are their lives saved; and before dawn the two boys are able to get home and appear the next morning as if nothing had happened.

But this freakish and terrifying experience does not dampen Pym's desire to go to sea. When Augustus' father makes ready a South Sea whaling voyage in the "Grampus," Pym is secreted in the hold with enough food and drink to allow him to survive until the ship is safely out to sea. Pym's incarceration is prolonged interminably: he undergoes the worst tortures of being buried alive and of suffocation in the stupefying hold. Awakening from one of his stupors, Pym is surprised to find his dog Tiger with him; but Tiger also nearly goes mad and threatens his master. After the two have suffered together for what seem endless days, the frenzied dog turns on Pym, who barely saves his life as Augustus comes through the darkness and shows the way out of the ship's interior.

Pym has lain for eleven days in the hold; in that time the ship had put to sea and a mutiny had broken out. Captain Bernard and a few faithful men have been put overboard and cast adrift in the lonely Atlantic; nearly all of the loyal sailors have been brutally murdered. Through the efforts of Dirk Peters, the leader of a minority faction of the sailors who are about to be murdered, Pym and Augustus plot to catch the mutineers off guard. When Pym puts on the clothes of and masquerades as the dead sailor, Hartman Rogers, the vicious sailors are overpowered and killed. Afterward only Pym, Augustus, Dirk Peters, and a repentant sailor named Parker are all that remain.

A terrible storm comes up, strips the "Grampus" of its masts and rigging, and leaves it a hulk floating in the sea. The four survivors endure the terrible suffering of thirst and hunger; in their extremity they draw lots for one man to die in order to save the rest; the lot falls on Parker, whom

Peters kills, and the others feed on his body. Augustus afterward sickens and dies; another storm comes and turns the hulk bottom up. Somewhere in the South Atlantic Peters and Pym, the only survivors, are picked up by the "Jane Guy," a sealer out of Liverpool. In a short time their strength comes back and they sign on as members of the crew.

Though the "Jane Guy" was bound for the South Pacific, its captain turns southward into Antarctica. The farther south the ship sails, the more temperate the climate becomes; and the natives on the islands appear to be very friendly. On one of these islands the whole crew is ambushed and annihilated in a very cleverly devised avalanche. Only Pym and Peters escape by having, on the moment, explored a crevice in the mountain. They remain hidden until hunger drives them out; they make their desperate way to the shore where, though they are nearly captured by the blood-thirsty natives, they get away in a long canoe and with a captured native as a guide. They sail ever southward to avoid the oncoming polar winter. At the end they are moving straight toward a blinding whiteness. There the narrative closes; in an "editorial note" Poe expresses regret that, though Peters is alive in Illinois, he cannot be located; and the only record of the extraordinary adventure is Pym's incomplete diary.

This plot summary is based on the assumption that not many readers, even readers of Poe, have read *Arthur Gordon Pym*. The intention here is not to resurrect a minor but hitherto unacknowledged masterpiece but to set the stage for an analysis of a work central to Poe's mind and thought, despite the admission of Poe himself that it was "a very silly book." [6] The book readily divides itself into five parts: a prologue which recounts the scapegrace night adventures of Pym and Augustus Bernard on the "Ariel," and four major episodes — Pym's incarceration in the hold of the "Grampus"; the sudden overthrow and destruction of the mutineers; the "Grampus" becalmed and the sufferings of the four survivors; and the voyage of the "Jane Guy" into Antarctica, followed by the brutal trickery of the South Polar natives and the escape of only Dirk Peters and Pym.

The first chapter, or prologue, of *Pym* is a highly dramatic yet abbreviated narrative of everything that the rest of the book will contain; it is very like "The Custom House" chapter as prefatory to *The Scarlet Letter* and the New Bedford–Nantucket episodes as prologue to *Moby-Dick*. In all three instances the opening episode is a microcosm of the whole action which is to follow. Each of the four main narrative episodes in *Pym* is, to some degree, a development of a theme suggestively treated in that night's adventure aboard the "Ariel" (even the association of that small boat with the ship in which Shelley drowned is for a purpose) — deception, self-loss, death, rebirth.

That first chapter, with Augustus maddened and then stupefied by alcohol, strikes one of the book's major themes, the theme of deception: nothing really is what it seems. Augustus can "imitate the outward demeanor of one in perfect possession of his senses"; the night storm capsizes the "Ariel," yet a whaler is happily nearby to pick up the boys; Pym's neck wound made by a grappling hook can easily be explained; and the boys readily trick their totally unsuspecting parents. Yet all the while this clever deception is being set forth almost as a valid rationale of behavior, we are made aware that everything is masked by innocence — the youthful mind's inability to grasp the meaning of what it has done and of the terror of the events through which it has passed. Pym is so compeltely unaware of any wrong-doing and of his own staggering ignorance that he does not know that his rescue was "brought about by two of those almost inconceivable pieces of good fortune which are attributed by the wise and pious to the special interference of Providence." On such an easy assumption are the terrifying moral problems of the first chapter acquitted. The garrulous sailors aboard the rescue ship, the "Penguin," told of "thirty or forty poor devils" who perished in the night storm, and the monstrous fabrication easily passed for the truth.

This is the boy's world of daring, of hurt, of deception, of forgetfulness: the pain leaves no mark, and the adventurer has learned nothing. Pym at the beginning shows none of the signs of the maturing American hero; he is no Ahab, certainly no Ishmael. Pym enacts, in that first chapter, the idyl of American boyhood and innocence most notably dramatized at a later time by Tom Sawyer, Huck Finn, and Joe Harper on Jackson's Island in the Mississippi: those three boys, as a climax to their scapegrace deception, were privileged to return in triumph to their own funeral. Even Tom's close brush with death on the night of Dr. Robinson's murder and his terrifying adventures with Becky in the cave taught him nothing. Tom remains to the end the boy-man who, even though he turns the social code upside down, makes a success by running away and then coming home again. Pym got back from the night adventure in the "Ariel" because, like Tom Sawyer and like the typical heroes in Sinclair Lewis' novels, he could cheat and connive and come home again. At the very end, however, Pym could never come back from Antarctica because he had undermined so many of society's rules that he no longer had any place in the world he had left. Pym is a curiously "American hero," uprooted, without a past, and yet determined to know himself. This knowledge is not easy; it must be a knowledge of absolutes, or else it is nothing. Through an eighteen-months' pilgrimage, from Nantucket to the South Polar icecap, the boy turns into a man.[7]

Having dealt with this prologue or introductory episode, we need not consider the other episodes in chronological order. A better way of investigating *Pym* is to disentangle the themes and ideas woven variously through the different episodes.

One of the themes of *Pym* which link it with a variety of writings in American literature, such as *Moby-Dick, Tom Sawyer,* or even Henry James's *American,* is the development of a simple youth into a mature man. Hitherto Poe had concentrated, in the poems and in the early short stories, on the psychic consciousness of a very young person of hardly more than adolescent perception — a perception sometimes almost infantile. *Pym* is Poe's masterwork in the evolving consciousness of a fully developed man. The tale begins, however, where most of Poe's tales and poems on this subject had begun, with the high degree of responsiveness of a young and simple-minded boy.

The first stage of this young person's awareness is his capacity to practice the lowest kind of cheating and deception. He is still able to practice the same vice at the end — except that he has discovered one noteworthy fact that the whole world of matter and man is constituted of trickery and deception. This sense of participating in a cosmic design does not alleviate the sins which Pym commits; it simply allows him to see himself and his actions by means of some cosmic comparative.

From the opening page, Pym and his friend Augustus unscrupulously practice the lowest guile. Their adventure on the "Ariel" turns into a way of further deceiving their parents; for, if they were able to hide that event, then Pym can be easily concealed aboard the "Grampus." On the way to the dock where the "Grampus" is moored, Pym and Augustus meet Pym's grandfather:

"Why, bless my soul, Gordon," said he, after a long pause, "why, why, — *whose* dirty cloak is that you have on?" "Sir!" I replied, assuming . . . an air of offended surprise, and talking in the gruffest of all imaginable tones — "sir! you are a summat mistaken; my name, in the first place bee'nt nothing at all like Goddin, and I'd want you for to know better, you blackguard, than to call my new obercoat a darty one." For my life I could hardly refrain from screaming with laughter at the odd manner in which the old gentleman received this handsome rebuke.[8]

This is preparatory to Augustus' hiding Pym in the hold of the "Grampus," and the eleven days during which Pym feigns death in "an iron-bound box . . . nearly four feet high, and full six feet long, but very narrow." Even death itself can be deceived and cheated; for as soon as Pym is released from the stifling hold, he again feigns death by dressing himself in the clothes of the dead sailor, Hartman Rogers, whose "corpse presented in a few minutes after death one of the most horrid and loathesome spectacles I ever remember to have seen." The mutineers, superstitious and fearful of the return of one whom they had murdered, are frozen with terror and easily ambushed when the hitherto unknown Pym suddenly appears in the "smock," "a blue stockinett, with large white stripes running across," and "a false stomach, in imitation of the horrible deformity of the swollen corpse."

Pym is himself able to practice deception so that, though danger is all around him, he is himself seldom in danger. There is one occasion when, marooned on the hulk of the "Grampus," Pym has dived into the submerged hold and brought up a bottle of wine. After a series of subsequent dives, Pym returns to discover that his three shipmates who are all that have survived have drunk the wine and cheated him of his share. This event is, of course, not the last nor the worst of the long catalogue of trickery; the worst is the climax of the narrative when the South Polar natives, who have hitherto appeared so innocent and guileless, send a whole mountainside crashing down on the men of the "Jane Guy" and destroy all but Dirk Peters and Pym. Their escape is owing to mere chance: they have just stepped inside a wide fissure in a mountain and, though buried inside, are eventually able to make their way to the light.

This theme of deception is applicable not only to the lives of men but, as Pym slowly comes to understand, to the very construction of the world itself. Man cannot live by cheating alone; he survives by virtue of some rationale of flux, infinite variety, and formlessness in the universe outside. Men are maddened, whether at sea or on land; but they are made mad, not because they live in a chill, rational, ordered world of fact and metaphysics, but because the invisible spheres themselves are formed in madness and insanity. Existence is a flux and an aimless war because there is no other procedural or definable rationale to the universe itself. Pym's chartless voyage is from an assumption that man lives by law and design, in his private life and in his society, to a realization that man lives only by illusion. Legality and social pressure maintain themselves only so long as the opposite pressures do not become too strong; but at any moment life breaks its bounds and threatens to destroy itself. Pym deceives and revolts against his parents and his grandfather; the sailors, as soon as they have left the legalisms of a land world, revolt against Captain Bernard; Pym and his allies, though outnumbered, revolt against and overthrow the mutineers; nature herself sends violent storms; the floating hulk of the "Grampus," though well stocked with provisions for a long voyage, resists Pym's best efforts to find any food; then the hull turns over — and its bottom is covered with succulent molluscs; finally, the simple-minded South Polar natives, revolting merely because of some motiveless delight, destroy the men of the "Jane Guy."

One does not like to push an interpretation too far; but *Pym* is truly a symbolic parable of how the mind moves from an assumed coherence and reality of things to a recognition that everything, even the most logically substantial, is an illusion; the mind makes its own reality. And the perceiving mind fails to act with precision only when it takes for granted a "reality" which is not real, as in the scarifying moment when the Dutch brig sails toward the becalmed survivors on the "Grampus":

> Of a sudden, and all at once, there came wafted over the ocean from the strange vessel . . . a smell, a stench, such as the whole world has no name for. . . . I gasped for breath, and turning to my companions, perceived that they were paler than marble. . . . As she passed under our stern at the distance of about twenty feet, we had a full view of her decks. . . . Twenty-five or thirty human bodies,

among whom were several females, lay scattered about between the counter and the galley in the last and most loathesome state of putrefaction. . . . Yet we could not help shouting to the dead for help!

A moment later "a huge seagull, busily gorging itself with the horrible flesh," rose lazily into the air and dropped a "horrid morsel . . . with a sullen splash" on the deck of the "Grampus."[9]

This theme of deception and revolt is widened beyond the range of mere human perception not only by such incidents as the appearance of the ship of the dead but by the steady recession of any "fact" world — the facts of ships and men, sequence of days, food and drink, society, law, justice, and honor — and the gradual domination of a chimera or the world as it really is behind the mask of ostensible reality: time recedes and ceases to have any measurable validity; food, the very basis of life, is just out of reach or becomes putrescent; wine, a normal drink, brings a ravening madness to the drinkers; and society itself never stays the same — it is killing and cheating, a massive investment of man's deception of himself and his fellows. Man, in truth, lives against society, for his primal condition is both loneliness and a perpetual war. Poe's clearest mirror of man's vaunted civilization is in the colony of penguins whose ponderous and clumsily oafish ways are a reduction of human society to its primitive, and therefore basically timeless, condition.[10]

Pym is, in this regard, an ever-widening of the focus from the sailing port of Nantucket and the life of Arthur Pym to the loss of individuality and, concurrently, the steady dissolution of the world of physical reality. The book is, in its way, a philosophical investigation both of the nature of the self and of the way by which the self comes to know. Like "Al Aaraaf" and "The Raven" and like "Ligeia" and "The Fall of the House of Usher," *Pym* is an inquiry not only into the iniquitous illusion that humankind think is real but also into a representative man who (put it "philosophically") proceeds through a set of stages by which he comes to understand something he or the rest of his fellows has never entertained before. We might now consider the idea not just who makes the journey or quest for understanding, through a sense of deception and illusion, but what the end of the journey is: what is it that becomes a blinding whiteness at the conclusion of the narrative?

3

The quest in *Pym* is for ultimates, for an abstraction; it is the same quest that, nearly a dozen years later and toward the end of his life, Poe would undertake in a long exposition called *Eureka*. The ultimate or abstraction is the idea of Unity, an idea which has already received some investigation in this study and will receive even more in subsequent chapters.

In *Pym* the idea or abstraction of Unity is left incomplete or unresolved because it is treated not so much as a theme as the terror-world of the protagonist, Arthur Pym himself. Pym goes through a number of stages and passes from innocent boy to mature man as though he were doing these things as representing all men. Yet we never really know what this pilgrimage is, inwardly or developmentally for Pym, because we are never admitted to the private recesses of Pym's own mind; we are always outside, in an external, almost allegorical, representation of those inner states of being. Every thought, every whim and mood becomes known through an instant figuration; the outside world enacts Pym's drama, and he is somehow, though knowing, relieved of responsibility or hardly there at all.

This method of externalization is not new to Poe; in fact, it is his method throughout his poetic and short-story career. The difference between *Pym* and other pieces is, however, that nearly all of Poe's inquiries into the impact of the horrific external world on one of his protagonists is, as it were, after the fact. Only infrequently, as in "The Raven," do we have the actual impact of the unseen and the terrible on a sensitive mind; in "Morella," "Ligeia," "The Fall of the House of Usher," and in other narratives the protagonist is there, but he is Poe's and our means of remaining outside the action and therefore unhurt. In a moment rare in Poe's artistic career, Poe broke through this discrete separation of his hero from the action and showed us, in Arthur Pym, not only the "afterward" of terror but the stages of passing through terror; for it would seem that terror is the way to a knowledge of the world's primal unity.

Generally speaking, Poe's horror tales are considerations of a human mind, whether knowing or not, lodged in a chance world of meaningless events. Anything may happen at any time; nothing is logical or rational, except as some perceiving mind, such as that of Dupin in the detective stories, is able to make sense of it. In *Pym* we begin with this state of man's and the world's madness — the low cheating, the burial alive, the insane reversals of life — and more and more we move into a horror-world which is an externalization of Pym's inner condition. Horror and the slippery illusion of things become the way Pym sees the event in which he is involved. The event is an external mirroring of his own mind. But reality tends to fade and to become simple division between black and white, earth and sea, man and man as Pym approaches the final understanding. All the while we know almost nothing about Pym himself; we know him only as the world around him is a mirrored symbol, even sometimes a fallacy, of what he knows inwardly. Nature becomes an embodiment of his idea — but the more he knows and grows, the more simple and even primitive those natural forms are rendered.

This movement toward simplicity and opaqueness is one of the curiosities of a book which, though it presumably deals with man's enlarging consciousness and with the steadily maturing effect a knowledge of the world has on an impressionable mind, the farther it moves the more it tends to reduce external objects and events to their simplest forms. This matter becomes especially apparent after Pym and Peters are rescued by the "Jane Guy" and begin their voyage into Antarctica. But this increasing awareness is not accompanied by any increase in Pym's ability to understand himself; in fact, the better he is able to control his existence, the less he is inclined to speculate on existence. He has none of the power of an Ishmael in *Moby-Dick* who could assay himself as he was more and more caught in the monomania of Ahab. The farther Pym goes, the more perception is external or is represented outwardly in action or horror or death. An act of perception is a fulfillment in physical sensation; nothing is known until it is felt or endured; the muscle and the brain are very close. Hunger and thirst are demonstrations of rational intelligence; killing is a measure of the mind's knowledge of survival; love and hate are realized only in the caresses of a dog or in the trickery or fidelity of a shipmate. All thought seems to occur outside the mind, as though the human mind were at every turn the victim of thought and action long anterior to itself. Thought is first known "somewhere," then it is manifested in some physical demonstration, and finally it is known as an idea and concept.

The horror-world of *Pym* is that we can never know what is going on in Pym's mind, unless in a point for point relevance the world is duplicating the mental functions of Pym himself. Yet the farther the story proceeds, the less relevance becomes demonstrable between physical fact and mental construct; or, to put the idea another way, as Pym matures and gains control over outward circumstance, the more the external world tends to dissolve. Early we have the frightening reality of a ship's stygian hold and the brutal and senseless killing of men aboard ship; later the compulsive outer world becomes less and less violent until, in the last chapters, we have stolid expositions of marine and animal life near the South Pole.

This movement from ignorance to comprehension is marked not only by the mind's making itself known in direct physical contexts but also by a general tendency to reduce these physical embodiments of inner being from complexities to simplicities. More and more the external world becomes a sharp distinction between white (of the sea, the polar bear, the sky) and black (the natives, the terrain), between the good and the bad, between, in short, the varieties of comprehensions which Pym has. The better he understands, the more simple become the pathways and conclusions of his understanding until he can, almost with prescience, know what is going on around him and what is soon to be.

With the lessening of complexity of physical forms and with the diminution of the dramatic action, *Pym* moves toward the same problem that had been apparent in the poetry, namely, the question of symbolic language. How does art or the word make reality known or even convey reality at all? Is the word a tonal equivalent for the real, or does the mind make known the real to itself by means of some sound or verbalism? Poe's method in *Pym* was virtually the same as it had been in the poetry: words are not things but ideas of things; the word-order of the writing is a progress of the mind and the imagination toward understanding. Words can create another reality, neither the mind's nor the thing's. It is in the direction of this sharp disjunction of thing from idea that Poe was moving in the last pages of *Pym:* his symbolic white and black, land and sea, barbarian and civilized man are the sharpest distinctions he can make as a means of setting the speculative intelligence apart from what it is speculating on. At the end of this journey Pym is sailing toward that whiteness whose center lies beyond first things and whose nexus may be the creative impulse of the universe itself. Faced with this bewildering and ultimate reduction, Poe can use only a word, an idea of whiteness, the negation of fact and shape. Melville's Ishmael came back from this side of the ultimate illumination; but Pym went all the way through and never returned. He, like the primal order of matter itself, was reduced to a blinding One — or chaos. There was no word or term which could further report the vision of nothing on the other side. Nothing was all; there was no other word for it but "white." "And now we rushed into the embraces of the cataract, where a chasm threw itself open to receive us. But there arose in our pathway a shrouded human figure, very far larger in its proportions than any dweller among men. And the hue of the skin of the figure was of the perfect whiteness of the snow."

4

Pym's symbolic journey is sustained longer than any other in Poe's writing, for one reason, because we have both the beginning and the end of that journey (as opposed to Poe's normal practice of giving us only the end) and, for another, because Pym himself, beginning as a distinct self, an arrogant young American go-getter, steadily loses that identification and becomes more a voice or a commentator. Just as the forms of the natural world become more and more simplified, so too does Pym's vision become clearer, its lines and demarcations drawn carefully between black and white, good and bad, man and world, mind and matter. The journey is a study in the depersonalization of the self: Pym passes through stages of deception, concealment, burial alive, the disintegration of food and drink, the shameless collapse of honor, and even the deaths of his shipmates and moves toward an unsubstantial yet knowing Pym whose final illumination is blocked only because there is nothing more to see and know. Similarly along that journey, others, like the powerful Dirk Peters, lose their identity and, like Pym, pass from the positive, assertive self to the lost or indeterminate self. As we approach the eschatos toward which Pym is driven, everything tends to blend and to go back toward first principles or become colorless, bland, shapeless, even mindless.

Two final themes emerge in this symbolic narrative. The first, and less important, is the struggle to reach and yet at the same time to avoid self-destruction. Like so many of Poe's characters, Pym is possessed by the death-wish, by the passion for annihilation. Yet this compulsion is a moral force: unlike Poe's other characters, Pym is a moral being because he realizes some purpose in the emergent shape of the universe and his own moral displacement. In destruction there is knowledge; in loss there is gain. To some extent the journey is, allegorically, very like the Christian journey from this world to the next: he that would save himself must first lose himself; he that would have eternal life must first be born again. Poe, however, puts nothing on the other side or in the condition of being reborn: the search for the self's true center ends in the death of the self. The idea is, of course, an anomaly which is implicit in much of Poe's writing: the romantic drive toward self-assertion ends in total self-destruction: the hero finds himself only at the moment he loses himself; he dies the instant he is about to be born again; the blankness of eternal mystery engulfs him the moment he faces the white light of revelation.

The anomaly, stated another way, is the idea that in a mindless, chaotic world the only final reality is the single perceiving self. Yet the moment this self begins the quest for knowledge and awareness, it is destined to become like and subject to the mindless chaos which is the world around it. The search for the self is the loss of self; the quest is the annihilation. To remain in ignorance is to maintain one's primal being; to be curious is to be suicidal. The world or reality constantly undergoes this cyclic metamorphosis, from life to death and back to life again; but man, though a creature submissive to the natural laws around him, can go only through death or perhaps to the ultimate "silence" of the sonnet on that subject, the silence of total annihilation.

The second theme is more implicit than obvious but it is a part of the narrative nonetheless. If Pym's quest is for selfhood, for first principles and primal being, it is also a moving backward through the natural order as it presently exists and into the world's original condition, as primal first cause. Pym moves not only through space and idea but also backward through time. He has reached, in Antarctica, not merely a geographical region still uncharted by the explorers; he has gone through and come out on the other side of the archeological discoveries of the latter eighteenth and early nineteenth centuries. Antarctica is the world that existed long before Pompeii was buried, before the valley of Arabia Petraea was left desolate, before the first crude monuments were erected along the Nile. What Pym saw at the South Pole was, metaphysically and symbolically as history, the most primitive source of man and his history on this globe. It was essentially a dead world in which there were ciphers and hieroglyphics, but no one, least of all the natives, could read them; vast structures rose up as witness to some still earlier civilization, a historical parallel to Baalbec and Gomorrah, but no one knew when they had existed nor what their signs betokened.

This region was, therefore, not only the physical world reduced to its primal origin and simplicity but man reduced to his. By a curious inversion, the noble savage became very like his civilized descendant: he cheated, stole, killed with a ruthlessness that would do credit to modern man. The quest for knowledge ended in futility: primitivism was as great a failure as civilization, just as the primal order of the natural world was as meaningless as the later evolutionary condition ("evolution" not in the Darwinian but in the Lamarckian sense).

Natural man or the long-sought primitive was, as Melville would soon discover in the Typee valley, a vast complexity into which later civilized man could not penetrate. Primitivism was itself a form of civilization, vastly different from but not lower than what Pym had left behind in New England. The quest for self-knowledge, backward through natural forms and downward through historical and archeological time, ended in mystery. Pym discovered only the whiteness of the purest unknown — a color without any body, a light without any prismatic reflection. Poe's imaginary voyage had left the meaning of the human mind as mysterious as before: the self might be One, but the term still had little meaning, chiefly because Poe, unlike Hawthorne and Melville and perhaps more like Whitman, was fundamentally uninterested in the inner drama. His usual method was to pictorialize or outwardly demonstrate the inner condition. What Poe did succeed in doing, to a rather remarkable degree, was to present a drama of natural forms: the world, as it had a complex physical history, became the main protagonist, and Pym himself was so far lost in the physical dimension that he nearly ceased to have any existence at all. The *Narrative of Arthur Gordon Pym* is a curiosity in Romantic symbolism: its main burden is the ultimate submergence and loss of man to the world of infinitely variable forms which Romanticism posited. In fact, the variables are so great that man, once he investigates his relation to them, slips away into nothingness. A Romantic mind like Wordsworth could posit an infinitely varying world which, however, could be made stationary for the moment of scrutiny: "Tintern Abbey" recounts such a moment wherein Wordsworth's or man's time can be various but the physical world can remain fixed. Poe's *Pym* has a coherence and consistency of maintaining an utterly variable universe and variable man in it. Only Coleridge's "Rime of the Ancient Mariner," its own drama not far remote from Poe's *Pym,* rests on such an accreditment of indetermination. Never again did Poe's imagination take him quite so far; afterward he was content to limit his view to a set of analyses of human motive and action based on surer principles of the world's stability.

VII

The Tale as Allegory

Poe has often been cited for his detestation of allegory and for his pungent remarks on the "heresy of the didactic." These comments must be taken several ways: in their own time and context they were Poe's rejection of the tale as "simply moral" — that attitude which made art into science, religion, morality, and anything else the artist may cover. He was attacking a view very common in his day and one especially noticeable in fiction or the prose tale which, ever since the eighteenth century, was a suspect form anyway. The tale had to assume that it was a narrative and then everything else too; Cooper, the outstanding novelist or tale-teller in Poe's day, was careful to include those lessons, moral saws, or outright sermons in the mouths of his moral mouthpieces like Natty Bumppo; and Hawthorne, as Poe himself quite corectly pointed out, had a tendency to lapse into allegory and thereby reduce and delimit those imaginative exercises which, with the purity of his "tone," made the Hawthorne tale itself an act of the imagination. Poe's war was, therefore, on the necessity of the tale to be allegorical and to be moral. The other direction of Poe's attack on allegory was no doubt more personal. He himself could not write "allegories"; he could not do that work which was so remunerative in the gift annuals and in the periodicals. They were merely sneers at a profitable commodity in the literary marketplace.

Yet Poe was an allegorist in spite of himself. An allegory was a means whereby his creative imagination undertook to solve certain problems of its own mind and art; they were ways of reducing reality to determinate and logical outlines. Together they formed a significant group — perhaps the most considerable demonstrations of Poe's art as it came closest to a consideration of the religious, social, political, and imaginative worlds in which it lived. They were ways of making a fractured and dismembered world obtain some form; for, truly speaking, Poe's world was utterly disorganized not only because Poe himself saw the world that way but also because his world was that way. We might well consider these tales as a group and analyze a few representative examples under a set of provisional hypotheses.

Poe's allegorical narratives might conveniently be examined under two major themes, one religious, the other social and political. The first, if it can be measured by the number of tales which were written around essentially religious subjects, probably occupied a larger space in his art and thought; the second is, however, of importance, if for no other reason than that it marks one more way by which Poe rejected the real world around him and set up a fictive, symbolic range of experience and expression. The "destructive tendency" was operative in both; it had more subjects and more ranges in the religious dimension than it had in the social and political.

2

Poe belonged to a select, though not unusual, group of writers in America, or in the world for that matter. It is a group which could exist at any time and in any place; it numbered in the nineteenth century such writers as Hawthorne, Melville, Emily Dickinson, and Henry Adams. One mark which characterized all these writers is that they came at a time when a once-powerful religion was in decline; yet this decline left "a detritus of pieties, strong assumptions, which afford a particularly fortunate condition for certain kinds of literature."[1] The "condition" was one which offered strong religious motives for thought and action but which exacted no requirement that the writers themselves adhere to any religious belief; yet all the while they were free to investigate and dramatize religious themes with a clarity which, to some extent, is denied the believer. Hawthorne's *Scarlet Letter* is a superb inquiry into the Puritan mind; it operates on basic Puritan dogmas of sin and regeneration — yet there is not the slightest indication that these codes and dogmas had any prescription for Hawthorne or for the times in which Hawthorne lived. A *Scarlet Letter* was impossible in the age of Cotton Mather; a *Scarlet Letter* was inevitable in the times of Melville and Whitman because men in New England still adhered to the whole program of sin and regeneration as set forth in Hawthorne's novel — and yet the heart of a once-great religion had gone out of their life. Hawthorne's generation, which was Poe's, was either struggling toward another religious formulation or in the act of losing the old.

In New England, the religious detritus was exhibited in a clash between soul and intellect (as it had been from the time of Jonathan Edwards to William Ellery Channing); intellect no doubt won the struggle, but while the struggle was going on, it was acutely dramatized in the nineteenth century by the clash between business and morality: morality was itself part of the running-down of a powerful religious impulse that had been on the wane ever since Franklin had penned the easy morality of Poor Richard. Throughout this tension the churches in New England and the best minds all the way through Horace Bushnell to Josiah Royce posited the final power of the percipient self; yet all the while the practical mind of New England was emphasizing and placing all its code of salvation on the humanly willed product of man's hands.

In the South, on the other hand, the decline of a religious force was not so precipitate or apparent. Especially in Virginia, where there had been for two centuries only one church, religion had too long been the support of the status quo ever to force an issue or to raise the dramatic specter of doubt. The church, in sum, was the final sanctification of the whole southern code of morals, slavery, politics, love, oratory, war, daily living, even of a pseudo-Greek revival in architecture; to break away from the church meant a total break with society itself—or, to put the matter conversely, to break with society spelled a permanent rift with the dominant religious mind of Virginia.

The church or religion in the South sanctified all of men's activities and put its benediction on all man's expressions except one — the arts; the church in Virginia had nothing to say or do for the arts except to encourage a weak classicism and an amiable sense of the deep past. The church had been sufficiently disestablished not to interfere in men's lives; yet religion was so much a part of the equipment of a Virginian that he could not personally get along very well without it. Religion offered no drama, no antagonisms, no tension; it did offer a set of worldly prescriptions. The church in the South never suffered from the attacks of Unitarians or Quakers or even the hell-fire Methodists simply because it had so long acclimated itself to the very air men breathed; however, to reject the church and its worldly-wise teachings was to make one virtually an outcast from what was the accepted mode of conduct and belief in the first half of the nineteenth century.

Yet far beyond the edge of this world of observed pieties were the camp meetings, the Negro prayers and songs, and the torch-lit revivals among lonely people on the frontier. Every southerner heard these wild voices in some strange cacophony which did not fit his experience in the white man's settled world. As one listened, these songs were the one poignant expression of a religion for the desolate and lost and not for the comfortable and accepted. Stephen Foster and other pseudo-folklorists domesticated those songs for the consumption of the circumspect; yet somewhere beyond the churches of Richmond a boy like Poe must have heard the uncontrolled wail of those whom his society regarded as trash and as lost.

These matters are conjectural only because we do not have the evidence which links Poe's home and early life with the tales he wrote when he became a man. This evidence could not be supplied, for Poe or any man, because it is part of the imaginative sediment a sensitive boy takes with him into manhood and can never tell where he got it. The best we can do is not to engage in suspect psychoanalysis of Poe the boy or Poe the man but to inquire into representative short stories which Poe wrote at the height of his career and see how the decline and loss of a once-strong religious motive helped to produce the *outré* situations and the half-demented human beings who are products of a curious and inquiring religious temper.

3

One of the primary marks of a writer whose imagination might be regarded as religious but whose temper has long removed him from any doctrinal or dogmatic religious content is that, whether poet or tale-teller, he becomes his own god, his own supreme maker of visions, prophecies, and parables. Yet all the while the baffling character of these projections is that they have no apparent relationship to any body of truth or revelation. They are, to put it another way, not anti- or pro-Christian; they are simply not Christian nor even pagan; they have, if such things can be, the character of being a wholly invented simulacrum of a religious action and faith. In this respect, to play god was one of the favorite excursions of the romantic mind: Shelley engaged in the adventure so far that he invented a universe of Idea which, in an instant, he could destroy; and Keats's private pleasure-dome of aesthetic dimension had all the requisites of a profound religious experience, while Keats himself was his own god and demon. In the end, the religious mind of the Romantics became demonic because it was ultimately destructive of what it had created.

Poe's assumption of the role of god took a form not quite typical of poets or imaginative seers in the nineteenth century but one characteristic of the spell-binders and projectors of new thought in that age. His role takes him into a religious primitivism, that is, back to the primary revelation or to the original moment when the revelation was given, just as Protestant enthusiasts have longed for a return to Apostolic times and to a re-creation of the true gospel as it was initially revealed by the Messiah. In another way, however, Poe is typical of certain expressions of the Romantic mind: his religious premise is essentially anti-intellectual and anti-ritualistic; he would return to the pure religion before it became contaminated by priestcraft and bell-ringing. Or, to state a corollary, he looks forward to the final Apocalypse, to the utter destruction of all things wherein the god finally achieves his justice or gets his awful revenge on the wicked.

In such an early tale as "The Conversation of Eiros and Charmion" (1839) we have this vision of the last day. A comet, in accordance with all the words of "the biblical prophecies," came within range of the earth and, by "a total extraction of the nitrogen" around the earth, rendered the air so combustible that the world was destroyed in one massive, blinding flash—"the entire fulfilment," Poe as vision-maker insists, "in all their minute and terrible details, of the fiery and horror-inspiring denunciations of the prophecies of the Holy Book." [2] We are not too far from the Puritan Wigglesworth's *Day of Doom* or the horrendous threats hurled against the damned by nineteenth-century evangelists.

Yet Poe's apocalyptic visions were not intended as denunciations; they were meant to be rationalizations or scientific expositions of what might be considered proved religious fact. In "The Colloquy of Monos and Una" (1841) the idea turns on not the end of the world as an inevitable fact in the logistics of nature but on the death of a single human being as a "swoon" or transfer from one form of perception to another. Monos, or the fractured and many-sided human being, passes through the three phases of being which, as we shall see, marked the upward progress toward personal fulfillment in Poe's hierarchy of insight: Monos proceeds through the physical or sensual, then through the intellectual ("a mental pendulous sensation"), and finally into pure spiritual being from which, the body having been resolved to dust, the mind and imagination can move, beyond "Place and Time."[3]

Poe's religious inquiry began, therefore, with simplicities. He took creation either back to its primal origin or forward to its ultimate consummation. Like religious myth-makers of long ago, he felt free to create his own cosmos in any form that suited him and to give it any function necessary to its fulfillment. Thus death was denied in the mere "swoon" from one stage of perception to the next, as in "The Colloquy of Monos and Una"; or he was privileged to evolve a universe in which all its atomic structures served only those purposes and intentions which he as god-player ordained. It was, in short, a child's magic world, and hardly religious at all; for it had no room for evil and no condition of tragedy; no souls were lost and none was saved. But it was at such an utter remove from the conventionalized religious world in which Poe moved that it seemed like a revenge on what, in its own terms, was a rigid and institutionalized body of thought and belief. Poe's universe in imagination was at least spaceless and timeless in contrast to the easy temporality of the church in Richmond, or Philadelphia, or New York.

This universe of Poe's is not merely a spaceless and timeless cosmos; people do inhabit it; yet they do not exist in it on the simple level of morality and belief that one might expect in such a primal world as Poe imagined. Poe's nightmare universe is one in which the world is itself either just begun or just finished but the people in it are condemned to live as if they are in some long after-time of belief and morality. They exist very like the South Sea islanders Melville found on Nukaheva: they live by a rigid code of the taboo, but they have long lost any notion of what the code means. They are forced to believe and exist for reasons that have long ceased to have any meaning. No one understands or can interpret, in this moral region of Poe's lost souls, why he must be punished; yet the penalty for any moral infraction is frightful and all the more terrifying because no one had enforced it and no one knows why it must be administered. The punishment comes not from a church, a law, or even from society: it comes from some inner compulsion of the evil-doer himself who suffers from what Poe otherwise terms "perversity": he must do evil, and yet he wants to be punished and to suffer. Thus he has willed his crime, and he wills his retribution.

These characters are themselves god-players. In "The Tell-Tale Heart" the narrator assumes the right to do away with the old man whose one "eye, with a film over it," becomes an object of loathing to him. It is not so much an old man that he kills as it is the "Evil Eye"; but this god-player made the mistake of thinking it was an eye which was so vexatious; all the while it was a sound, the beating of the old man's heart, which kept pounding in the murderer's ears after the man was dead. The police who make a routine investigation are not ministers of justice; they are mere expressions of the narrator's compulsion to unmask and destroy himself by finally admitting the crime he had committed. In this respect the god easily passes into the devil and becomes his maker and slayer both.

"The Black Cat" (1843) is even more pointedly addressed to this theme "of perverseness . . . this unfathomable longing of the soul *to vex itself*—to offer violence to its own nature—to do wrong for the wrong's sake only." The sins the protagonist committed were so "deadly" that his "immortal soul" would be placed "even beyond the reach of the infinite mercy of the Most Merciful and Most Terrible God." When the criminal had reached the completion of his iniquity and had walled up the body of his dead wife, he had, of a necessity beyond his comprehension, buried alive the cat which would betray and condemn him. No other god but the self as god can wreak such vengeance as when the criminal is his own judge and executioner.

In these ways, therefore, Poe removed all moral and religious considerations as far as possible from any social code or body of religious warrants. This method was not so much an overt attack on the society of his day as it was his tacit assumption that a moral and social code had so little cogency that he would have to discover or invent a rationale of existence as remote as possible from it. The otherwise baffling tale, "The Man of the Crowd," (1840) is a consideration of man's abandonment of the moral prescription within which he is supposed to live. We have the modern metropolis and a man so typical as to be almost an Everyman; we never know, however, whether this Man is an individual who cannot bear to be alone or whether he is, in reality, the narrator and protagonist of the story in a cringing, fearsome guise that the narrator will not admit even to himself. That the Man is some embodiment of evil in the modern world which has long lost any belief in evil is suggested by "an expression . . . never seen before, . . . the pictorial incarnations of the fiend." This nameless and almost faceless Man may be several things: he could be that human being who really has no inner being at all; the horror he faces is that he might be thrust into the private world of mind or spirit; if such an event were to happen to him, he would go mad of desperation and loneliness. The other matter of interest in "The Man of the Crowd" is that we can never be sure whether we are following a mere Man or whether we are pursuing the narrator himself, who is so terrified of admitting who or what he is that he projects himself into this desperate and wholly imagined fugitive. It is interesting to note that the "I" is never at a loss to follow the Man through the darkest byways of a vast metropolis; and he knows the Man so well that he can easily see through "a rent in a closely-buttoned and evidently secondhand *roquelaire* which enveloped him" and gave him "a glimpse both of a diamond and of a dagger." Whoever or whatever he is, the Man is the lost soul which never knows it is lost. He is, like Hawthorne's Wakefield, an "outcast of the universe," one who has somehow taken a single step awry and has thereafter lost any sense of belonging to the human and material worlds.

If the subject of "The Man of the Crowd" concerns the inability of a Man either to belong in a world of evil or to acknowledge to himself that he is one of "the Crowd" which is the world, the tale does not seek out these ideas in the Man himself. As so frequently happens in Poe's writing, inner moods and ideas are consistently externalized; the city itself, the labyrinthian streets, the noise and garish colors — these are the pictorial and frenzied manifestations of states of mind which would presuppose that the world is a mirrored chiaroscuro of the human psyche. Yet what Poe was further attempting to suggest was that whatever has happened to the Man or whatever he has done is a monotonous repetition of the crime of the human race: its implacable indifference to suffering, its bland ignorance that evil exists at all. The Man is, however, an outcast because he does suffer and because he wants to discover some similitude to his suffering among the millions who swirl about him.

If there is a moral system in these stories, it is nebulous indeed. Poe consistently attacked the Utilitarians of his day, with their idea of "happiness" and "the greatest good to the greatest number."[4] Yet, while he could not locate the moral sense in mankind itself, he was unwilling to make the individual responsible. Even more interestingly, he did not consider that the universe itself was God's primary mistake or the outward manifestation of a cosmic tragedy; for him "the invisible spheres" were not "formed in fright." Evil or good is each man's right and his willing; each one saves or damns himself. But the ultimate reason why man chooses or wills one or the other is far beyond anyone's knowing; the sinner is compulsively driven by some motive to be malignant, by some maggot in the brain which he cannot anticipate or understand but the penalty of which he is more than willing to suffer. This need to do evil Poe placed in the idea of "perversity," man's tendency to act "for the reason that he should not." The "assurance of the wrong or error of any action," Poe continued, "is often the one unconquerable *force* which impels us, and alone impels us to its prosecution. Nor will the overwhelming tendency to do wrong for wrong's sake admit of analysis, or resolution into ulterior elements. It is a radical, a primitive impulse — elementary." Here then was the rationale for man's moral system and the answer to his bewildering actions which, in so many crimes, went diametrically against any Utilitarian theory of man's willing and seeking his own happiness or the greatest happiness to the greatest number.

Poe was content to lodge this faculty in man alone and apparently leave him a moral freak in the world of mind and God. Yet this "principle, the antagonist of bliss," is, however, similarly found in the universe itself: what man is, as a fractured and disjointed being, is but a miniature of imperfection and dispersion in the cosmic order. By a curious variation on the myth of Adam and Eve, Poe demonstrated that man had willed his own degradation; the earth had suffered the fatal flaw, and throughout the rest of the world's time-span this condition of evil and suffering steadily worsens. Owing to this defect in man and in the universe, "the world will never see . . . that full extent of triumphant execution, in the richer domains of art, of which the human nature is absolutely capable." Evil and suffering have become, therefore, the capacity and measure of man to feel and know: moral sensitivity is not an act or even a thought but the knowledge all the while that pain is the basis for life and death is the only release from this grotesque condition of "perversity," or man's determination to hurt and destroy himself. Thus the Poe protagonists so eagerly will their own deaths; they must plunge into "the common vortex of unhappiness which yawns for those of pre-eminent endowments"; only in death can they find release and peace.

Each character in Poe's moral inquiries is his own moral arbiter, lodged in a total moral anarchy. Society has invented law and justice, but these are mere illusion and exact no true penalty. The Poe hero or villain is never in revolt against them, as the Romantic hero so frequently is; the Poe hero acts as if the laws of society had never even existed. The moral drama is, however, all the more terrifying because it has no rules and no reason for bringing about the end that eventually comes. It is not even a comfortably deterministic moral scheme in which whatever happens must happen; it is a moral world of an inscrutable calculus in which any one of an infinite number of results might occur.

This, then, so far as it can be sketched with any consistency, is Poe's moral cosmology, a universe of such individualism that virtually every atom has its own right and rule to exist. Within it is, of course, lodged man; but man is himself, in an almost Shakespearean way, a mirror of the universe, or the universe is a macrocosmic extension of man. The universal metaphysic is tripartite: body, mind, and soul. Every element and form in the cosmos, as Poe had suggested in "Al Aaraaf," is constituted so that it has three separate organisms and functions at the same time that these three parts are intricately interrelated to form the one and the many, the "monos" and the "una" of a universal design.

Poe's final exploration of this subject was *Eureka,* written in the last years of his life.

However inexact Poe was in his outline of the tripartite organization of the material universe, he was quite explicit concerning man: man is a being formed of three separate and yet interacting forms, body, mind, and spirit. The transitions between them are so slight as sometimes to be almost indistinguishable; they form the one total "machine" that is the complete human being; they also constitute absolutely distinct functions and even parts of the human organism, and one may become, as we shall see, hypertrophied or atrophied at the expense of the other. The sources and bases for these ideas have been sufficiently well explored that we need not consider them here; suffice to say, this scheme of the human being was derived from the popular psychology of Andrew Combe and Spurzheim early in the nineteenth century. Poe was content to assume that all of his readers were so well aware of it that he did not need to go into explanatory detail; several of his noteworthy moral investigations of men are, however, built around this psychology of the tripartite organization and functioning of man.[5]

The normal, healthy human being is one in whom these three faculties are in balance; none dominates the other. But in the mysterious and chaotic condition of the universe, which is itself a duplicate of man's state of being, anything at any moment may occur in order to tip the human psyche either way, into sanity or into madness. And like the universe, the human organism, so delicately is it made and so intricately adjusted are its parts, can be turned in an instant into any one of an infinite possible conditions or states. The mind itself, the second or midway faculty of reason and direction, has no power to control either its own condition or the responses of the body and the soul; its only capacity is to speculate on whatever state of being it finds itself in at a particular moment. Neither the body nor the soul has this power: the body functions only as brute, insensitive existence; the soul, with only rare moments of perception, has the power of penetrating far beyond the limits of this sensual existence; chiefly the soul sleeps or is moribund.

In "The Fall of the House of Usher" (1839) we have an early exposition, and one of the best, of this psychic drama, a summary of Poe's ideas and method of investigating the self in disintegration.[6] The story was a study of the tripartite division and identity of the self. It was, to go even further, an attempted demonstration of the theory that spirit is extended through and animating all matter, a theory confirmed by the books which Poe, and Usher, had read: Swedenborg's *Heaven and Hell,* Campanella's *City of the Sun,* and Robert Flud's *Chiromancy,* to name only a few listed in the narrative, all of which consider the material world as manifestation of the spiritual. From the opening sentence of the story we have the point-for-point identification of the external world with the human constitution. The House is the total human being, its three parts functioning as one; the outside construction of the house is like the body; the dark tarn is a mirror or the mind which can "image . . . a strange fancy," almost "a dream." The "barely perceptible fissure" which extended "from the roof of the building . . . until it became lost in the sullen waters of the tarn" is the fatal dislocation or fracture which, as the story develops, destroys the whole psychic being of which the house is the outward manifestation.

Turning now from the material to the human realms, we find that the tripartite division of the faculties is even more clearly evidenced. Usher represents the mind or intellectual aspect of the total being: ". . . the character of his face had been at all times remarkable. A cadaverousness of complexion; an eye large, liquid, and luminous beyond comparison; lips somewhat thin and very pallid but of a surpassingly beautiful curve; . . . a finely moulded chin, speaking, in its want of prominence, of a want of moral energy." Madeline is the sensual or physical side of this psyche: they are identical twins (Poe ignores, and so may we, the fact that identical twins cannot be of differing sex); her name is derived from Saint Mary Magdala, which means "tower"; therefore she is the lady of the house.[7]

The tale is a study of the total disintegration of a complex human being, not in any one of the three aspects of body, mind, and soul, but in all three together. Roderick Usher suffers from the diseased mind which has too long abstracted and absented itself from physical reality; in fact, the physical world, and even the physical side of himself, fills him with such repugnance that he can maintain his unique world or self of the mind only by destroying his twin sister or the physical side of himself. Madeline sickens from some mortal disease and, when she is presumed dead, is buried in the subterranean family vaults or in a place as far remote as possible from the place of aesthetic delight wherein the mind of Roderick lives. Yet Madeline is not dead; she returns from the coffin and in one convulsive motion brings her brother to his death: the body and the mind thus die together. Very shortly afterward the House collapses, for it has all the while represented the total being of this complex body-mind relation which Poe had studied in the symbolic guise of a brother and sister relationship: "and the deep and dark tarn . . . closed sullenly and silently over the fragments of the 'House of Usher.'"

One of the curiosities of Poe's tale is that, while we have a study not only of the interrelationship of mind and body in the phychic life of a human being but also of the rapid disintegration of that being when one aspect of the self becomes hypertrophied, we have a narrative of presumed psychological inquiry with everything presented, as it were, "outside." We know no more of Roderick or of Madeline, or of the narrator for that matter, at the end than we knew at the beginning. The method is entirely pictorial, as though external objects and the configuration of the intricate material world could themselves assume a psychic dimension: not only is the material world an outward demonstration of some inner and cosmic drama but it is at every moment exhibiting that drama more strikingly than can the human actors. The two realms, material and immaterial, coexist in such exquisite balance that one can be read as a precise synecdoche of the other. The convulsive aspect of Poe's writing becomes nowhere better apparent than in his method of making the physical world of nature experience the drama more intensely than can any human being.

Another tale in which this theory of the multiple character of the self is treated is "William Wilson" (1840). In "The Fall of the House of Usher" the being of Roderick in its vital body-mind condition suffered complete deterioration and death; in "William Wilson" we have the converse theme of the nature of the self in its desperate necessity to preserve itself; in that act of self-preservation Wilson is not the prey to outward circumstances nor does he abstract himself from them, as did Usher. William Wilson is the clever man of the world who, however, in order to succeed in the world, must destroy an essential part of himself, his soul or spirit.[8]

At almost every point "William Wilson" poses a different question from that set forth in "The Fall of the House of Usher." The central problem of "William Wilson" is the nature of self-identity: is the self born isolated and alone, as was the early theme of "Usher," or is it permissively designed to order its own way in the world? From the beginning Wilson is endowed with freedom; as a child, he says, "My voice was a household law; and at an age when few children have abandoned their leading-strings, I was left to the guidance of my own will." This is not mere childish petulance and willfulness; it is, we are informed, a "hereditary temper" which makes impossible any submission to control. For a time the young Wilson is confined within the "iron" control of Dr. Bransby's school — it is interesting to note the images of iron and rigidity in the description of the school itself and of the narrowly confined lives of the students; but all the while this boy is living with only his mind to guide him. Society and religion have no force over him; and even the whispering voice of another boy also named William Wilson is not really a moral conscience (for conscience depends on some spiritual determinant in order to have any force at all) but is merely another being in the moral wilderness of Wilson's life. He is his own moral arbiter in a world wherein the only criterion is success; for no action of Wilson, not the cheating at cards nor even the attempted seduction of the Duke di Broglio's wife, is really bad; it is simply a failure in some materialistic ordering of the world which rewards success and punishes failure. Wilson is a moral incompetent and Utilitarian who assumes that the cosmic design is as materialistic as he is; the awful revenge comes when the realm of spirit, whose existence he has more and more denied, overcomes and destroys him.

Wilson also makes a progress down the ladder of private being. He begins as a complex body-mind-spirit whose first exercises are expressions of that total self in the games, studies, and prayers at Dr. Bransby's school. He is early able to hear his conscience or spirit breathing and speaking to him; he even makes a nightly visit to that other side of himself in order to be certain that it exists. Then he moves downward into the mind-side of himself: his cleverness in cheating and in impressing his fellows makes him for a time a success, until finally he is unmasked as cheating at cards. Thereafter he moves from the rational or mind elements to the merely physical when, in the last action of the tale, he tries to effect a seduction which would be almost a rape. Then the body and spiritual aspects of Wilson have become so far separated that one can exist only at the expense of the other; and Wilson, as a being, destroys himself.

In this psychic drama it is interesting to note that, unlike "Usher," none of the elements of the inner self is dramatized outwardly until Wilson stands appalled before a mirror that gives back to him what he really is. The reason for this incapacity in Wilson to find anything in the world which is an extension of himself is not that such extensions and manifestations do not exist but that Wilson so lives by the anarchy of his own private godlike will that he is only his own mirror and manifestation. Usher saw around him the infinite interrelations of the self and the world outside; he lived in such terror that his private mind-being might be destroyed that he created the outer protective shell or the House. Wilson, on the other hand, is the Romantic individualist for whom the world is nothing but the externalization of the self: at any instant what the self wills the world must become; his journey to extinction is only a few thousand miles shorter than that of Captain Ahab, who had to go from New Bedford to the central Pacific before he too was annihilated.

"The Cask of Amontillado," coming in 1846 toward the end of Poe's mastery of the short-story form, is the tale of another nameless "I" who has the power of moving downward from his mind or intellectual being and into his brute or physical self and then of returning again to his intellectual being with his total selfhood unimpaired. It is as though one might separate the physical aspect from the mind and then restore at will the harmony again. But this "I" has one power which was denied to Usher, Wilson, and others: he is from the beginning master, even god, of his circumstances: "I must not only punish," he ruminates, "but punish with impunity. A wrong is unredressed when retribution overtakes its redresser. It is equally unredressed," he concludes, "when the avenger fails to make himself felt as such to him who has done the wrong." The tale delineates the mastery which the controlling self, when it concentrates all its energies in one of its three faculties, can obtain and maintain over the world around it. The "I" does not function as a mind; we never know what has made him hate Fortunato nor are we aware that he has ever laid out any plan to effect his revenge. All we know is that we descend into the brute world "during the supreme madness of the carnival season," and there, in motley and drunkenness, we watch Montresor play on Fortunato's weakness—his connoisseurship of wines, his jealousy of a rival Luchesi, and his indifference to the evil effects of the nitre in the subterranean depths. There is nothing intellectual here; everything is mad and improvisatory—and Montresor succeeds just so far as he is able to adapt himself to a mad, improvisatory world. In short, he descends from one faculty to another and then returns to his former condition, all the while having suffered no detection from society or the world around him. The other protagonists destroyed themselves because they could not completely dissociate one faculty from another; Montresor is the rare example in Poe's studies of the variable self who succeeds because he could, for a time, live in distinctly separate functions.

"The Cask of Amontillado" raises, however, another question pertaining to the multiple character of the self, a question which has been implicit throughout Poe's other studies of this theme. There is no verifiable consistency in any of these treatments of the human will and behavior; no one character is very much like any other and no single motive or action has very much relation to others. The fracture or dislocation of human faculties is different every time such an event occurs. The only permission Poe may have for such a curious psychology of human behavior is the apparent conviction he had that life consists of the disjunction of sides of the self: various elements in the human psyche or being are forever at war with each other; tragedy is always present because, in the inevitable bifurcation, one element is bound to obtain control and thereby exert such dominance that the human being is separated not only from the normal condition of a balanced selfhood but from his fellows and from the world around him. The Poe protagonist, in another respect, is compulsively driven toward death because, if life is the condition of fatal separation of the human body, mind, and spirit, death or whatever afterlife there may be is the unification of these faculties. The narrator of "The Tell-Tale Heart," who suffers and commits a crime because of the excess of emotion over intelligence, is impelled to give himself up and pay the death penalty because he may thereby return to full selfhood or primal being. Death is the completion of the life cycle; it restores that totality of being with which one began existence or which one might have had in some prior existence but which, in the inevitable chaos of this earthly life, is more and more destroyed. The tragedy (if it is a tragedy) of the Poe heroes is that they suffer from a war between their own faculties, body and mind, or mind and soul; and once that struggle has begun, it ends only with death. This disease of being is the enormous distension of any one perception or faculty at the expense of the others; and the Poe protagonists nearly all have in common the death-wish: at the end the tripartite self is able to realize its total selfhood. In death comes the full comprehension toward which Poe had moved in the poems but which he could more artfully treat, as process and intellectual activity, in the short stories.

Religiously, therefore, Poe postulated that mind is the only reality; physical nature is the total, unrelieved chaos of natural forms which, if they ever had design, have long been condemned to insensitivity in the general decay of the world. Man is forever lodged in this dualism, the double worlds of nature and of mind. The only way the mind can make order out of nature is either to make nature a total illusion of the mind, as in "The Fall of the House of Usher," or else to conceive of nature as the demonstration of *a* mind, perhaps some other mind, and then trace the natural world back to some primal order which coexisted with the beginning of time; this task of tracing backward Poe assumed in *Eureka*. In the short stories of his middle and late career he resolved the problem in the death of the mind and its return to its own presumed condition of unity.

In a sense, Poe's poetic career declined as he more and more renounced or destroyed the natural world and sought ways for the imagination to go beyond or, as it were, into the limitless regions of thought which are the domain only of poetic inquiry. His short-story writing career developed and his mind matured, on the other hand, the more he sought ways for the creative imagination to come to some terms with the real or phenomenal world outside. Yet he could not help wavering in his purpose: by turns he asserted the insane condition of the natural world and the accompanying insanity of the human mind; again, he formulated some interaction between mind and reality as the mind struggled for full awareness; and, still again, he established the primacy of the mind as the only knower and doer, as capable of knowing only its own experience and ideas.

Poe was too much a child of the eighteenth century not to abandon the rationally ordered universe without a struggle. Yet he was well aware that the new science of his own day was steadily undermining the sense-world of the Enlightenment — his own curious fumbling between Leibniz's monads and Kantian ideal forms displays this tension. The psychology of Hartley and the popular phrenology of Combe and Spurzheim, much as they emphasized the rational interaction of object and mind, steadily moved in the direction of the mind's capacity to know only itself and its private ideas and to reduce the world more and more to an illusion.

Poe's moral and religious ideas, for all their presumed rationality and coherence, are anti-rationalistic. If the only reality is mind, then reality slips away and distorts its shapes. The strangely disorganizing, even destructive, element in Poe's mind and writing was that he posited an organic world which had evolved from some primal, generative idea but that he was never able to account for man as having a vital, creative place in it. He had the choice of an invariable, deterministic world somehow existing apart from man or of the mind of man as itself a pure determinism whose speculations had nothing to do with external reality. He could subscribe to neither view, and thus he was left with a moral system which somehow granted to man the right to create his own moral anarchy and suffer as a result of it. Man's rule cannot be nature's, and man's mind is the reflector and initiator of no order other than its own. Melville and Poe are both crises in this dislocation of man: they both put the final moral responsibility on man, but the measure and degree of that responsibility are no longer capable of any assessment by any standard man has so far discovered.

Like Melville too, Poe had not made the major transition which the later nineteenth century would make, namely, that of lifting the burden of moral responsibility from the individual and imposing it on society. Poe's moral world was the "agony" of men who are morally responsible but who have somehow lost all awareness of and any reason for their responsibility. Guilt and evil are all the more appalling because they exist in the ever-worsening condition of the world, and yet no one is to blame. Men are forced to exist in this drama of terror and death as though there were some long-enduring and consistent regimen of action and judgment; all the while, however, they must improvise on the moment whatever is their action and moral justification. Roderick Usher, William Wilson, the man in the crowd, Montresor in "The Cask of Amontillado"—all these and others comport themselves and are necessarily judged as though there were a massive tradition or morality behind them, but they have themselves never known what it was. They are like Kafka's man in *The Trial* who never knows the charges contained in his indictment.

Here was one more in a central intellectual problem of the nineteenth century. Every time it occurred it took a different form. Gerard Manley Hopkins, a Catholic, could live in his own agony world and rely on a solid body of dogma and religious refreshment; his emotions and his mind pulled him in two directions at once. Emily Dickinson had long lost hold on the Puritan-Protestant world into which she was born, and yet she could use all the phrases and formalisms of that faith as the vocabulary of her own invented world. Melville renounced faith and yet was unable to accept science; Mark Twain tried to grasp science and was unable to let faith go. Poe, for his part, tried to swallow the new science whole and make it a substitute for the ritualized and dying faith in which he was reared. But what he thought was "science" was, after all, only his own private reconstruction of reality, not a system, not a logic, not even a moral scheme. It was a continued act of will which attempted to make reasonable a wholly irrational world. Thus "reality" and man's good and evil were not a science or an order at all but an imaginative construct; whatever moral or religious system there was must be contained only within a single knowing mind which faced a different situation every time it had a thought.

4

Our second major premise in this treatment of Poe's moral tales is that Poe represents the decline or death of a once-powerful social idea. What had been in the seventeenth and eighteenth centuries the force for social action, for reform, for the raising up of distinguished public servants had, so far as Richmond, Virginia, was concerned, deterioriated into a number of still-observed social pieties behind which was only a powerful code for preserving the status quo. We might briefly consider several of these social determinants and then undertake to show how Poe's erotic world was either derived or in flight from that place and time in which he lived.

First of all, Poe was reared not in the tradition of democratic liberalism sanctified under the names of Jefferson and Jackson but under a powerful conservative or Whig reaction. Jeffersonianism and Jacksonianism were vulgar and frontier; the conservatism of Tidewater Virginia, especially dignified by John Marshall, was polite, urbane, and strongly anti-democratic and anti-reform. This political situation might have done several things to Poe: it could have made him a rebel and radical or a staunch, complacent supporter of the Virginia hierarchy. It did neither; for all that apologists have tried to show, it left him indifferent to the political contentions of his time. If he occasionally expressed an idea that might be labeled "social" or "political," it smacks so discreditably of the stale windbaggery of southern politicians and racists as to be embarrassing.

Another social determinant in Poe's early life may well have been the tension between the code of the Virginia landed aristocracy, with its emphasis on family, lineage, leisure, and social position and the still-unwritten but newly developing code of the trade and business class.[9] This tension was rare in ante-bellum Virginia; but Poe happened to be reared in it because his foster father, John Allan, was a new-rich representative of the merchant class who would someday, perhaps not until the twentieth century, set the direction which Virginia and the rest of the South would go. In Poe's young manhood this tension appeared when the code of the gentleman who gambled at the University of Virginia met head-on the code of the penurious Scotch businessman. Part of Poe's personal tragedy was that he was carefully reared through the first eighteen years of his life to conform to the manners and code of the aristocratic, landed gentry in the fashionable circles of sophisticated Richmond; then he was suddenly thrust into the business world where the only money he ever made came from that otherwise discredited instrument in the world of finance, a writer's pen.

The result of this situation in Poe's life was not, as so many sympathizers have tried to make out, to reduce Poe to a forlorn leech on his not very understanding foster father or on society at large but to turn him to a lifetime's consideration of the place of an artist in a busy world which has no use or reward for artistic production. As early as 1836 he was asking rather stridently: "When *shall* the artist assume his proper situation in society — in a society of thinking beings? How long shall he be enslaved?" Then Poe went on to hope for an artistic "Revolution" which would free the spirit of man. Such a program readily led Poe to consider the artist as not like ordinary people: "That genius should not and indeed cannot be bound down to the vulgar common-places of existence, is a maxim which, however true, has been too often repeated. . . ."[10] Poe was never consistent in this idea of the place of the artist in society: sometimes the artist is a dreamer utterly remote from the practical affairs of men; sometimes he is the brilliant man of precise and practical genius whom society is only too happy to reward. At any rate, Poe was in the generation of Romantic writers who, as Jacques Barzun has shown, were the first to consider what an artist is and what he does in the act of making works of art. Some of Poe's tales, as we shall see, are treatments of this theme of who an artist is and what he does.

A third and final social determinant was the code of the gentleman. No one, least of all in Virginia or Baltimore before the Civil War, could or need define a gentleman, for everyone knew precisely what or who he was.[11] From all evidence that survives, Poe was himself a gentleman, an impeccable gentleman in speech, manner, dress (his wearing simple black clothes is indicative here), and certainly in his addresses to the ladies, many of whom found him so affecting that their hearts were touched. More important than the fact that Poe was a gentleman is the obvious conclusion that all of Poe's heroes and protagonists are gentlemen too, even when they indulge in murder or vent their criminal emotions on helpless animals. Yet the very fact that Poe's heroes, however cultured and well-mannered they may be, are driven to desperate actions and crime is suggestive that something is vitally wrong with the code they live by. The difficulty with Poe's gentlemanly protagonists is that, as with their religious behavior, they are required to conform to a code and to a set of pieties from which any meaning or purpose has long been lost. They are socially adrift in a world where nearly everyone behaves in a most correct manner for reasons beyond anyone's comprehension. In the end, if a wrong is done, society never punishes the criminal; he is caught by a malignant fate which had long foreseen the tragic event; the punishment comes from the unfathomed moral being of the criminal himself, for he becomes, as in "The Tell-Tale Heart," his own judge and executioner.

All his life Poe considered himself an outcast; from the beginning he was the child of strolling actors and therefore of mean origin; he could feel that he belonged neither in the Richmond society in which he was reared nor in the larger worlds of Philadelphia or New York.[12] Yet, as a writer, he had strong convictions about the theory and practice of writing and the proper place of the writer, not as in society, but as really beyond any social judgment. Thus in a way he tried to get his revenge, a revenge which took several forms. One was his setting up the gentleman-hero who should be not so much in revolt against society as contemptuous of it. The other was his elevation of the brilliantly technical hero, the man of astounding brilliance in law, science, or detection.

In America, as De Toqueville long ago pointed out, we have always been made uneasy by too much artistic and imaginative brilliance; we do applaud and favor any form of mechanical and technical ability. Poe's heroes were allowed to triumph in both respects: they are all victorious because, primarily, they can shape every turn of the drama to suit their own ends; and, moreover, they are most extraordinarily dazzling and victorious at the very moment when society's code and the laws of men have nothing more to do with them. They have actually been above society all the time; but they have been privileged to demonstrate their scorn and revenge by pretending to take seriously what they knew, as behavior and social morality, was fraudulent all the time.

Yet anyone looking for profound or caustic social commentary in Poe's tales is bound to be disappointed. Poe's tendency to fooling and hoaxes led him constantly to write uncomely grotesques which contained some of his most inflated and absurd writing and some of his most humorless puns: Dr. Ponnoner, Count Allamistakeo, Peter Proffitt, and others. Some critics have remarked that Poe's social ideas were wholly conservative and conventional. The unpleasant grotesquerie of Poe's social commentary may have derived from his indifference to if not contempt for politics, or, more likely, his unwillingness to use art to treat seriously a subject which he considered beneath the true value of art anyway. In part, then, because he early became convinced that society itself, especially the business and financial aspects of it, was contemptuous of artists and writers, the artist's only avenue was to reduce to the ridiculous what relegated him to a condition of inconsequence.

A tale like "The Man That Was Used Up" is a piece of

uncomely fooling which takes a popular, oracular military idol, in this case Brevet Brigadier General John A. B. C. Smith, who had made a fabulous reputation in the bloody Kickapoo campaign, and reveals him finally as a mechanical man whose arms and legs are screwed to his torso and whose beautiful baritone voice is a phonographic apparatus in his throat. "The Business Man" is the scapegrace, and not very funny, life of the very "practical" Peter Proffitt, who, like Mark Twain's more famous Colonel Sellers, is infinitely fertile in thinking up schemes to cheat the gullible public but who somehow never makes his fortune or becomes the success that society intends every man to be. The more pointed social commentary of "Some Words with a Mummy" and of "Mellonta Tauta" is directed haphazardly at man's vaunted theory of inevitable progress or at the illusion that freedom and education work toward human perfectibility.

Perhaps because he believed that the practical mind of man was totally inimical to the imaginative and artistic and because the marketplace had scant reward or use for art, Poe tended more and more as his career lengthened to treat social problems within the narrowest and most private contexts. In many respects these problems are not "social morality" or commentary at all but are concerned entirely with man's relation to his own private psyche, to his innermost secret being. In this respect we therefore enter a moral realm of what might be termed "utilitarian anarchy" or a form of hedonism so individual or unique that a generalization can hardly be made about it. Whatever is "good" is whatever allows a human being to exist with a minimum of pain; whatever is "evil" is that which destroys a man or brings about a distension of one faculty of his being at the expense of another. In a larger consideration of man's social and moral responsibility, Poe tried to relate man to the total order of the universe: the mind of God, from creation to the end of His scheme of time, is exerted throughout all space; each part and element of creation is a manifestation of God's mind and will and, throughout whatever existence it may have, tends to move toward unity or some knowable identification with the divine, primal order. But this was Poe's vision in *Eureka;* it was not his moral vision in the poems and tales of his mid-career.

5

In the tales of ratiocination or the detective tales are presented Poe's most consistent social and moral views, all together amounting almost to a "system." Though these tales have their antecedents in the hoaxes and in such exercises as "The Unparalleled Adventure of One Hans Pfaall" and "MS. Found in a Bottle," their ideas reach completion in "The Murders in the Rue Morgue," "The Mystery of Marie Roget," "The Gold-Bug," and "The Purloined Letter." They form a curious linkage between certain premises set forth in the allegorical tales and the ultimate *summa* in *Eureka.* They were moral, philosophical, and as autobiographical as Poe ever became. And, as everyone knows, they contributed to, if they did not actually bring into being, the modern detective tale and novel.

There are several interesting matters concerning the hero of these tales. From his first appearance as the all-knowing "I" in "MS. Found in a Bottle," he is fully grown and wholly in command not only of himself but of all the events through which he must go: sometimes he even exercises control beyond his own death. In fact, he is so wholly master of all situations that, despite all of Poe's efforts to make him special and different, he conforms to a very general American type. He is the perpetual American boy-man, the smart aleck, the sharper who really hurts only the foolish and evil, the Tom Sawyer, the traveling salesman: he is the most frequently duplicated young man in American legend and worship from the jaunty adventures of Captain John Smith, that first modern supersalesman, to the gods of comedy in the twentieth century.[13]

Yet this hero has another, and less frequently noted, qualification which makes him part of the American dream: he is the lonely one; he is the image of longing to get away, which is so much a part of Davy Crockett, Abe Lincoln (lonely whether in the log house or the White House), Natty Bumppo, Captain Ahab, Thomas Sutpen. He belongs to the people and yet he must make his great decision or undergo the major trial in the waste places or in the solitude of the anguished soul. He is one of us; yet he must, to express himself, go above, away from, or beyond our commoner range of experience in order to bring his message, the fire from heaven, the solution to the crime. This is the Dupin who figures in the three memorable stories in which he is the hero-god: he reverses the clock and lives vividly while the rest of the world sleeps; he is outside the range of society, and yet he can solve the greatest mysteries in society. In sum, we feel more comfortable with him than we do with any other of Poe's heroes.

Poe's hero-god Dupin did not, however, try to "corrupt"

anything or anybody. He was, furthermore, a nineteenth-century fulfillment of what Benjamin Franklin so ably defined in *The Way to Wealth* and in his *Autobiography;* but Dupin demonstrated what might happen to the myth of success, all the way from Franklin through Andrew Carnegie's *Gospel of Wealth* and beyond, when there would be no more ethical limits or productive restrictions to man's acquisitive instincts. It was the world of a commercial mind existing beyond any law of supply and demand, payment and price; it was as if man had conquered all his physical and economic limitations and had nothing more to produce except a perfect method of production; nothing would remain but the pure theory of making and doing. Hitherto, as Franklin had demonstrated, man had to control his own instincts and mind; then he had to gain control of the methods of acquisition. Poe's Dupin had long passed through and come out on the other side of the commercial formula: he had been able to make the commercial designs of society conform precisely to his own private ethic; yet he has made himself indispensable to society by being able, at will, to reduce society's madness and murder to a logic so simple that, if people were but aware of it, they could be Dupin too. But that measure of difference was Dupin's triumph: anyone who followed Franklin's thirteen precepts for living could achieve and be a Franklin; no one else could be Dupin, not even the worshipful "I" who accompanies him on all his exploits. The difference was measured, as Poe remarked, between "simple ingenuity," which anyone can possess, and "analytic power," an ability granted only to genius. Franklin's was a logic for every man; Dupin exhibited "a degree of acumen which appears to the ordinary apprehension preternatural. His results, brought about by the very soul and essence of method, have, in truth, the whole air of intuition."

Dupin's method is actually the grotesquerie of any rational system — and was no doubt so intended in terms of Poe's calculated attack on the sacred institution of money-getting. The mind of Dupin began with the assumption that the world was in total disorder. His is the unproductive sterility of a mind which can solve every ethical problem by acts of irrational, unethical intuition. The Lockean world of sensation and reflection became mere impulse and the flight of imagination; the countinghouse of John Allan would no longer be addition and subtraction but the calculus of ultimate improbability.

Poe's Dupin gets one more revenge on his own or Poe's time-world: he is not only a lonely man and a success (however much his "success" reduces logic to absurdity), but also a man of intellect for whom other men's problems are matters of mere and momentary amusement; apart from the amusement, the struggle and the solution are not worth the bother; Dupin is excused from any moral intention. He has thereby turned the ethic of success into pure hedonism: the mind alone can enjoy its own operations; it has long passed beyond industry and frugality or stewardship (in Calvin's, Franklin's, or Carnegie's terms) and can speculate on its own nature. He is the ultimate dream of the artist who has nothing more to do but enjoy his art.

Dupin was the triumph who could satisfy several needs at once: he was the faraway Prince for the periodical reader (he appeared first in *Graham's, Snowden's Lady's Companion,* and *The Gift*) who longed to see Paris, and he was also the American analyst, the inventor, the clever promoter who, given a different playground, could conquer a continent. Poe suited the same demand which, in other ways, Longfellow complied with — the domestication of the longed-for foreign culture. The American before the Civil War wanted to go abroad; he also wanted to feel that he was part of what Fiske called the "transit of civilization" from the Old World to the New. Poe satisfied that longing by inventing an extremely clever American, neither Southern nor Yankee, who was already abroad and already thoroughly cultured. The irony was that this grotesque Frenchman-American could get anything he wanted by never working but by simply thinking. Dupin was that total success who, as an exponent of an artistic inquiry, admitted no flaw; he was what Poe wanted the artist and his art to be with such completeness that, as an extreme, Dupin ended not in art or as an artist, but as an analyst and businessman.

Poe therefore posited, behind all of his tales of ratiocination, a final relationship between reality and the ideal, the seen and the unseen, the perceived and the imagined. These two realms of being and cognition never seem to coincide in the normal world of man's experience. A crime is, however, a sudden and startling thrust of what lies behind the bland surface of existence into the presumed reality; that reality instantaneously breaks down and, while in its fragments, sustains or reveals the "ideal." A crime is a disruption of the ostensible order of things — their temporal and physical relationships in which man puts his trust — and is, therefore, a glimpse into ideality, into the very nature of things. It is an instance whereby "Accident is admitted as a portion of the superstructure" of the world of things. A "true philosophy," Poe elsewhere stated, "will show, that a vast, perhaps the larger, portion of truth arises from the seemingly irrelevant." At such a moment the detective-philosopher sees the total relevancy not only of being but of non-being; he can begin to relate the irrelevant and seemingly meaningless action in the brute world to the total, primal calculus of relationship which can be apprehended only by the creative imagination. The man who solves a crime is a poet: he is a re-creator of things as they truly are, not as they seem "in reality" to the common gaze.

Any human problem or crime thus required, to be understood, a reduction of the common and generally false ideas of human nature to a basic, primordial simplicity, which is itself identical with the primal order of the natural world. Every human idea or action is, if it is truly known, a simulacrum of the universal metaphysical and physical realms of being; every activity of a human mind is a paradigm in little of the function of the universe. Dupin read the criminal mind by reducing all its exercises to a fundamental, primordial simplicity, its basic "Calculus of Probability." [14]

Yet it must be insisted that the human mind does not conform naturalistically to the laws of physical science; the two exist in separate realms of being, and a law of one cannot be directly applied to the other. But both mind and physical reality conform to an "ideal" set of logical determinants which, as though in a third realm of being, reach toward identity and unity. Just as the scientific laws approach a single Newtonian or transcendant formulation, so human intelligence and behavior, no matter what the background and experience, move toward uniformity and respond to stimuli in identical ways. Once this pattern of behavior or thought can be traced to its origins, the outcome or solution is open to precise exposition.[15]

Poe's term for this unitary characteristic of both mind and world was "simplicity" or the unvarying nature of the human mind to conform to a pattern of behavior which can at every stage be anticipated or discovered. In order to explain this calculus of relevance whereby human behavior could be explained as not like but ultimately parallel to scientific law, Poe set up a formula by which the several modes of human thought and action might be understood. First, there was the action of the commonplace, ordinary mind — the "real" side of man — which conformed to a calculus of probability simple to unmask merely by putting one's own mind in logical reference and identification with it: Poe's analogy was the boy who could easily outwit his fellows by guessing in which hand the marble was held. Next, the more complex, original mind was impelled toward simplicity, toward final and ultimate comprehension. It was the character of this mind to conceal itself, as did Minister D——— in "The Purloined Letter," behind some other or inverted calculus of relevance. This reach toward simplicity approached, however, the original and primordial simplicity of nature, itself based on the organization of the universe in some logical, all-knowing mind. What appears so baffling to the ordinary or rational mind is, in this category, the ultimate simplicity and relevance.

The third category of human perception led Poe straight to a unitary theory of mind and nature — unified not *in* nature or the world about man but in the ultimate order of mind and matter in the total "simplicity." "The material world," Poe asserted in "The Purloined Letter," "abounds with very strict analogies to the immaterial. . . ." Note that Poe insisted on "analogies," not identities. The ordinary mind is physically dimensioned and behaves according only to normal, material contours of reality: an object in the mind is supposititiously the thing seen, a rose is a rose, a letter is a letter. But shift ever so slightly the position of an object in relation to the observed "calculus of probability," and it may become something other than what it was. If it penetrates far enough behind the illusion of ostensible reality, the human mind has the capacity to destroy the world of confusion in which its normal experience is gained and reach toward a wholly new keying of reality whereby the appearances of things are dispelled and the total coherence is revealed. A tale of ratiocination is very like the poem: each in its special way proceeds from multiplicity and confusion to the primal "simplicity"; just as the material world chemically and metaphysically moves through its various phases from Unity to Multiplicity and back again, so the human mind may struggle to return to the functioning Idea behind the mask of appearances.

The tales of ratiocination are one direction of the artist's quest: by renouncing the actual world, Poe was free to construct a totally fictive playground of the mind which could still maintain workable likenesses to the world of common affairs. At the end, Poe came to a concept of God, part mind and part craftsman, who existed at one time in and then removed Himself from His creation. God and nature are thus dual; through nature, however, man essays to arrive at truth; but all the while he discovers in nature a frightening variety of discordant and cancelling propositions. "In their origin," Poe stated, "these laws were fashioned to embrace *all* contingencies which *could* lie in the future." Man perceives these laws as special in place and time, and thus he is forever confused by the jarring discrepancies between what is and what his mind tells him is "probability." What appears as an "accident" is merely a misapprehension of what is: "Modern science has resolved to *calculate upon the unforeseen.*" Poe's "Calculus of Probabilities" is a solution to his need of admitting that the mind is the only reality and that all it can know is itself and its operations which are concordant with the primal laws of the universe. The ratiocinative exercise of the detective is simply an allegory of how the mind may impose its interior logic on exterior circumstance. Dupin is the supreme artistic ego: everything external to himself can be made to fit the theoretical, the ideal logic.

Thus these tales of ratiocination were a number of expressions of Poe, the man and the artist. They were part of his struggle to conform by assuming more than a normal human share of certain faculties he otherwise held in contempt: he could assume the roles of natural scientist and "success," and then he could go much further and accomplish much more than the mere "businessman" of the nineteenth century could gain. He would go so far, in fact, that he would be contemptuous of the money he found in the pirate hoard in "The Gold-Bug" and care only for the imaginative exercise which made mere gold ludicrous. These tales are Poe's war on his age: he could not front his age in any truly critical terms, as did Hawthorne and Melville;

he could only ridicule by pretending to take seriously certain values and then destroy them at the very moment of treating them with reverence.

But in a larger sense, these tales were excursions into a philosophy of knowledge as, in their differing ways, were *Pym* and the allegories. They were attempted rationalizations not only of what nineteenth-century man held sacred but of what Poe regarded the central question of the relation of the mind to ultimate reality. They worked toward a final statement of his otherwise amorphous idealism, toward, in short, a unitary theory. They were aspects of that haunting question: what does man know and how does he represent to himself what he believes he knows? The poems were assumptions that mind and reality coexisted in some total design; the moral tales sought ways of measuring man against that rationale of the schematic universe; the ratiocinative stories destroyed the normative world and opened the suddenly revealed "ideal" in the crime and in its solution. In *Eureka* Poe would summarize and try to make coherent these approaches to a logical science and philosophy.

VIII

Eureka

Poe's *Eureka* has, for more than a century, been denounced as a farrago of nonsense or the last maudlin ruminations of a diseased Romantic mind.[1] It is, however, science, and it is poetry too. It should be taken, as Poe himself stated, "as a Romance; or, if I be not urging too lofty a claim, as a Poem; . . . it is as a Poem only that I wish this work to be judged after I am dead."[2]

Eureka was also science, a term that we must understand as, in the early sonnet, designating the whole body of discrete knowledge which man may know. It would be, Poe hoped, an elaborate yet simple theory out of which might come some new significant formulation for the comprehension of men. The philosophy of empiricism seemed to be rapidly going to pieces; and there was no new synthesis or schema that would make the world intelligible except perhaps to the most exalted mind of the age. For all Poe's scorn for Bacon or "Hogism," this would be a *novum or-*

ganum, a new compendium and system of knowledge wherein the first half of the nineteenth century would find mirrored not only its guiding hypotheses but also its sense of poetic and imaginative beauty as well.

In the strict terms of "science," *Eureka* is hardly a scientific treatise at all, but, like other imaginative projections of man's knowledge of the world, such as Lucretius' *De rerum natura* or Goethe's *Faust,* it is a poetic frame on which a great body of scientific information is hung. We must, therefore, first understand its basic "science" before we can undertake to discover its other philosophic and imaginative contexts.

The book is concerned with three scientific problems relating to the physical universe: first, the concept of creation (or, how did matter become what it appears to be?); second, the nature of matter (or, what is matter and how is the observed physical universe energized?); and third, the prospect for the natural world (or, toward what end is the ever-changing universe moving?).[3] Around these three points Poe's argument is set forth and joined.

The preamble to *Eureka* consists of a whimsical attack on Aristotelian, Baconian, utilitarian, inductive logic which would abandon the guiding hypothesis as a means of investigation and substitute the collection of sense data as facts. Yet, by contrast, Poe could not rest comfortably on the deductive method: as a choice between the two, he considers the intuition as the surer way to truth and cites Kepler's discoveries as examples of the way scientific advancement has been made through mystical insights into the laws of nature: "Yes! — these vital laws Kepler *guessed* — that is to say, he *imagined* them."[4] Then Poe undertakes the first major question of his discourse: what is matter or substance in the universe? Varying Newton's law which described merely the present observed condition of things, Poe attempts to return to an origin and to describe both the known condition of matter and its problematical beginning. He posits two contending forces in the universe. One is attraction or gravitation, a physical principle operating as the data or patterns of what the sense perceptions tell us are occurring. The other is repulsion or electricity, a spiritual principle: this is a curious modification of Kant's idea that known laws are forms introduced by the means of perception provided by the recipient himself.[5] Matter exists as expressions of only these two forces; spirit is extended throughout, is individualized in matter and assumes special forms which may be far removed from the laws or forms known to man, and reaches its highest development in the conscious and intuitive intelligence of man.

The second part of *Eureka* concerns the present observed constitution of the universe. In the beginning God, or the first cause, existed only as spirit; in that condition of thought there was made known the principle of "Diffusion," which, when it occurred, caused matter to be created at some focal point and then dispersed throughout the universe. During that process of dispersion, God exists in diffused matter and as spirit in His universe; when the dispersion is completed and the universe has reached the forms which accomplish God's design, then God's thought is to be withdrawn, and there will commence a reverse process, a necessary conflict of the powers of attraction and repulsion. Eventually, by its tendency to return to a single center, matter and spirit will be perfectly unified again: "The Body and the Soul will walk hand in hand." As a support for his thesis, Poe employed not only the Newtonian law of motion but the wave-theory of light and the nebular hypothesis of Laplace: all of these demonstrate, for Poe, that once the dispersing power has reached its climax and the motivating spirit is withdrawn, then the reaction or return to center will begin. "The Thought of God is to be understood as originating the Diffusion — as proceeding with it — as regulating it — and, finally, as being withdrawn from it upon its completion."[6]

Thirdly, Poe considers the nature or unity or the eventual prospect of the universe. Once the conflict between attraction and repulsion has ceased and matter has returned to its primal form as spirit, God, at present existing variously as matter and spirit, will again be as He primordially was, purely spiritual and individual, that is to say, as Unity. Then the "inconceivably numerous things which [we] designate as His creatures, but which are really but infinite individualizations of Himself," will become molded into one; and afterward will commence still another creative act of diffusion and a wholly new cycle of universal existence.

This mere summary in no way does sufficient justice to a work on which, despite its strange mélange of science, pseudo-science, and plain wishful thinking, Poe expended a great deal of effort and which he did regard as offering a *summa* of human thought in his own time. Our concern will be more with the imaginative and artistic implications of *Eureka* than with its science; yet we might initiate our inquiry by considering its "science," however suspect that science may be.

2

It would be both easy and difficult to say exactly where Poe had obtained his ideas for *Eureka*.[7] Many of these ideas were in the common and popular currency of scientific thought which, like the scientific thought of any time, is a bewildering compound of popular science, of the still-surviving science of a past age, and of the diverse blends which men make of their religious faith and their assumptions of what science is or ought to be. Poe's science is also a religion — not the religion of any formal churches but the religion of what a few men thought would be a scientific hypothesis concerning God at a time in Western thought just before the impact of Darwinian evolutionary ideas. *Eureka* might in one term be regarded as a treatise in "scientific religion" at a moment in intellectual history when the ordered universe of the eighteenth century was still a self-explanatory fact, when the Deity could obviously be conceived as the original and the still-continuing force in His universe, and when man — his history reaching back only to the starting-point of recorded time — was a creature that existed as the highest order of beings in a universe which had been designed expressly for his pleasure and perfection.[8]

The basic hypothesis to account for that universe is, in *Eureka,* a machine. It is a mechanism which is very like the cosmological system of Newton, Locke, and the eighteenth-century empiricists — with those happy variants introduced by Poe himself in order to make the universe an "unknown known" or a poem. Poe conceives of the universe as matter, motion, and force in a succession of instantaneous configurations of matter. He acknowledges Newton's law as a description of the presently observed condition of things, but he seeks to go beyond the Newtonian formulation in order to posit a law not only for the observed condition but for the origin of matter: *"Every atom, of every body, attracts every other atom, both of its own and of every other body, with a force which varies inversely as the squares of the distances between the attracting and attracted atom . . . ; the general result being a tendency of all, with a similar force, to a general centre."*[9] Then he appended the theory of Laplace as a further proof for the origin of the material universe in some generating principle or thought: matter was radiated from a source into nebula; the particles of the nebula were themselves dispersed into a steadily increasing complexity and heterogeneity. The process can be expressed by the following formula:

Unity →	Irradiation →	Diffusion
(The aboriginal state)	(The creative process)	(The present condition or multiplicity)

At some moment in God's historical time this process will be reversed: the force of dispersion will be withdrawn; the force of attraction, basic to all organic and inorganic life and even to human consciousness, will become sufficiently powerful to overcome the force of disunity and dispersion, and all those infinitely various forms will move back to their original state of homogeneity; the whole universe will once more be in its primal "concentricity" or unity.

Like his age, Poe found another support for his theory of unity in heterogeneity or animism in mechanism. The discoveries in electricity from the age of Franklin onward had argued the presence of a primal energy or an "ether" inhabiting all the spaces of the universe and dispersed even between the infinitely minute particles of observed matter. This ether, sometimes confused with electricity, was the means of transmitting light and energy from the sun, of holding atoms in the physically observed forms, and even of transferring sense data from one mind to another. Electricity was, therefore, the force which seemed to function in the universe as the clearest physical demonstration of "spirit" or the animating and diffusive power of God. We might now consider how the observed forms of the world, man's place in the world, and even man's thought could be explained according to the then current theories of electrical energy.[10]

Matter, once dispersed throughout the universe, now exists in gradations; some of these distinctions between kinds and degrees of matter man at present knows and assigns to scientific and logical organizations; others are so remote or "pure" as to be beyond his comprehension. The reason why matter is in these various gradations is the "electrical principle" which governs the form all substances assume. Matter is never in a state of rest; its motion is, however, not merely an observed fact or a logical, causal shift of constituent parts. The direction of motion is an act of mind expressing itself through the agency of the electrical energy that animates all things. Motion cannot therefore be called "thought," for the electrical force which is the energizing of thought is long antecedent to that thought and that action. Behind all observed matter and behind all thought is a primal electrical force; thinking is the conscious paralleling of an individual thought with that universal direction. Behind even thought is unity. What man terms "thinking" is merely his instinctive, inevitable conformity to an elemental principle which is the one principle animating all motion and matter. Matter and mind are one in the total design. Thought in man is the same as the mechanism of the universe.[11]

What, then, is the condition of man, and why does man seem to be the one being who is somehow disfigured and out of place in the cosmic design?

Man encompasses both spirit and substance and consists of two forms of "bodies": one is a rudimentary or simply physical existence; the other is a variable component which governs man's conformity (even though man himself may be unaware of this condition) to the ultimate configurations of matter and motion as they existed once in the primal order of God. Throughout the passage of time or the corrosive action of the dispersive force in the human realm, man has become more and more separated from his long-ago conformity to the unity of matter, motion, life, and spirit; he has become incapable of perceiving more than a mere fraction of what exists. Only, as it were, by working back from disunity through dispersion to unity in thought can man ever penetrate the small circle of his present existence and reach the aboriginal concept which is the unity of the universe.[12]

Man's mind and being are not alone in this tendency; all forms and all created matter conform to the law of "simplicity" or the law of unity from which everything has come and to which everything will inevitably return. In support of this thesis of "simplicity," Poe borrowed a rule of Keplerian physics which had stated, in effect, that atoms are drawn toward each other and thus eventually toward some coherent design or unity. Just so, Poe reasoned, the human mind, itself a form lodged in the universe, tends toward "concentrality" and is continually expressing its "tendency always to return to unity." By the very nature of this tendency or struggle, the material world is incomplete or abnormal: man's mind, necessarily in conformity with the known laws of matter, is also functioning in diversity, in multiplicity, in crude approximations to the true nature of things. And, just as the atoms and the material forms "struggle back" to the center, so too does the human mind move toward the primal order of final being. But this struggle is difficult: so far as it can ever go toward ultimate completion, the mind is permitted, in its present state, only rare flashes of brilliant and fragmentary illumination, such as at moments of scientific discovery or of poetic insight, into the absolute reality which lies behind this illusory structure of the material world.

The basic science in *Eureka* is directed, therefore, to set up some kind of monism. Mechanism can be a monism, as William James pointed out, because it arises from a theory of causal unity: things hang together as substance and as force.[13] But Poe was not content with a simple mechanistic world-hypothesis: he worked toward a teleological unity, a purposive monism. He would go even further and posit an ontological and epistemological unity: things hang together because our minds perceive them in association. For him this postulate was further proof that the whole universe, of matter, mind, and spirit, was monistic: things both are and seem together. Man's rational and intuitive exercises of the mind conform to the one "supremeness . . . of symmetry.

. . . Poetry and Truth," Poe concluded, "are one. A thing is consistent in the ratio of its truth — truth in the ratio of its consistency. *A Perfect consistency* . . . can be nothing but an absolute truth." Neither sense impression nor idea exists except as unity and "perfect Simplicity." Man is not ultimately dislocated or fractured; he is not even subject to the mechanism of which he is a part. He is indeed All, and everything he does or thinks reflects and even drives toward that absolute center from which the whole radiating process had come and toward which all things must return: ". . . are we not, indeed, more than justified in entertaining a belief . . . that the processes we have here ventured to contemplate will be renewed forever, and forever, and forever; a novel Universe swelling into existence, and subsiding into nothingness, at every throb of the Heart Divine. And now — this Heart Divine — what is it? *It is our own*." [14]

Thus Poe established the total similitude of scientific reality as conforming to the very being of God; matter is but the extension of thought; a scientific law is a symbolic approximation, however crude and fumbling, to the primal Idea of God. God manifests Himself by degrees; the more thought, the more there is a knowledge of God and of the absolute unity in the universe. But this "thought" or science is not man's only way toward a comprehension of the One or of truth; there are, implied or explicit in the determinations of *Eureka,* two other avenues: one is philosophical and the other aesthetic. We might, for ease of analysis, consider the epistemological and philosophic premises which underlie the theory of "simplicity" and the content of Poe's "poem."

3

Although some minds in the nineteenth century clearly understood the difficulties that positivism had left, they were mostly committed to the Newtonian, Lockean, rationalistic program which was best expressed in Hume's great question: "What *can* we experience?" The answer was obvious: the data of experience are the patterns of sense impressions provided by the sense organs.[15] This doctrine led to the assumption that man has only a few avenues of direct communication with the external world, namely, the five sense organs. The search for data and for knowledge was thus narrowed to the further question: What data are directly provided by the activity of the sense organs? The answer was, quite properly, those data which the mind knows as fundamentally uniform and continuous and not subject to the vagaries of the individual percipient himself. Poe's theory of "simplicity" or the ultimate coherence of sense data and ideas was based on the assumption that there was a uniform, unvarying world which presented these data to the senses; were the material universe variable and capricious, then there would be no consistency or uniformity in man's sense impressions and ideas.

Poe, like his age, brushed aside or ignored this question of the world as uniformity: if it were as unvarying as some men assumed, then sense data and ideas, stimulated by that "world," would never change; man could not evolve, and each generation of men would have to recapitulate the history of ideas. A further confusion was apparent in this scheme of thinking, a difficulty which Poe himself was quick to perceive.

There are, in corroboration, two kinds of refined data: empirical data, which are pointer readings capable of reduplication (as with thermometer indications and other matters of physics), and logical data, which are evidence for the validity of numerical and mathematical transitions; they are considered coherent and logical to such a degree that men have for a long time regarded them as legitimate. Rationalism and positivism in the eighteenth century developed from a theory of knowledge and of the world based only on empirical data; but that system of thought was ever ready to use logical data, existing only as constructs and propositions of the mind, as though they were demonstrable fact. Eighteenth-century empiricists, and their nineteenth-century followers at whom Poe sneered in the opening pages of *Eureka,* could not keep their categories in order, or else they employed one criterion as a means of proving an idea which pertains to quite another datum of experience. Therefore, they made knowledge identical with science; all thought was referred to refined, organized, empirical data. The fallacy of Comte and Mill was that they overestimated the state of knowledge: except in chemistry and physics, it is doubtful that the cognition of belief can ever exist in any empirical form. There seems to be little indication that, unless some new method of corroboration is discovered, we can ever approach an "ideal" of known data. Positivism ended in skepticism, as with Hume, or dogmatism, as with Comte and Mill, who erected a variety of structural evidences which presumed to rest entirely on mere common sense.[16] Poe's attack on Mill and on the positivists, despite his flamboyant rhetoric, is not without meaning and reason.

Furthermore, positivists are notoriously scornful of metaphysics. Since their hypotheses are based only on common sense, they consider that systems of thought and of ideas are methods merely of keeping facts in order and thus have no cognitive value. To memorize the multiplication table is a means of facilitating human thought, but in itself it does nothing. Some positivists would even deny the guiding hypothesis or theorem because it would be, in its primary stages of cognition, beyond common sense and should be applied only to an extended mass of corroborative evidence. Kepler would never have been able to prove that the motions of planets describe ellipses, not circles, because, as Poe suggested, he would never have dared to formulate an hypothesis which went against common sense regarding the motions of bodies in space.

Metaphysics or systems of thought serve the purpose not only of organizing thought but of providing logical transitions from one system to another. One may begin with common sense, proceed to a hypothesis, and end with mathematics and symbolic logic. The eighteenth-century positivists betrayed their unwillingness to deal satisfactorily and logically even with what common sense informs us is the full extent of existence and experience. In this respect William James was their most devastating critic.[17] What, for his part, Poe was attempting to do, especially in the first part of *Eureka,* was to fill out the metaphysical and logical structure which positivism and common sense refused to deal with.[18]

Poe's science and metaphysics, positing matter and mind

as originating in a central Idea and then undergoing dispersion throughout space and time, argued that the material universe was not fixed or rooted in "common sense." Quite the contrary: in *Eureka* the world assumed the form of a chimera whose every moment might exhibit some new condition of things which had almost no relevance to an antecedent condition. What Poe did was to set up a rational, empirical order of things as those things are assumed to exist in common sense and in sensory experience—and then posit a concurrent order of things-as-ideas existing in a totality of experience beyond empiricism and abstract logic. There was, there must be, the "unknown" in human thought toward the comprehension of which man is moving, else there would have been no change in the past intellectual history of man. In the end, we do rely on the experience of our sense impressions—and we do not. Poe's denial of the methodological value of either inductive or deductive logic and his positing of the superior capacity of the intuitional faculty cut straight through the Lockean or positivist philosophy of knowledge and left him with a "mechanistic animism." True, he involved himself in so many contradictions that *Eureka* can be accounted only as "imaginative metaphysics" at best; yet, as we shall see, its imaginative approach to problems of thought may have transgressed logic but pointed the way toward a poetically conceptual idea of man and his mind.

There were several avenues of solution to this question of an animate machine, a mechanistic organism, in the pre-Darwinian thinking of the nineteenth century. One favorite device was the analogy, an incisive and deceptive tool in the hands of a positivist logician like Herbert Spencer, who may have been the last to use it with any real faith in its value; it was also a clever device which Poe employed in order to reach what is a form of "empirical animism." Its argument would be somewhat as follows:

Man and the universe had a beginning and thus a beginner whom man calls God. The universe is an extension and a symbolization of God; it is contained within observed data and form; so too is man. God, or idea, and man are made known to each other both through empirical data and through logical data, through facts and through symbols. If everything existing as this continuum of man and the universe could be formulated into one law or symbol, then the total reality or the unknown would be revealed. Poe termed that law "simplicity" and thus reduced all knowledge and the whole universe to a sentence: "I now assert—that an intuition altogether irresistible, although unexpressible, forces me to the conclusion that what God originally created—that that Matter which, by dint of his Volition, he first made from his Spirit, or from Nihility, *could* have been nothing but Matter in its utmost conceivable state of—what?—of *Simplicity*."[19] Poe ended where such systems of thought, whether positivist or animist, usually end, in utter dogmatism; for he could never bring any sense data or categories into logical conformity with his system. At that point, however, where philosophy or science failed him, Poe could move far onward—to the "poem" which would itself be a method and system of thought.

In addition to the analogy as a means of escaping or avoiding the mechanist dilemma, there was the method of defining knowledge and experience wholly in terms of sense data and then of going beyond that range in order to find proof for the data which sense itself could not have supplied. This argument ends with a universe of sheer accidence, every one of whose accidentals can somehow be logically explained. Laplace and his followers (of whom Poe was certainly one) posited that every particle can be defined in space and time.[20] That such a particle happened to meet and collide with some other particle and form a substance is an accident; the result might have been any other of an infinitude of conditions. The universe, as Berkeley showed, would thereby tend to become ever more irrational and causeless until one would arrive at a subjective mechanism which denies any existence whatever except to what takes place in the mind itself. The mind would thereby become the ultimate accident, conforming only to the unknown and unpredictable accidence of irrational matter. This skepticism of the sensory world found its classic statement in Hume's *Treatise of Human Nature:* "When both the objects are present to the senses along with the relation, we call *this* perception rather than reasoning; nor is there in this case any exercise of the thought, or any action, properly speaking, but a mere passive admission of the impressions through the organs of sensation. According to this way of thinking, we ought not to receive as reason any of the observations we may make concerning *identity* and the *relations* of *time* and *place;* since in none of them the mind can go beyond what is immediately present to the senses, either to discover the real existence or the relations of objects."[21] The whole force of this passage, as Whitehead has suggested, depends upon the mind as "a passively receptive substance" and the "impression" as a very "private world of accidents." Thus objects and impressions have no real existence whatever; they are simply highly individual impressions of the mind.[22]

This solution to the paradox of whether the mind knows things or knows only itself led to still another, a corollary assumption, namely, that there is one law for everything that happens in the physical world (Poe's term was the oft-repeated "simplicity"), and yet, contrariwise, there are different laws for different conditions. Laplace set forth the startling theory, of which Poe must have been aware, that we should be able to know the configurations of all matter for any time whatsoever.[23] We come back, however, to the same conclusion that we had before: these presumably separate laws may not be "laws" at all but are only human constructions or approximations to the actual relations in nature. Mechanism passed readily into subjective idealism and even into nominalism. Not until the full impact of evolutionary biology was felt did this curious form of "mechanistic idealism" (to employ an impossible term) finally collapse.

Poe was speaking for the urgency of his age which had, for more than a century, committed itself to a mechanistic universe — yet it was a universe which had God or an animating intelligence in it. It was a unity with every sign and behavior of multiplicity; it was a world of absolute fixity and predicability which was nonetheless undergoing a continuous process toward the consummation of a grand design. *Eureka* was the positing of an invariable machine — and it was a protest against everything mechanistic and empirical.

So far, then, we have followed two themes in the structure of ideas in *Eureka,* the scientific and the philosophic. We are now ready for the third and last. These themes, it must be stressed, are not separate designs which are argued back and forth as they appear in the treatise: they are organic to the very concept of the One or "simplicity." Each belongs to and supports the other.

The third major problem which is undertaken in *Eureka,* and the one which may be more germane than the other two, is the question of art and the artist. Poe was seeking some way of avoiding the admission that there was, after all, a final rift between science and art and between the world of things and the artist. He conjured up the known pluralisms of the universe — scientific and philosophic — and then posited an ultimate monism. So too art must be, in this term, regarded as but another extension and demonstration of "the plot of God" and the artist as a god-player. Poe's argument may be one more example of the forlorn hope of establishing any relationship between the data of experience transmitted into the life of practical affairs and those transmitted into art. As Hume long ago pointed out, philosophic and artistic doctrine fails to justify the practice of daily life. Nevertheless, whatever fallacy he may have invited, Poe set forth a dialectic of the autonomy of art and of expressive symbolism. We might now consider some of the implications of that urgent demand that somehow the artist does belong in the universe and that what he communicated is not just word, line, or tonality.

4

Eureka ought to be significant in modern metaphysical and artistic history for one reason alone: it made no attempt to investigate the bases of physical and astronomical law or of man's mind and place in the world on the basis of Experience. In fact, the constant insistence is that any search for understanding, of any kind, is outside or beyond experience. The experience or history of science or art is not the history or experience of man. Art and science have their own histories; society or human experience is a quite separate narrative. André Malraux's study of "The Metamorphoses of Apollo" is not an account of laws governing man's experience from the fourth century B.C. to the twelfth century A.D. out of which came the change in the sculpture of the human head. Apollo's head became the heavy-lidded Buddha of India because of the special quality and character of Hindu art; and it became the agonized, upward-staring face of the crucified Christ in medieval Europe because of fundamental artistic designs in sculptors' minds, not because of any historical events in Christendom or Western Europe in those years.[24]

"Experience" is always a dangerous norm to apply to art. Dr. Johnson, in the age before Poe, asserted that poetry and criticism are rooted in experience. However variously he used the term, he meant some means by which the mind makes order out of existence — how the mind makes its own "history" — and he conceived that the more general or typical the experience, the greater the design and therefore the greater the art of the poem. Like Dryden, he castigated the Metaphysical poets not because they brought into the poem too much experience but because their poems did not succeed in organizing experience around some particles.[25] To a certain extent Poe was a metaphysical artist: he knew that art could not be a substitute for living or for experience; art might well be another experience, another existence; it was not necessarily an escape from living; it was a totally different kind and expression of living. Therefore, the presumed norms of human existence and experience could no more be applied to the understanding and judgment of art than they could to the supposition of the law of inverse squares, to a theory of infinity, or to the square root of minus-one.

Yet Poe's position in *Eureka* is almost a commonplace of romantic art theory and history: from Lessing's *Laokoön* (1766) to the manifestoes of the French Impressionists toward the end of the nineteenth century, the philosophy of art has rejected art's representational function in the world. The aesthetic philosophy of Romanticism announced two salient concepts: one, that the world of art is an autonomous realm and has its own special rules and methods quite distinct from other functions of man and his mind; and two, that art and the artist come not from "life," that is from a personality who has relevance in historical place and time, but from other precedent art and artists. The inquiry in the *Biographia Literaria* took Coleridge back, not to his life or experience, but to the roots of his imaginative being alone.[26] So too did Poe's *Eureka* essay the search for man's total intuitive perception.

But is that perception, the question kept recurring, derived somehow from the world, even remotely from experience, or is it a construct only of the mind? Poe pondered the meaning and function of the word "infinity": is that a transference of the idea of infinity to a verbal equivalent, or is it only a reference or tag for the mind when it gropes for the meaning of limitless space which it can never really "know" at all? Are these verbal constructs ways by which the mind *seems* to make things known to itself, or are they what exist only in the mind? Are words realities of the world? are they realities of the world and mind together? or are they realities only of the mind? We might pursue this epistemological question a little further before we come back to more pointed concerns of Poe's theory of art and the artist.

Like other Romantic artists, Poe, while addressing himself to the total autonomy of art and art's disconnection from daily life, was yet all the while disturbed by this wide separation. Later artists and critics were to be concerned with the history of this fracture, all the way from Henry Adams to Ortega y Gasset; the chief impetus of the Romantic inquiry was, on the other hand, to discover the implications of this rift for the Romantic artist himself, in his own world and work, and then try so to reconstitute the world (note: the emphasis is on "world," not on the artist himself or on his art) that the two might somehow exist in coherence again. In short, if there is no connection between experience and art, there must be some unifying principle which lies behind even their apparent dichotomy.

Poe sought ways of escaping the final acknowledgment of a split between imagination and fact, between mind and world, or, to put the problem in more central terms, to escape the dilemma whereby the artistic imagination, a creative faculty, would come finally to rest in a mindless universe and thereby be forced to admit that the only permanent reality was the reality it made for itself. For all his sneering at Mill, Bentham, and logical positivism, Poe was aware of the mind's dead end which the following hypotheses would impose: "Ability or inability to conceive is no case to be received as a criterion of axiomatic truth"; or again:

"Contradictions cannot *both* be true — that is, cannot exist in nature. . . . A tree must be either a tree or *not* a tree." If these contradictions do exist, then only the most subjective and capricious imagination of man can have being. Illusion would be the only reality; art would consist simply as the ephemeral report of the mind's most willful, momentary impressions. If Mill were right and if his syllogism held, then the poetic imagination — even the whole range of imaginative discourse — would be relegated to the limbo of nonsense.[27]

Poe passed this question by with his graceless sneers at Mill in the opening sections of *Eureka* and was happy to rephrase a solution to the dilemma according to the Kantian and Coleridgian concept of the double truth of both exterior and subjective knowledge: the tree which seems a speck is both a speck to the viewer and a tree in fact. The report, or the poem, can treat either the speck or the tree; whatever its subject, it is a real report on a real thing. Ideas exist even if there is no mind (except possibly God's) which can know of their existence; thus contradictions can be true and can coexist in nature. The paradox can be phrased still another way: the universe is a mechanism which nonetheless has soul and mind, whose atoms do not blindly run; and yet the cognitive evidence for this assumption rests only in the human mind which is somehow itself not dependent on such primary categories of space, time, and location. Poe ends with a solipsism or a subjective idealism — a mechanism with a mechanic but without a machine.

There were several possible solutions to the fear that there is an unbridgeable gap between mind and reality, between art and world. One was to posit that the human mind is somehow, mysteriously even, a part of the universal mind. On this point Whitman fixed all his thought and his poetic career. The other was to advance rules of art or imagination which are not identical with the laws of the natural world but which are somehow similar to or parallel with the empirical evidence of the world and thereby attain to a "science" of poetry, of art. Poe's long search for the laws in his criticism was a sign of this necessity. The tree as a scientific fact conforms to scientific law; the tree which seems a speck is a mental construction which is not "like" the empirical evidence for the tree as a reduced object but is an imaginative maneuver which has arranged the ever-varying process of reality into a comprehensible, even a "true" metaphor. The symbolic speck which the artist reports as a tree is just as "real" a tree as the tree which the botanist analyzes and describes. Both the artist and the botanist have followed the laws of their own method of inquiry; yet they in no way reach the same end.

This paradoxical resolution of the double dimension of reality — that which is true both to exterior knowledge and to subjective perception as well — led to another problem which Poe faced with a certain amount of acuity. This was what might be called the art object in its "time context": can a poem or any work of art have existence and duration beyond or apart from the time in which it is made? Or does the art object have existence, like a headless statue uncovered from the dust of centuries, only as an antiquarian detail in the history of man? Romantic artists and critics were among the first in the history of art to discover that works of art have a time-duration both coterminous with the period in which they were made and also projected into a future whose dimensions the work of art itself might define: the carved head of Apollo formed two major expressions of art long after a being known as Apollo had ceased to exist.

The scientific inquiry in *Eureka* was a study of the laws of diffusion from the unified center; by implication, science became a study in dispersion, in dis-unity, in things as they are according to the determinable laws of empirical knowledge. The artistic and imaginative inquiry into the universe differs not only in its positing of the truth of subjective knowledge but in its awareness of what might be termed "the universe as time backward": art is man's only means, beyond his own private memory, of knowing the world in all its temporal complexity—what was, what is, and what is to be. Art is the way, forward or backward, to unity in a process parallel to that of God's when He removes His force and all things drive back toward "concentrality." The imaginative power is able to extract from the confusing illusion of reality "little by little . . . their chaff of inconsistency—until at length there stands apparent an unencumbered *Consistency*." [28]

Yet, really to be complete, the imaginative activity needed both its own expression and its attendant explanation—a "science," in short. Thus painting and poetry always required criticism: the poem was the way through things to essence or ultimate reality analogous to the creative activity of God; criticism was the necessary analysis, even science, of the method of that imaginative journey: "The Raven" was not complete until Poe had written the explanatory "Philosophy of Composition." The essay did not, could not, recapitulate the imaginative journey from sanity to madness, from this dimensioned world of sense to the dark beyond of mystery which the poem had exposed; but the essay could set up the procedure in this present temporal world of dispersion as a starting-point for the imaginative thrust toward a region beyond. If an artist were able to follow Poe's prescriptions in "The Philosophy of Composition," he would not write another "Raven"; he would, however, seek within himself and within the temporal fluidity that art and the imagination define and compose some other journey toward further understanding beyond this region of diffusion and "inconsistency."

At this point in the argument the poet, or Poe, was back with his central question: How does the artist in the act of making art simulate God? We have so far seen that the imaginative activity of the artist is like the creative energies of God and that the work of art is itself a paradigm of metaphysical reality; we have also seen that the artist is not so much against the scientist, or the scientist against the artist for that matter, as that the artist is a "maker" in the fullest sense in that his art is a continual drive toward "simplicity," "consistency," and the primal order of things in the total universe or the mind of God. Poe was fond of quoting an aphorism of Baron Bielfeld: "To understand God one must be God Himself." Several implications of this theory of the artist as god-player are crucial to Poe and to the history of nineteenth-century Romanticism.

5

The artist may be, like God, a timeless mind or a being who can transcend time. Yet he is of a time and he addresses himself to that time. He is a citizen of the fourteenth, the seventeenth, or the nineteenth century; if his art can escape and exist beyond time — time backward and time forward in the symbolic ordering of the total universe — he cannot. As Poe himself wrote:

> Now, it is clear, not only that what is obvious to one mind may not be obvious to another, but that what is obvious to one mind at one epoch, may be anything but obvious, at another epoch. . . . It is clear, moreover, that what, to-day, is obvious even to the majority of mankind, or to the majority of the best intellects of mankind, may to-morrow be, to either majority, more or less obvious, or in no respect obvious at all. It is seen, then, that the *axiomatic principle* itself is susceptible of variation, and of course that axioms are susceptible of similar change.[29]

Romantic artists felt this burden of duality of time — this living both in and out of time — in several significant ways. *Eureka* is a document typical of this thought, in that it reaches far into metaphysical and abstract time by means of employing the tools and scientific insights of its own special, limited time-world. But the time-world is not the empirical range of experience to which one man is confined: in Romantic theory, the artist, as an autonomous being, was endowed with the principle and the authority to encompass the whole scope of time and experience. He had several things to aid him: one was a psychology, which, as we have seen, made the artist the microcosmic responder; another was a concept of history which granted him the privilege to reach backward through history not as a fact but as an abstraction; still another was the paradoxical view that the artist is and is not like ordinary men. In the end the only autonomous rationale and source for art was in the artist himself: the artist was a god-player who "imitated" his own mind, who found all the determinations for his art in his own being and in the historicity of art itself, and who was free to seek whatever imaginative realm of being his unique insights gave him. The world of "selfish solicitude" he left to science or to "fancy," for it was essentially an illusion anyway; the ultimate real world was that of art, or the way man had of paralleling the originating and structural mind of God.

This theory of Romantic art has often been exposed; Poe's *Eureka* is one in a long line of documents from Hegel through Schelling, Coleridge, Carlyle, Emerson, and Baudelaire. But Poe also posed two further problems of the artist as god-player which one does not find in general Romantic theory of art. One was whether or not the artist was like other men; the second was whether art and the artist exist differently in this later time of the world from what they had been in remote times.

In its early stages the Romantic poet considered himself just like other men; perhaps he was endowed with a special faculty of expression, but that faculty set him apart from other men no more than did the ability to lay brick or to make a speech. Gradually, however, the Romantic poets, especially as they found that the world of normal experience had little use for them, considered the gaps between themselves and their fellows. This gap they measured not so much because they were different as human beings as that what they said was different from what other men said; and as they more and more projected their art into the gray and nether world of imagination and disclaimed the world of ostensible reality, they tended to find the distinctions ever more apparent. The truth "to *David* Hume," as Poe frankly expressed the matter, "would very seldom be a truth to *Joe.*"[30] These several kinds of "truth," the one empirical and the other abstract or imaginative, marked the difference; the longer the artist in the nineteenth century pursued his aims and sought further means of expressing his special version of imaginative truth, the further he tended to draw away from his common audience; the inheritors of the Poe tradition to the end of the century virtually granted the right of its audience to reject or ridicule them.[31]

The other problem of the artist was the relation of the work of art not only to its own time-concept or range of expression but to the variable time-views of critics and viewers in its own time and in the time to come. Following the analogy which Poe used in other relations between empirical science and critical theory, we can see the implication of the idea of dispersion of force: just as the world ages and becomes more chaotic, so the older art becomes, the more it must somehow project a vision of the lost unity. In "Al Aaraaf" Poe had an early glimpse of this view of the lost centrality of things; in *Eureka* he tried to expand the whole concept in order to demonstrate that, while empirical science and the rational mind of man drive toward diffusion and the comprehension of itself in particles, the imagination is impelled toward a unitary determination. And the older the time, the wider the separation between the two. In their origin, science and art were one; in the dispersion of man's faculties and his knowledge, the two have become an intellectual and metaphysical universe apart.

This bifurcation of man's original insight into two ways of thought, the one empirical and the other imaginative, while it brought a remarkable sharpening of the factual and discursive, nonetheless caused a virtual atrophy of the imaginative insight, or else, in the passage of time, relegated poetic exercise to a mere plaything. Scientific inquiry becomes easier with advancing times; imaginative and artistic discourse becomes more difficult, if not virtually impossible. The reason is not only that the struggle toward a unitary idea becomes increasingly difficult with the onrush of the dispersive tendency toward multiplicity, but the language problem becomes more onerous. The romantic writer like Poe felt an almost desperate necessity to recapture the lost sense of the oneness of things and to vivify language as a means of re-creation of man's aboriginal insight. In Romantic terms, men once spoke poetry; and, as Emerson stated, the farther we go back in time, the language of prose more closely approached the precise images which only imaginative discourse can render. But the passage of time slowly extracts clear meaning from language until men in a later time, not themselves knowing the meaning of words and discourse, must have the meaning reattached to the language for them.

Men have lost their capacity for image-making; they have similarly lost their ability to understand images: the relationship, once so clear in their minds, between the object and its stimulus, has long been reduced to a monontonously repeated sound. Therefore, in the latter ages of man, the artist or writer must undertake the burden of rediscovering and then making the relevances for his fellowmen. The later the time, the more terrible this burden becomes. With Poe we have almost a formulation of the theory of modern symbolism: namely, the artist must recast and make relevant the long-separated dualism of man's mind; he must bridge between the chaotic, particularized world of empirical data and the instinctive, cognitive awareness that mind and matter cohere in a disclosed design. Poe as a symbolist was among the first to formulate a theory—and *Eureka,* itself an extended symbol, is the central statement—that art is man's one instrument for making some order out of the infinitude of empirical formlessness. He also understood the perilous dichotomy which is the paradox of the symbolist method: symbolism is the way of the mind and the imagination to make coherent an infinite variety of impressions, ideas, and forms which might otherwise remain totally disordered; yet the order which the imagination enforces is only that order alone which is in the picture or the poem; "reality" is as chaotic and fractured as ever; only the word, the metaphor, the tonality, the imposed coherence make a design out of what still is, empirically, shapelessness. Art and science are not one; they are not so much at war as they are worlds apart in their ways of understanding and inquiry; they may both drive toward that "one," but in the present order of created things, they only suggest the gap which has been widening ever since man entered the realm of logical positivism and relegated poetry and myth and even the arts to superstition or to mere entertainment.

What, in the end, Poe was forced to acknowledge was that, in order to remain "pure," art had to disavow any connection with science, with the world as it is, with the forlorn hope that it can in any way direct the lives of men. *Eureka* was one more in the considerable line of Romantic protests against common sense and against art as morality; it affirmed that the work of art is like the creative act of God: a special, a private autonomy, a unique disclosure of idea and fact, word and idea. After the poem or the art-work had been made, the maker was absolved from any further responsibility; it ceased to be his as soon as he had made it; he was not, as was God, granted the power to explain himself. Nor would his readers or viewers be given the right to find him in it. Criticism and philosophy met at this point at which the "personality" of the thinker and maker was of no consequence, for the work of art had a life of its own long after it had left its maker's hands. By investigating the abstract laws of nature one might find the teleological being called God; by studying the poem one might find, not the poet, but "the rationale of verse" or the method which poetry, or art, allows in seeking the meaning of time and man, history and art (for art rests on its precedence), man and the total abstract design of the universe. The "meaning" could never be finally stated; the "way" was always through the imperfect range of discourse, metaphor, analogy, symbol. But if the artist could somehow establish a provisional set of relevances and then, as it were, grant his symbolic order the right to have a life of its own, as Poe did in "The Raven" and in "The Fall of the House of Usher," to name only two of a dozen, then art opened a further range of expression and understanding beyond the limits which empirical data insisted were all that existed. Poe therefore wrote *Eureka,* supposedly a scientific treatise, in order to demonstrate that knowledge was not science but intuition, that the artist must free himself from the moral and from the empirical, and that the artist must admit to himself that he can pursue his "forlorn demon" alone or only in terms of the history of his art.

IX

A Final Word

Despite the excellence of analytical and investigative research which has been directed into the life and works of Edgar Poe, the reputation of Poe, except at the popular level of adolescent reading confined to secondary education, is today quite low. His poetry is regarded as not very complex nor artful rimes by a poet who took the subject of poetry more seriously than his poetry demands. His short stories have their admirers, but the number of tales which still seem great are, at most, a mere half dozen; and his criticism, however much excitement it has always aroused in France, is considered to be based on a totally false methodology in terms of contemporary critical theory: Poe made the egregious mistake either of taking critical concepts into the "psychology" of the writer himself or of considering that a work of art is not only an autonomous but a unique creation which, as it were, is like the universe: it must be discovered as though nothing like it had ever appeared before.

Apologists for Poe try to make a case for Poe's "influence":

he is the "founder" of modern symbolic writing; without Poe, there could have been no Baudelaire, Verlaine, Rimbaud, Gide, or even Eliot and Pound. Others regard him as the proper spokesman for the modern theory of the essential autonomy of art: art is not politics, sociology, history, morality; it is only art, a pure domain of its own. This judgment has varying effects on the reputation of Poe; sometimes he is placed unfavorably in the art-for-art's-sake school; at other times such a placement inflates his reputation, as it might in our own time — except that Poe really did not take the question of art far enough into the "pure serene" of imaginative exploration. Somehow, it is said, he left art still tainted either with a false methodology, as Yvor Winters has charged, or with an insufficient maturity, as T. S. Eliot has suggested.

There is still another attitude which puts Poe somewhere below the first rank of writers. In our time we have become profoundly aware of what might generally be called the "American experience"; that is to say, as Constance Rourke long ago pointed out, not all of our culture and art were brought to America by the transit of civilization from Europe to the New World; a good deal of what we call our American culture was, frankly speaking, created here out of the merest hints of English or European ideas. This conception of the American experience is not local or contemporary chauvinism; it is quite old; it can be traced from F. J. Turner's "frontier thesis" at the end of the nineteenth century; it was given an extraordinary literary and cultural demonstration in F. O. Matthiessen's *American Renaissance,* which significantly changed the course of American studies and the American critical sensibility; and it is being given innumerable explorations by a host of young American critics and scholars in the mid-twentieth century.

Edgar Poe seems far removed from this principle that the great American writers of the nineteenth century — Emerson, Thoreau, Whitman, Hawthorne, Melville, Twain, James, to name only a few — had their artistic and intellectual birth and being in the fullest American experience. Poe does not conform to any general or basic American design or character; he represents the danger of the literary spokesman who was all his life convinced that nothing existed in the native world about him but that only by the most arduous transplantation of the European culture can the New World effect any artistic competence and distinction. Thus Poe represents the hypertrophy of an imagination which had only its imported culture to feed upon. This charge does not mean that, like Whittier or Garrison, he should have been inflamed to champion causes of his day — posterity always takes its vengeance on an artist who lowers his art to merely contemporary issues — but that he should have missed so many of the vivid explorations which, perhaps all unaware, Emerson, Thoreau, Melville, and Hawthorne were following: the questions of man in the new mass world of democratic society, of the new "American Adam" whether in the wilderness or in the driving urgency of success, of the lonely self struggling to understand himself, his world, his God — these and many others Poe merely touched and passed by or even ignored.

The question of Poe will never be settled; no question pertaining even to an artist ever is. But one might make one generalization about the mind and art of Poe to account for the intensity of his expression and its narrowness. Poe belonged to the Romantic age; he could be considered almost an archetype of the Romantic mind; yet Poe himself never had a "Romantic revolution." That is, he never in his own mind and experience passed through those stages of self-awareness and development which have always made the "Romantic mind" so fascinating to watch and its artistic products so wide-ranging in their imaginative scope. Poe never changed; he never grew; he remained to the end of his life an exponent of the hypostatized self-as-subject with which Romantic artists necessarily begin. Poe's last and most mature work *Eureka* was simply another version of that plot of the percipient "I": if the universe existed as a unitary design, then the self exists as a total organic being too. Philosophy and science proved what had earlier been the thesis of "Tamerlane" and "Al Aaraaf."

Yet Poe was a "Romantic," and some of his major insights are a portion of the age in which he lived — or the property of the artistic, exploratory mind of any age. One certain premise in which Poe's mind and art were centered was that art, whether poetry or prose, was not a "form" of expression or a means of reducing the variables of idea and existence to order but that art was "another life." In the mind of Poe this precept had enormous consequences. If art *is* reality — more "real" than sensible reality itself — then art is a world of thought and design in the very act of being made; it is a construct and similitude of God which proceeds through the universal paradigm of chaos to order. A poem is a microcosmic universal creation, and the poet has made "a plot of God." But this creative action must always have its exegesis: the poem must have a prose analysis, a philosophic spectrum and insight. Somehow art, existing in its pure domain of the creative imagination, needs the act of inquiry coming from, as it were, the other side of misconception and confusion. The poem, short story, or any other work of art is a virtual negation of existence as man lives it; but it must have the lower dimension, the commentary, even a "philosophy" to link it somehow with the variable minds of men.

By means of this double system of value, Poe imposed on the creative imagination and on art itself a burden greater than they ought to bear. Need the life of the imagination be such a terrifying confrontation of the single mind with the universe of speculation and Idea? Might not art and the imagination be permitted to take a "holiday" and justifiably assume that much of the life of art is unconscious and most of its activity a mystery? In the age of Poe, however, the principle was strong that art is somehow divine. Therefore, in order to fulfill its divinity, the artistic quest must break down and transform the massive obstructions to understanding and perception. No wonder the poetic imagination of Poe was suicidal: its every act entailed a removal from the world of experience as well as a total transformation of experience. It held a mirror, a lamp, and a pulverizer to nature.

Art and the life of the imagination were not, therefore, mere substitutes for living; they *were* living. One did not escape from or deny sensory existence; one merely had, as it were, "another existence." Out of this principle which directed so much of the Romantic inquiry, there came another: the Romantic's discovery of the terror implicit in continually posing the self as subject. Wordsworth's *Prelude,* Keats's "Ode to a Nightingale," Poe's "Raven" — these were realizations not only of self-scrutiny but also of the artistic self-consciousness. What gave the poet his subject could also destroy him. It is one of the ironies of literary history that what was a new discovery — the concept of the artist's selfhood or his autonomy — should have been an instrument of stifling the very art it might have produced. The artist looked "within" and wrote; but what he too often found there was only the detritus of his own imagination which could not forever poetize itself. Unless he found a subject other than the self or a further extension of private being, then the artist was reduced to intricate meditation: witness Melville, the supreme victim of the soliloquy which kept going farther and farther into the recesses of its own being. Every Romantic artist — from Berlioz, who put intellectual Faust in insensible matter, to Goethe, who made Faust a symbol of moral man — had to come to terms with the Romantic dilemma of self-awareness and its attendant, self-annihilation.

The aspect of Romantic dualism was a subject of profound importance to the whole of the nineteenth century, so long as the duality was that between mind and nature, self and external reality, or being and nothingness. Coleridge has become in our time virtually an exponent of this dichotomy, for he faced it in all of its ramifications. Yet the dualism of Poe was not of that order, however beguiling that split may appear in "The Fall of the House of Usher" or in *Eureka*. The central bifurcation in Poe was between two sides of the self, between emotion and intellect, feeling and the mind. Much of what Poe wrote stemmed from a feeling self, a Romantic consciousness deeply moved to make some adjustment between itself and insensate reality; but Poe was literally ashamed to let that self-awareness go too far; he was continually putting a brake on imaginative exuberance; he was constantly making poetry the stimulus for a prose analysis and then setting prose as a means of explicating the poem. In the end it was prose against poetry, thought against emotion. Feeling was intense, bewildering, terrifying; thought or mind was rational, comprehensive, and fascinating to watch in its processes. The split was, finally, disastrous, for the wider it became, the less the imagination had to do except to do over what it had already done.

Poe's greatness lies in his few explorations into the dark underside of human consciousness, and subconsciousness—that variable world of thought, dream, and terror beyond life and knowledge. Poe best limned this world in incompleteness, in the gray dimension of our never knowing why the student in "The Raven" or Roderick Usher were driven mad or why the Man of the Crowd was obsessed to wander the streets of a modern city. Poe's art was the spectrum of symbolic irresolution; but then who could be final and complete in dealing with the mind's dark terror world of which it is itself unaware? His weakness was that he seldom thrust this drama of the haunted mind into the commonplace world where, as in Hawthorne's "Young Goodman Brown" or "Wakefield," the greatest terror exists. Poe's greatness lay in his projection of that horror in wholly new terms; he charted the way for farther, deeper ranges of symbolic extension. That "way" and the range of artistic perception will always be farther than any interpretive speculation can reach: with writers like Melville and Poe, there is no end to what the symbolic imagination can disclose.

NOTES
INDEX

Notes

I have not employed a footnote every time I have quoted from or cited the writings of Poe. The texts are sufficiently identified and available to allow anyone to find the lines or passages for himself. When I have referred a quotation to one of the editions of Poe, I have done so because I am making use of one particular text which, because Poe was an inveterate reviser of his own pieces, has been employed for a specific purpose. That is, the 1827, 1829, or 1831 version of a poem may be vastly different from the final text which Poe established in the 1845 volume. Unless there is some statement to the contrary, the text of Poe's poems is that of his own marked copy of *The Raven and Other Poems* (New York, 1845), the last revision of his verse which he left before his death. This corrected version, known as the Lorimer Graham copy, has been reproduced by The Facsimile Text Society and edited by Thomas Ollive Mabbott (Columbia University Press, 1942). The text of the short stories and critical works, unless otherwise noted, is that of *The Complete Works of Edgar Allan Poe,* edited by James A. Harrison (17 vols.; New York, 1902), which is hereafter cited as *Works.*

I. The Necessary Demon

1. Preface to the 1845 poems; *Works,* VII, xlvii.

2. This oft-repeated idea that Poe "did not *know* enough" was first offered by Sidney Lanier; see *The Poems of Sidney Lanier* (New York, 1884), pp. xxxv–xxxvi; J. M. Robertson, *New Essays Towards a Critical Method* (London, 1897), p. 106; Killis Campbell, *The Mind of Poe and Other Studies* (Harvard University Press, 1933), pp. 3f. The idea has been revived more recently by T. S. Eliot,

"From Poe to Valéry," *Hudson Rev.*, II (Autumn 1949), 327–342.

3. See *Baudelaire on Poe,* trans. and ed. by Lois and Francis E. Hyslop (State College, Pennsylvania, 1952), pp. 38f. The question of Poe and Baudelaire has always been of considerable interest. The major inquiries are Paul Valéry, *Variété* (Paris, 1937), II, 145–165; L. Seylaz, *Edgar Poe et les premiers symbolistes français* (Lausanne, 1923); L. Lemonnier, *Edgar Poe et les poètes français* (Paris, 1932), and *Edgar Poe et la critique français de 1845 à 1875* (Paris, 1928); Regis Michaud, "Baudelaire et Poe: une mise au point," *Revue de littérature comparée,* XVIII (1938), 665–683; Marcel Françon, "Poe et Baudelaire," *PMLA,* LX (September 1945), 841–859. A recent glimpse of how little Baudelaire knew Poe's writings is provided by W. T. Bandy, "New Light on Baudelaire and Poe," *Yale French Studies,* no. 10 (1953), 65–69.

4. Professor Floyd Stovall has made the interesting suggestion that the quality of discordance in Poe's early poetry was in Poe's "struggle for emotional tranquillity. He was a man of passionate temperament, but in his art as well as in his personal conduct he attempted to impose on the liberty of impulse the restraint of law" ("Poe as a Poet of Ideas," *Texas Univ. Studies in English,* XI [September 1931], 57–58). On the whole question of self-revelation in Poe's poems and tales, see Campbell, *Mind of Poe,* pp. 126ff. D. H. Lawrence's telling remark was that Poe was "absolutely concerned with the disintegration processes of his own psyche" (*Studies in Classic American Literature* [New York, 1923], p. 93).

5. See *The Complete Poems of Edgar Allan Poe,* ed. J. H. Whitty (Boston and New York, 1911), pp. 161–165. The best discussion and first authentic printing of this poem was by Jay B. Hubbell, "'O, Tempora! O, Mores!' A Juvenile Poem by Edgar Allan Poe," *Univ. of Colorado Studies,* Ser. B, II (October 1945), 314–321. Killis Campbell did not think the poem Poe's; T. O. Mabbott and Hubbell do; their evidence seems to be conclusive.

6. Poe's unfortunate love affair with Sarah Elmira Royster attracted considerable attention and stimulated some minor literary effusions within a short time after the event. It inspired Henry Poe's "The Pirate," published in the Baltimore *North American* for 1827, and Lambert A. Wilmer's "Merlin," a verse play, which was published in the *North American* on August 12, 25, and September 1, 1827, and separately on September 22. See Lambert A. Wilmer,

Merlin; Baltimore, 1827; Together with Recollections of Edgar A. Poe, ed. T. O. Mabbott (New York: Scholars' Facsimiles and Reprints, 1941). See also A. H. Quinn, *Edgar Allan Poe: A Critical Biography* (New York and London, 1941), pp. 90–93.

7. From his flamboyant and tasteless attack on Wordsworth and the "Lakers" in his "Letter to B——" prefatory to the 1831 volume of poems, we know that Poe was well aware of Wordsworth's poetry and critical ideas. At what point in his career Poe read Wordsworth we do not know; certainly he knew the *Lyrical Ballads* (1798 and 1800) and the *Poems in Two Volumes* (1807) as well as the various prefaces through 1815.

8. "Tamerlane," though it underwent a number of revisions in the 1829 and 1831 editions, was reprinted in 1845 almost identical with its first version; the 1845 text is the one which is analyzed in this study and will form the texts of all subsequent poems, unless there is a note to indicate that another version is being used.

9. This important question of the philosophical and epistemological formulations of Poe's poetry and critical theory are discussed in Chapter II.

10. *Tamerlane and Other Poems,* ed. T. O. Mabbott (New York: Facsimile Text Society, 1941), p. 29. *Works,* vii, 150.

11. *Tamerlane,* p. 30. *Works,* VII, 151. I have intentionally read "sigh" instead of "sight" in line 8.

12. Allen Tate, "The Angelic Imagination: Poe and the Power of Words," *Kenyon Rev.,* XIV (Summer 1952), 455–475.

13. *Al Aaraaf, Tamerlane, and Minor Poems,* ed. T. O. Mabbott (New York: Facsimile Text Society, 1933), p. 11.

14. The major investigations of "Al Aaraaf" are by W. B. Cairns, "Some Notes on Poe's 'Al Aaraaf,'" *MP,* XIII (May 1915), 35–44; Floyd Stovall, "An Interpretation of Poe's 'Al Aaraaf,'" *Texas University Studies in English,* IX (July 1929), 106–133; Quinn, *Poe,* pp. 156–161.

15. Prefatory to the poem in its first printing was the following headnote which Poe afterward revised and placed among the explanatory notes: "A star was discovered by Tycho Brahe which burst forth, in a moment, with a splendor surpassing that of Jupiter—then gradually faded away and became invisible to the naked eye" (*Al Aaraaf,* p. 9; see *Works,* VII, 158). Because the poem underwent major revisions in its subsequent reprintings and because we are

here considering Poe's poetic mind in its early years, all quotations from "Al Aaraaf" are, unless otherwise noted, to the 1829 version of the poem.

Poe may well have known any one of a number of references to Tycho's comet; that of Laplace will indicate the nature of these descriptions: "Such was the star observed by Tycho Brahe in the year 1572, in the constellation Cassiopeia. In a short time it surpassed the most brilliant stars, and even Jupiter himself. Its light then waned away, and finally disappeared sixteen months after its discovery. Its colour underwent several changes; it was at first of a brilliant white, then of a reddish yellow, and finally of a lead coloured white like to Saturn" (*The System of the World,* trans. and ed. H. H. Harte [London, 1830], II, 334).

16. Poe's botanical references are not entirely poetic or evocative for prettiness of name only; they are physical exemplifications of his theme that the Idea and especially the Idea of Beauty manifest themselves in shape and form. Behind this view are not only Plato and successive philosophers but the whole "concept of life" as recently set forth by Dr. John Hunter, his student and propagandist, Dr. John Abernethy, and the numerous articles in *Philosophical Transactions.* Very cogent to this point, and perhaps the summary and source of Poe's idea, is a long footnote in Coleridge's *Friend,* of which the significant parts are as follows: "The Hunterian idea of a life or vital principle independent of the organization, yet in each organ working instinctively towards its preservation . . . demonstrates that John Hunter did not . . . individualize, or make an *hypostasis* of the principles of life, as a something manifestable *per se,* and consequently itself a *phaenomenon;* . . . but that herein he philosophized in the spirit of the purest Newtonians, who in like manner refused to hypostasize the law of gravitation into an ether, which even if its existence were conceded, would need another gravitation for itself. The Hunterian position is a genuine philosophic idea. . . . Is not the progressive enlargement, the boldness without temerity, of chirurgical views and chirurgical practice since Hunter's time to the present day, attributable, in almost every instance, to his substitution of what may perhaps be called experimental dynamics, for the mechanical notions, or the less injurious traditional empiricism, of his predecessors?" *The Complete Works of S. T. Coleridge,* ed. W. G. T.

Shedd (New York, 1884), II, 446n–447n. Poe was to return to the "concept of life" theory in *Eureka;* see Chapter VIII.

17. These lines are quoted from the last or 1845 version; *Works,* VII, 29. Interestingly, their rather heavy theological implication is underlined in one of the earliest versions which appeared in John Neal's *Yankee* for December 1829; there (p. 262) the significant lines read:

> Silence is the voice of God —
> Ours is a world of words; quiet we call
> "Silence" — which is the merest word of all.

Perhaps owing to his knowledge of the biblical prophetic books Poe made use of a more definite identification of the source of the "word" ("In the beginning was the word") than he would afterward employ in the final version of the poem. God spoke the Word and things came into existence; man has a word "silence" which is mere air and has no form.

18. Poe's very considerable indebtedness to Milton, not only in "Al Aaraaf" but elsewhere, has been ably summarized by Thomas P. Haviland, "How Well Did Poe Know Milton?" *PMLA,* LXIX (September 1954), 841–860.

19. There is a source for this episode of Ianthe and Angelo, long ago pointed out by Killis Campbell, *The Poems of Edgar Allan Poe* (New York, 1917), pp. xlvi–xlvii. It is in Thomas Moore's "First Angel's Story" in *The Loves of the Angels* (1823). On the surface, Moore is retelling once again the legend of the god who saw the earth-woman (in this case her name is Lea) and fell passionately in love with her. (Poe simply has reversed the sexes of the lovers and made the goddess fall in love with the earth-man.) What Moore fully grasped, however, as the Preface to his poem demonstrates, is that such a myth as the one he is retelling is but one among the many by which man has attempted to account for (1) "the fall of the Soul from its original purity"; (2) the descent of the soul through long ages into this material world; (3) "the loss of light and happiness which it suffers, in the pursuit of this world's perishable pleasures," coupled with its attempt to return to the regions it once inhabitated (Thomas Moore, *Poetical Works,* ed. A. D. Godley [Oxford University Press, 1929], p. 537). Moore's narrative in the "First Angel's

Story" is, except for the reversal of the sexes, a parallel to Poe's; only the end of Moore's legend is different: there the god, though earth-bound, is able to will the earth-woman's ascent upward into immortality while he remains contentedly below in a brute human form. Both poems are, in their several ways, trying to say the same thing: that Idea, god's or man's, manifests itself in physical form but that man's vision is clouded by man's own willingness to remain insentient. For still other influences of Moore on Poe see Hoover H. Jordan, "Poe's Debt to Thomas Moore," *PMLA,* LXIII (June 1948), 753–757.

20. *Works,* VII, xliii.

21. For the very interesting lines of the 1831 version, afterward discarded, see *Poems* (New York: Facsimile Reprint, 1936), pp. 34–35; *Works,* VII, 164.

22. "Dejection: An Ode," *The Complete Poetical Works of Samuel Taylor Coleridge,* ed. E. H. Coleridge (Oxford, 1912), I, 365.

23. One or two commentators have seen in some lines Poe added to the 1831 version and deleted from the 1845 volume the earliest admission of Poe's drinking:

> For, being an idle boy lang syne,
> Who read Anacreon, and drank wine,
> I early found Anacreon rhymes
> Were almost passionate sometimes . . .
> And so, being young and dipt in folly
> I fell in love with melancholy . . .

(*Poems,* Facsimile Reprint, p. 54; *Works,* VII, 164.)

The reference is quite probably not to alcholism but to an "Anacreon" in the only form in which Poe would have known the Greek lyrist's verses — the translations of Anacreon's odes by Thomas Moore, whom, as everyone knows, Byron dubbed "Anacreon Moore." Anacreon, by way of Moore's translations, was far more poetically stimulating to Poe, as of 1831, than the whisky bottle. The young men of the 1820's chanted the lyrics of Moore's translations much as a generation a century later might have recited A. E. Housman or Dylan Thomas. Anacreon's Forty-Fifth Ode, in Moore's version, might well stand for what Poe "early found" in "Anacreon rhymes":

> Within this goblet, rich and deep,
> I cradle all my woes to sleep.

Why should we breathe the sigh of fear,
Or pour the unavailing tear?
For death will never heed the sigh,
Nor soften at the tearful eye;
And eyes that sparkle, eyes that weep,
Must all alike be seal'd in sleep.
Then let us never vainly stray,
In search of thorns, from pleasure's way;
But wisely quaff the rosy wave,
Which Bacchus loves, which Bacchus gave;
And in the goblet, rich and deep,
Cradle our crying woes to sleep.

(*Poetical Works,* p. 24.)

24. This is the fourth stanza of the 1829 version; see *Al Aaraaf,* Facsimile Reprint, p. 69; *Works,* VII, 168.

25. Mrs. Sarah Helen Whitman was the first to discuss Mrs. Stanard as the "image" of Helen in the poem, a point which has caused much discussion in the years that have passed; see *Edgar Poe and His Critics* (New York, 1860), pp. 42–43. For an account of Poe's memories of Mrs. Stanard, see Quinn, *Poe,* pp. 85–87.

26. Most of this discussion of the women who may have been prototypes for Helen is summarized by Paull F. Baum, "Poe's 'To Helen,'" *MLN,* LXIV (May 1949), 289–297. See also T. O. Mabbott, "Poe's 'To Helen,'" *Explicator,* I (June 1943), 60.

27. The genesis of the poem probably lies in "Al Aaraaf," Part II, lines 36–39:

Friezes from Tadmor and Persepolis —
From Balbec, and the stilly, clear abyss
Of beautiful Gomorrah! O, the wave
Is now upon thee — but too late to save!

In a canceled footnote to the 1829 version, Poe suggested: "It is said (Tacitus, Strabo, Josephus, Daniel of St. Saba, Nau, Maundrell, Troilo, D'Arvieux) that, after an excessive drought, the vestiges of columns, walls, &c. are seen above the surface. At *any* season, such remains may be discovered by looking down into the transparent lake, and at such distances as would argue the existence of many settlements in the space now usurped by the 'Asphaltites'" (*Al Aaraaf,* Facsimile Reprint, p. 27; *Works,* VII, 31n).

28. *Poems,* Facsimile Reprint, p. 51; *Works,* VII, 177.

29. *Poems,* Facsimile Reprint, p. 63; *Works,* VII, 179.

30. This split in Poe's career has so far been noted only by Alterton and Craig: ". . . we may say that in 1831 [Poe's] youthful opinion defined poetry almost entirely from the standpoint of imagination. . . . In 1836, in providing for both imagination and reason in poetry . . . he paid particular attention to reason" (*Representative Selections,* p. lix).

31. In a footnote to the sketch of N. P. Willis in "The Literati," first published in *Godey's Lady's Book,* May 1846, there is one of Poe's longest and most illuminating derivations from Coleridge concerning the distinction between the "fancy" and the "imagination": "The range of imagination is thus unlimited. Its materials extend throughout the universe. Even out of deformities it fabricates that *beauty* which is at once its sole object and its inevitable test" (XV, 14n). For further inquiries respecting Coleridge and Poe, see Floyd Stovall, "Poe's Debt to Coleridge," *Texas Univ. Studies in English,* X (July 1930), 70–127, and Harry T. Baker, "Coleridge's Influence on Poe's Poetry," *MLN,* XXV (March 1910), 94–95.

II. Aspects of a Philosophy of Poetry

1. Studies of Poe, like those of J. W. Krutch, *Edgar Allan Poe: A Study in Genius* (New York, 1926), and Marie Bonaparte, *The Life and Works of Edgar Allan Poe: A Psycho-Analytic Interpretation* (London, 1950), however stimulating they may be, rest a complete interpretation of Poe's writings on a single aberration of the man himself: find the aberration or the psychic dislocation and the total design of the writings becomes clear. Mme. Bonaparte represents an extreme of this mode of interpretation: Poe's imagination operated most characteristically in terms of his latent sado-necrophilism; thus the phthisic shade of the mother who died when he was an infant holds the key to the neurosis and to the art of the writer.

2. Profesor T. O. Mabbott has made some interesting conjectures on the vision of Poe's foster mother, Mrs. Allan, as she became embodied in the vision of Helen; see "Poe's 'To Helen,'" *Explicator,* I (June 1943), 60.

3. The "histrio" aspect of Poe has been the subject of N. Bryllion Fagin's absorbing study, *The Histrionic Mr. Poe* (Baltimore, 1949).

4. See A. N. Whitehead, *Science and the Modern World* (New York, 1926), chap. v: "The Romantic Reaction."

5. Treatments of this philosophical and artistic question are numerous. A summary mention might be made of these important discussions of the question: F. W. J. Schelling, *Concerning the Relation of the Plastic Arts to Nature,* 1807 (a convenient reprinting is in Herbert Read, *The True Voice of Feeling,* New York, 1953, pp. 323–364); Coleridge, *Biographia Literaria,* especially chaps. xiii and xiv. See also Ernst Cassirer, *The Philosophy of Symbolic Forms,* vol. I (Yale Univ. Press, 1953); Susanne K. Langer, *Philosophy in a New Key* (Harvard University Press, 1942), and *Feeling and Form* (New York, 1953); Martin Foss, *Symbol and Metaphor* (Princeton, 1949); Charles Feidelson, Jr., *Symbolism and American Literature* (Chicago, 1952); Philip Wheelwright, *The Burning Fountain: A Study in the Language of Symbolism* (Indiana Univ. Press, 1954), pp. 8–100; S. C. Pepper, *World Hypotheses* (Berkeley and Los Angeles, 1948), chaps. viii and ix; F. O. Matthiessen, *American Renaissance: Art and Expression in the Age of Emerson and Whitman* (New York, 1941), especially "The Metaphysical Strain" and "The Organic Principle," pp. 100–140.

6. *Character & Opinion in the United States* (New York, 1920), p. 22.

7. Important to an understanding of this problem in the mind and art of Poe are Margaret Alterton, *Origin of Poe's Critical Theory* (Iowa City, 1925), pp. 155–156, *et seq.; Representative Selections,* pp. xiii–xvi; and Marvin Laser, "The Growth and Structure of Poe's Concept of Beauty," *ELH,* XV (March 1948), 69–84.

8. *Symbolism and American Literature,* pp. 162–212.

9. *Critique of Pure Reason,* trans. by N. K. Smith (London, 1933), pp. 257–275, *et seq.*

10. *Critique of Judgment,* trans. by J. H. Bernard (London, 1931), pp. 45–100.

11. Coleridge wrote: ". . . grant me a nature having two contrary forces, the one of which tends to expand infinitely, while the other strives to apprehend or *find* itself in this infinity, and I will cause the world of intelligences with the whole system of their representations to rise up before you"; *Biographia Literaria,* ed. J. Shawcross (Ox-

ford, 1907), I, 196. See also M. H. Abrams, *The Mirror and the Lamp* (New York, 1953), pp. 167–177.

12. Coleridge coined the word "esemplastic," to mean "to shape into one," "because having to convey a new sense, I thought that a new term would both aid the recollection of my meaning, and prevent its being confounded with the usual inport of the word, imagination." Coleridge's fullest statement (and one very close to Poe's conception) of how the imagination works "to shape into one" was the following:

"The poet, described in *ideal* perfection, brings the whole soul of man into activity, with the subordination of its faculties to each other, according to their relative worth and dignity. He diffuses a tone and spirit of unity, that blends and (as it were) *fuses* each into each, by that synthetic and magical power, to which we have exclusively appropriated the name of imagination. This power, first put in action by the will and understanding, and retained under their irremissive, though gentle and unnoticed, controul . . . reveals itself in the balance or reconciliation of opposite or discordant qualities: of sameness, with difference; of the general, with the concrete; the idea, with the image; the individual, with the representative; the sense of novelty and freshness, with old and familiar objects; a more than usual state of emotion, with more than usual order; judgment ever awake and steady self-possession, with enthusiasm and feeling profound or vehement; and while it blends and harmonizes the natural and the artificial, still subordinates art to nature; the manner to the matter; and our admiration of the poet to our sympathy with the poetry" (*Biographia Literaria,* II, 12).

In so treating the imagination, we are necessarily concerned more with poetry than with prose. The imagination is not absolutely confined to poetry: Romantic theorists of literature thought it was, for they tended to assign poetry to the unifying and prose to the dispersive functions of the mind. Therefore, they judged poetry — Poe certainly did — against an indefinable and absolute standard which was the *quality* of the poet's imagination; and once having assumed that this special, expressive imagination was in *a* poet, then they easily veered away from criticism and into psychology as a means of finding what the poetry was and how it had been written by the special person, the poet; Romantic impressionistic criticism was born in this transfer.

13. *Biographia Literaria,* I, 202.

14. D. G. James, *Skepticism and Poetry: An Essay on the Poetic Imagination* (London, 1937), pp. 17–18.

15. *Works,* XIV, 198.

16. Poe's first major presentation of these Coleridgean ideas was in his review of J. R. Drake's *The Culprit Fay* and of Fitz Greene Halleck's *Alnwick Castle,* in the *Southern Literary Messenger* for April 1836; see *Works,* VIII, 281–284; see also XII, 36–37. Poe continued to elaborate and extend these ideas of the tripartite, yet unified, qualities of the mind until his most complete statement in "The Philosophy of Composition."

17. See *Works,* X, 61–62, 65; XIV, 187, 189–190; XV, 13n–15n.

18. Washington Allston, whose critical theories closely paralleled Poe's, similarly divided imaginative originality, first, "by the combination of forms already known," and, secondly, "by the union and modification of known but fragmentary parts into a new and consistent whole." Originality is the degree of sovereignty the artist maintains over either "the purely physical" or "the moral and intellectual." Allston was concerned with the history and criticism of art, chiefly among artists themselves; Poe was concerned with how art came to be. See Washington Allston, *Lectures on Art,* ed. R. H. Dana, Jr. (New York, 1850), pp. 75–110 *passim.*

19. Baron Bielfeld, *The Elements of Universal Erudition,* trans. W. Hooper (Dublin, 1771), I, 222–225, 236.

20. *Works,* X, 65.

21. *Ibid.,* p. 66.

22. *Lectures on Art,* p. 86.

23. Allston, himself reared in the same aesthetic tradition as was Poe, denoted artistic or imaginative truth as of two kinds: "first, that the Idea of the Whole contains in itself a pre-existing law; and secondly, that Art, the peculiar product of the Imagination, is one of its true and predetermined ends." Simply stated, the theory is very old, that of the microcosm and the macrocosm: the particle is a replica of the universe and the universe is itself sign and cipher of the particle. Whether one contemplates a planet or a grain of sand, he is instinctively impelled to move toward an awareness of something beyond that object: it is the whole or the All in which that object exists, not as separate, but as functional in a total design. The single object has the potential to call up a timeless, an absolute

relationship with every other object and existence. This relationship is "absolute" in that it obtains only as a universal fact beyond human knowledge, beyond even good and evil. The human mind, by acts of its imaginative exploration and synthesis, is aware of this unity—a "law of Harmony," "that mysterious power, which is only apprehended by its imperative effect."

24. *Skepticism and Poetry,* pp. 8–9.

25. *Works,* XIV, 195.

26. *Biographia Literaria,* II, 6.

27. *Science and the Modern World,* pp. 74ff.

28. See W. M. Urban, *Language and Reality: The Philosophy of Language and the Principles of Symbolism* (London and New York, 1939), pp. 25–27. Urban noted: "This is one possible answer to the question of the relation of language to reality. Language is *not* 'moulded on reality,' to use Bergson's terms. It is either a veil that has been woven by practice between us and reality, and which must be torn away, or else it is a distortion of reality which must be corrected by the invention of other instruments and symbolisms" (p. 51).

29. Wordsworth, in analyzing the imaginative domain of language, employed the metaphor of the stone with telling effect in order to demonstrate that a poet uses language not merely to indicate objects but to compel his readers to create in their imagination the object as he himself imagined it. See Preface to the Edition of 1815; *Poetical Works,* ed. E. de Selincourt (Oxford, 1944), II, 438–439. See also James, *Skepticism and Poetry,* pp. 75–81.

30. Although there are many expressions of this language problem in Jonathan Edwards's ministry and thought, his major statements are in *A Treatise of Religious Affections* (1746) and in *Images or Shadows of Divine Things,* ed. Perry Miller (Yale University Press, 1948), pp. 44, 65, 93, 97, and esp. 119–120, wherein Edwards differentiates between the "liveliness" not only of "things" but of "images" by which man truly knows things.

III. "The Raven" and Afterward

1. A stimulating and controversial analysis of "Ligeia" is Clark Griffith, "Poe's 'Ligeia' and the English Romantics," *Univ. of Toronto Quart.,* XXIV (October 1954), 8–25.

2. *The Letters of Edgar Allan Poe,* ed. by John W. Ostrom (Harvard University Press, 1948), p. 161.

3. *Works,* XIV, 201–202.

4. "Ulalume" has aroused much critical comment, the chief of which are the following: T. O. Mabbott, "Poe's 'Ulalume,'" *Explicator,* I (February 1943), 25, and *ibid.,* VI (June 1948), 57; Lewis Leary, "Poe's 'Ulalume,'" *ibid.,* VI (February 1948), 25; James E. Miller, Jr., "'Ulalume' Resurrected," *PQ,* XXXIV (April 1955), 197–205.

5. Yvor Winters, *Maule's Curse: Seven Studies in the History of American Obscurantism* (Norfolk, Conn., 1938), pp. 93–122.

IV. Death, Eros, and Horror

1. See Robert A. Aubin, "Behind Steele's Satire on Undertakers," *PMLA,* LXIV (December 1949), 1008–1026: "Modern funeral undertaking arose in the last two decades of the seventeenth century from a materialistic conception of man's posthumous condition. The Church of England taught that at death occurs a temporary separation of body and soul: the latter passes to a preliminary and incomplete state of glory in Abraham's bosom while the body rots — and sleeps. On the Day of Judgment the body will undergo a physical resurrection and a transformation, will be reunited with its soul, and will pass to its final place of reward or punishment" (p. 1008).

2. In this connection Poe once made the following comment on the effects of a lack of any aristocracy of taste in America: "It is an evil growing out of our republican institutions, that here a man of large purse has usually a very little soul which he keeps in it. The corruption of taste is a portion or a pendant of the dollar-manufacture" (*Works,* XIV, 106).

3. See Kenneth Burke, *A Grammar of Motives* (New York, 1945), p. 450. D. H. Lawrence considered this Eros theme in Poe as a split between physical love and spiritual love; see *Studies in Classic American Literature,* pp. 95–99.

4. See Scott's Introduction to *The Heart of Mid-Lothian,* wherein he relates not only the source of his novel in the life of Helen Walker but the point of view which he had in mind throughout the writing — "A pleasing view of the moral dignity of virtue, though unaided by birth, beauty, or talent."

5. *Works,* II, 32.

6. *Works,* VIII, 233. Perhaps the most telling inquiry into the erotic, suffering woman is Mario Praz, *The Romantic Agony* (London, 1933), pp. 95–164.

7. For the strong interfusion of democracy and Protestant evangelicalism in the first half of the nineteenth century, see R. H. Gabriel, *The Course of American Democratic Thought* (2nd ed; New York, 1956), pp. 28–39.

8. For an interesting set of generalizations on Poe's art in respect to this school of painting, see *Chivers' Life of Poe,* ed. R. B. Davis (New York, 1952), pp. 86–87. For a general treatment of this school of painting, see Christopher Hussey, *The Picturesque: Studies in a Point of View* (London and New York, 1927); and for a discussion of the Hudson River school and genre painting in the United States, see Matthiessen, *American Renaissance,* pp. 596–613.

9. For a very stimulating study of the "catastrophe" motif in art and archeology, together with the reflections in literature of the interest in the excavations at Herculaneum and in Pompeii, see Curtis Dahl, "Bulwer-Lytton and the School of Catastrophe," *PQ,* XXXII (October 1953), 428–442.

10. William Gaunt, *Bandits in a Landscape: A Study of Romantic Painting from Caravaggio to Delacroix* (London and New York, 1937), p. 100.

11. See Gabriel, pp. 22–25.

12. The only hitherto noteworthy study of Poe's idea of horror or terror is in H. P. Lovecraft's chapter on "Poe" in *The Supernatural Horror in Literature* (New York, 1945), pp. 52–59. For general studies of the horror cult of Poe's time, see Oral S. Coad, "The Gothic Element in American Literature before 1835," *JEGP,* XXIV (January 1925), 72–93; Edith Birkhead, *The Tale of Terror* (London, 1921); P. E. More, "Origins of Hawthorne and Poe," *Shelburne Essays,* First Ser. (New York, 1904), pp. 51–70; Napier Wilt, "Poe's Attitude toward His Tales," *MP,* XXV (August 1927), 101–105. The Gothicism of Poe's horror is the subject of Margaret Kane, "Edgar Allan Poe and Architecture," *Sewanee Rev.,* XL (1932), 149–160.

13. In the early short story "Berenice" (1835) Poe investigated the monomania of a man who, in the face of all intelligence and rightness of behavior, was bent on hurting or destroying himself and of turning whatever of "pleasure" in his reach into pain. Egaeus suffered from

the profound wretchedness of a man compelled to live as though there were no moral rules whatsoever, or if they were still in existence, they had become so distorted that they were instruments of man's self-torture. Only on this basis could Poe explain that from "beauty" Egeaus "derived a type of unloveliness — from the covenant of peace a simile of sorrow," from systems of ethics, evil, and from love, murder. Later Poe would simplify this idea into what he called "perversity" — the very need of a man to do wrong and to hurt himself because he knew he should not and would have to suffer.

14. One of the most remarkable expressions of an interest in how a person died is Emily Dickinson's inquiry concerning the death of her friend, Ben Newton, an inquiry which has often been mistaken for passionate love; for a correct interpretation, see George Whicher, *This Was a Poet* (New York, 1938), and Thomas H. Johnson, *Emily Dickinson: An Interpretive Biography* (Harvard University Press, 1955), pp. 72–73.

V. The Short Story as Grotesque

1. On the question of Poe's turning to the short story in order to make money, see Campbell, *Mind of Poe,* pp. 161–162.

2. In that biographical tissue of lies and half-truths, Griswold stated that, after his removal from West Point, Poe reëntered the army and spent the year 1832 again in military service. No one has been able otherwise to account for this year in Poe's life. My friend, Professor Thomas O. Mabbott, has carefully searched the army records for any listing of Poe's name as "Edgar Perry," the name he assumed during the earlier enlistment, or for any other alliterative variant, and has found nothing. Griswold so often was half right that one is strongly tempted to assume that he knew more than Poe ever cared to reveal. At any rate, I am suggestively placing the beginning of Poe's short-story writing career a little later than the date usually ascribed. I do not mean to make a complete case for the haphazard nature of Poe's writing the early tales; I merely offer the opinion that the first steps in the "Tales of the Folio Club" were perhaps more casual or even more calculating than they have generally been considered.

3. Poe wrote in 1836: "At different times there has appeared in the Messenger a series of Tales, by myself — in all seventeen. They

are of a bizarre and generally whimsical character, and were originally written to illustrate a large work 'On the Imaginative Faculties'" (*Letters,* p. 103). Earlier Poe had stated that there would be eleven tales (see *Works,* II, xxxvii). By 1836 Poe had printed in the *Messenger* a total of fourteen tales; of these Quinn accepted all with the possible exception of "Hans Pfaall" as belonging in the series (see *Poe,* pp. 745–746). J. S. Wilson accepted only twelve; see "The Devil Was in It," *Amer. Mercury,* XXIV (October 1931), 214–220. See also T. O. Mabbott, "On Poe's 'Tales of the Folio Club,'" *Sewanee Rev.,* XXXVI (April 1928), 171–176.

4. Poe made heavy levies on *Blackwood's* for material which he wove into these grotesques; see D. L. Clark, "The Sources of Poe's 'Pit and the Pendulum,'" *MLN,* XLIV (June 1929), 349–356; K. L. Daughrity, "Notes: Poe and *Blackwood's,*" *Amer. Lit.,* II (November 1930), 289–292; Margaret Alterton, *Origins of Poe's Critical Theory,* p. 11; and Napier Wilt, "Poe's Attitude toward His Tales," *MP,* XXV (August 1927), 101ff. Poe himself acknowledged that his aim in the Folio Club Tales was not only to satirize "lionizing" and literary puffery but "the extravagances" of *Blackwood's* as well; see *Letters,* p. 84, and Campbell, *Mind of Poe,* pp. 164–165.

5. *Letters,* p. 84.

6. *Baudelaire on Poe,* pp. 159, 162.

7. Concerning frontier life as stimulating the special American character of cruelty and terror, see Lewis Mumford, *The Golden Day* (New York, 1926), pp. 77–79. That Poe was aware of and sensitive to this matter is obvious in his comments on the frontier amusement of "gander pulling" and in his condemnation of the cruelty and violence in the novels of William Gilmore Simms: see *Works,* VIII. 262ff.

8. Poe's friend Chivers made the following interesting comment: "Mr Poe wrote about seventy Tales — all of which appear to me to be the faithful records of some peculiar phase of his own being, or mental rapture, at the time of their composition . . ." *Chivers' Life of Poe,* ed. R. B. Davis (New York, 1952), pp. 78–79.

9. *Works,* IV, 281.

10. Both the manner and the content of Sterne's "Slawkenbergius's Tale," which opens Book IV of *Tristram Shandy,* as well as the whimsical chapters on "noses" in Book III (chaps. 31 and 32), are

strikingly close to Poe's early device of hiding some not very clever pornography behind the bland appearance of innocent double-talk.

11. For these revisions and deletions, see *Works*, II, 323–330.

12. *Ibid.*, IV, 222.

13. For these variants, see *ibid.*, II, 378–379.

14. *Ibid.*, p. 379.

15. The most forceful statement in defense of Poe as a critic of his times is that of Campbell, *Mind of Poe*, pp. 99ff. See also Ernest Marchand, "Poe as Social Critic," *Amer. Lit.*, VI (March 1934), 28–43, and *Representative Selections*, p. lxix and note.

16. The question of the writer as satirist or writer of grotesqueries and his place in the world of men is the subject of Robert C. Elliott's stimulating "The Satirist and Society," *ELH*, XXI (September 1954), 237–248, wherein the point is made that the satirist, once having been the magician and fire-bringer, has become the victim of society's censorship and legal retribution until, from the time of Swift onward, he has been forced to masquerade behind an elaborate set of literary and mythic deceptions. Poe was himself aware of the risks of being attacked or misunderstood by a public that did not know how to respond to these satirical jests. J. P. Kennedy wrote him on February 9, 1836: "Some of your *bizarreries* have been mistaken for satire . . ." (XVII, 28). Poe replied on the 11th: "You are nearly, but not altogether right in relation to the satire of some of my Tales. Most of them were *intended* for half banter, half satire — although I might not have fully acknowledged this to be their aim even to myself" (*Letters*, p. 84).

VI. *Arthur Gordon Pym*

1. For Poe's levies on Irving's *Astoria* and on *The Adventures of Captain Bonneville* as well, see Woodberry, *Poe* (1909), I, 191, 236; Hervey Allen, *Israfel*, II, 419, 463; H. Arlin Turner, "A Note on Poe's 'Julius Rodman,'" *Texas Univ. Studies in English*, X (July 1930), 147–151. Poe also drew on *The History of the Expedition under the Command of Captains Lewis and Clark* (2 vols.; Philadelphia, 1814), especially on Jefferson's memorial of Meriwether Lewis; see Polly Pearl Crawford, "Lewis and Clark's *Expedition* as a Source

for Poe's 'Journal of Julius Rodman,'" *Texas Univ. Studies in English,* XII (July 1932), 158–170.

2. Woodberry first drew attention to a number of Poe's sources for *Pym;* see *Edgar Allan Poe* (Boston, 1885), pp. 33, 49, 106; later, in his edition of Poe's works, brought out in collaboration with E. C. Stedman, he mentioned still others; see *The Works of Edgar Allan Poe* (Chicago, 1895), V, 355–361. These might be accounted Poe's chief sources for *Pym:* James Cook and James King, *A Voyage to the Pacific* (2 vols.; London, 1784); Benjamin Morrell, *Narrative of Four Voyages to the South Seas and Pacific, 1822–1831* (New York, 1832); J. N. Reynolds, *An Address on the Subject of a Surveying Exploring Expedition to the Pacific Ocean and South Seas* (New York, 1836). For other studies of Poe's sources for *Pym,* see Robert Lee Rhea, "Some Observations on Poe's Origins," *Texas Univ. Studies in English,* X (July 1930), 135–145; D. M. McKeithan, "Two Sources of Poe's 'Narrative of Arthur Gordon Pym,'" *ibid.,* XIII (July 1933), 116–137.

3. The only attempt so far really to analyze *Pym* is the brilliant study by Patrick F. Quinn, "Poe's Imaginary Voyage," *Hudson Rev.,* IV (Winter 1952), 562–585, reprinted in *The French Face of Edgar Poe* (Southern Ill. Univ. Press, 1957), pp. 169–215.

4. *Ibid.,* pp. 579–585.

5. *Works,* II, 27.

6. *Letters,* p. 130.

7. Some of these themes are illuminated elsewhere in American writing of the nineteenth century in R. W. B. Lewis's provocative study, *The American Adam: Innocence, Tragedy, and Tradition in the Nineteenth Century* (University of Chicago Press, 1955), especially chaps. 5, 6, 7.

8. *Works,* III, 20–21.

9. *Ibid.,* pp. 111–113.

10. See *ibid.,* pp. 153–157.

VII. The Tale as Allegory

1. Lionel Trilling, *The Liberal Imagination* (New York, 1950), p. 300. This discussion of religion in the pre-Civil War South leans heavily on W. J. Cash, *The Mind of the South* (New York, 1954), pp. 65–70, 89–93.

2. *Works,* IV, 5, 8. Mr. Allen Tate has considered at length these apocalyptical tales; see "The Angelic Imagination: Poe and the Power of Words," *Kenyon Rev.,* XIV (Summer 1952), 455–475.

3. See *Works,* IV, 200–212.

4. The most pointed of Poe's attacks on the Utilitarians are in the tale, "Mellonta Tauta," 1849 (see *Works,* VI, 201–205) and in *Eureka, Works,* XVI, 188–195; see chapter VIII.

5. For this popular version of the "science of mind" or psychology in Poe's day, see Edward Hungerford, "Poe and Phrenology," *Amer. Lit.,* II (November 1930), 209–231.

6. Two months before Poe's "Usher" was printed in *Burton's Gentleman's Magazine* there appeared a short article entitled "An Opinion on Dreams"; though unsigned, it was from the hand of a certain Horace Binney Wallace, known to Poe only as "William Landor." Wallace argued that the reason nothing had hitherto been known about dreams was that there had never been a correct distinction made between Mind and Soul. "I believe," Wallace went on, "man to be in himself a *Trinity,* viz. *Mind, Body,* and *Soul.*" Then he made a distinction between "dreams," which are of the mind and "proceed partly from the supernatural, and partly from natural causes," and "visions," which are of the soul and are "immaterial . . . alone." "Thus *three* portions of the *one* man seem to be most essentially different, in this way; that the body often sleeps, the mind occasionally, the soul never." The mind is situated, therefore, at center mediating between the two opposites, body and soul. The soul is continually reporting its "visions" to the mind which, in turn, though it remembers only a small fraction of them after sleeping, is still the only link between those two opposing faculties, the body and the soul. If the mind were not forgetful and so much subject to the sleepy control of the body, then we should all be aware of the illuminations and revelations which have come so vividly to saints and mystics — and sometimes to writers and poets. [H. B. Wallace], "An Opinion on Dreams," *Burton's,* V (August 1839), 105. This identification was first made by T. O. Mabbott, "Poe's Vaults," *N & Q,* no. 198 (December 1953), 542–543. The critical writing on "The Fall of the House of Usher" has always been stimulating; in recent years it has become almost an arena for critical warfare. Of the many pieces in this debate, the following are perhaps the most stimulating: Darrel Abel, "A Key to the House of Usher," *Univ. of Toronto Rev.,* XVIII

(January 1949), 176–185; and D. H. Lawrence, *Studies in Classic American Literature* (New York, 1923), pp. 110–116.

7. Further suggestive relationships between the House and the inhabitants thereof are ably treated by Maurice Beebe, "The Fall of the House of Pyncheon," *Nineteenth-Century Fiction,* XI (July 1956), 4–6.

8. The source for "William Wilson" is Washington Irving's "An Unwritten Drama of Lord Byron," which appeared in *The Gift: A Christmas and New Year's Present* (Philadelphia, 1836), pp. 166–171; the volume also contained a reprint of Poe's "Manuscript Found in a Bottle." In a letter to Irving, dated October 12, 1839, which has recently come to light, Poe acknowledged this debt; see John Ostrom, "Supplement to *The Letters of Poe,*" *Amer. Lit.,* XXIV (November 1952), 360.

9. See Cash, *Mind of the South,* pp. 42–49. A. H. Quinn clearly delineated these social and financial stratifications; *Poe,* pp. 94–96.

10. Review of Henry Chorley, *Conti, The Discarded, Works,* VIII, 230, 231.

11. Poe's own description of a southern gentleman, Brevet Brigadier General John A. B. C. Smith, despite its obvious whimsey, is not very far from the ideal: "He was, perhaps, six feet in height, and of a presence singularly commanding. There was an *air distingué* pervading the whole man, which spoke of high breeding, and hinted at high birth. . . . His head of hair would have done honor to Brutus; — nothing could be more richly flowing, or possess a brighter gloss. It was of a jetty black; — which was also the color . . . of his unimaginable whiskers. . . . Here were the most entirely even, and the most brilliantly white of all conceivable teeth. From between them . . . issued a voice of surpassing clearness, melody, and strength" ("The Man That Was Used Up," *Works,* III, 259–260). See also Cash, *Mind of the South,* pp. 19–22, 71–77.

12. *Letters,* pp. 458, 461. In 1841 when he was trying to found *The Penn Magazine* in Philadelphia (a project which was never realized) Poe wrote "that what I most need for my work in its commencement . . . is *caste.* I need the countenance of those who stand well not less in the social than in the literary world" (*ibid.,* p. 154).

13. In this connection an exchange of opinions with Philip P. Cooke has some bearing on the supposititious autobiographical

identification of Dupin with Poe. Cooke wrote in August 1846: "I think your French friend, for the most part, fine in his deductions from over-laid & unnoticed small facts, but sometimes too minute & hair-splitting. The stories are certainly as interesting as any ever written" (*Works,* XVII, 263). Poe replied five days later: "You are right about the hair-splitting of my French friend: — that is all done for effect. These tales of ratiocination owe most of their popularity to being something in a new key. I do not mean to say that they are not ingenious — but people think them more ingenious than they are — on account of their method and *air* of method. In the 'Murders in the Rue Morgue,' for instance . . . the reader is made to confound the ingenuity of the supposititious Dupin with that of the writer of the story" (*Letters,* p. 328). The obvious self-identification is apparent; Poe wanted readers to "confound" the hero and the author.

14. In "A Chapter of Suggestions" (1845) Poe wrote: "The theory of chance, or as the mathematicians term it, the Calculus of Probabilities, has this remarkable peculiarity, that its truth in general is in direct proportion with its fallacy in particular" (*Works,* XIV, 186).

15. Poe insisted that laws of science are not laws of human behavior: "Mathematical axioms are *not* axioms of general truth. What is true of *relation* . . . is often grossly false in regard to morals. . . . In this latter science it is very usually *un*true that the aggregated parts are equal to the whole. . . . In the consideration of motive it fails; for two motives, each of a given value, have not, necessarily, a value when united, equal to the sum of their values apart" ("The Purloined Letter," *Works,* VI, 44–45). For interesting insights into Dupin, see Robert Daniel, "Poe's Detective God," *Furioso,* VI (Summer 1951), 45–54.

VIII. *Eureka*

1. See Woodberry, *Poe,* pp. 290–292. See also Hervey Allen, *Israfel,* p. 591.

2. Preface to *Eureka; Works,* XVI, 183.

3. In his way Poe conformed to the design Emerson had set in the chapter entitled "Spirit" in *Nature* (1836): What is matter? whence did it come? wherto is it going? See Emerson, *Complete Works* (Centenary Edition, Boston and New York, 1903), I, 61–65. It seems unlikely that Poe was in any way aware of Emerson's epoch-

making book published twelve years before his own essay; yet the line of similarity is apparent: both were attempting, poetically and rationally at once, to bring back to philosophy and even to the daily lives of men, what presumptuous natural science and positivism had come to regard as their province alone.

4. *Works,* XVI, 197.

5. *Critique of Pure Reason,* trans. N. K. Smith, pp. 44ff. "Now it is easy to show that there actually are in human knowledge judgments which are necessary and in the strictest sense universal, and which are therefore pure *a priori* judgments. . . . But what is still more extraordinary . . . is this, that certain modes of knowledge leave the field of all possible experiences and have the appearance of extending the scope of our judgments beyond all limits of experience, and this by means of concepts to which no corresponding object can ever be given in experience."

6. *Works,* XVI, 238. In the nebular hypothesis, especially as it was outlined by Laplace, two problems became apparent: (1) If matter were broken off from the sun, dispersed through space, and formed into stellar bodies, then what was the origin of the sun's matter? (2) what was the end of the "dispersion"? How far could the process go and what would stop it if it were to end in anything but the disintegration of the sun's energy and substance? Here Poe introduced the idea of the reverse of irradiation, namely, "a determinate irradiation," or the reactive process, whereby all substances would return to their primordial source.

7. Though Poe made numerous references to and quotations from a variety of scientific works, the following titles might be considered basic to the formation of his ideas on cosmology and physics; the dates of publication are not necessarily those of the first editions but of the printings in America which Poe would most likely have read:

Thomas Dick, *Celestial Scenery; or, The Wonders of the Planetary System Displayed* (New York, 1838); *The Sidereal Heavens and Other Subjects Connected with Astronomy* (New York, 1840).

John F. W. Herschel, *Preliminary Discourse on the Study of Natural Philosophy* (Philadelphia, 1831); *A Treatise on Astronomy* (Philadelphia, 1834).

Pierre Simon, Marquis de Laplace, *The System of the World,* trans. and ed. H. H. Harte (2 vols., London, 1830).

John Pringle Nichol, *Views of the Architecture of the Heavens*

(London, 1838). This very popular work went through a number of editions, each so different from the others as to constitute an almost separate book. I have not been able to determine which edition Poe read. — *The Phenomena and Order of the Solar System* (New York, 1842).

In addition to these primary works there should be mentioned some of the "Bridgewater Treatises" (on these Poe wrote an extended comment in "Marginalia," *Works,* XVI, 9–10), of which the following are pertinent to the scientific content of *Eureka:*

Thomas Chalmers, *The Adaptation of External Nature to the Moral and Intellectual Condition of Man* (2 vols.; London, 1833).
John Kidd, *On the Adaptation of External Nature to the Physical Condition of Man* (London, 1833).
William Whewell, *Astronomy and General Physics Considered with Reference to Natural Theology* (London, 1833).

The important recent studies in the science and thought of *Eureka* are:

Alterton, *Origin of Poe's Critical Theory,* pp. 112–122, 132–169, and *Representative Selections,* pp. xxv–xlii.
F. D. Bond, "Poe as Evolutionist," *Popular Science Monthly,* LXXI (September 1907), 267–274.
Frederick W. Conner, "Poe's *Eureka:* The Problem of Mechanism," *Cosmic Optimism* (University of Florida Press, 1949), pp. 67–91.
Clayton Hoaglund, "The Universe of *Eureka:* A Comparison of the Theories of Eddington and Poe," *Southern Lit. Messenger,* I (May 1939), 307–313.
George Norstedt, "Poe and Einstein," *Open Court,* XLIV (March 1930), 173–180.
Floyd Stovall, "Poe's Debt to Coleridge," *Texas Univ. Studies in English,* X (July 1930), 120–127.
Philip P. Wiener, "Poe's Logic and Metaphysic," *Personalist,* XIV (October 1933), 268–274.

8. It is interesting to watch the change in Poe's thought from the rather obtuse, trusting rationalism of 1839 in the Introduction to

The Conchologist's First Book (see *Works,* XIV, 98–100) and *Eureka.*

9. *Works,* XVI, 215, 221.

10. Poe relied for further proofs of his cosmological system on such electrical and magnetic theories of his time as Sir John Herschel's four determinations: (1) Electricity is not limited to a few substances but is found in all; (2) magnetic and electrical phenomena conform to the same principles of inverse squares as does gravitation; that is, the force of electrical energy increases as the square of its distance from its source; (3) electricity, according to Volta, is generated by contact between different substances; and (4) there is a direct relationship between electrical and nervous phenomena. These principles supplied Poe with a set of laws and, when they could not function satisfactorily as laws, of analogies which explained not only the constitution of matter but the interaction of matter and mind.

In the age of Poe there were many expressions of this interconnection of the sciences with thought. Perhaps a typical example might be taken from a very popular pre-Darwinian handbook by Edward Hitchcock: "The records of zoology and botany afford endless illustrations of [the equilibrium of organic nature]. But the great truth which they all teach is, that so intimately are we related to other beings, that almost every action of ours reacts upon them for good or evil. . . . But does not this law of mutual influence between organic beings extend to other worlds? Why should it not be transmitted by means of the luminiferous ether to the limits of the universe? Who knows but a blow struck upon a single link of organic beings here may be felt through the whole circle of animate existence in all worlds?" (*Religion of Geology and Its Connected Sciences* [London 1851], p. 433). As early as 1841 in "The Island of the Fay" Poe had expressed a similar idea: "I love to regard [rocks, waters, and forests] as themselves but the colossal members of one vast animate and sentient whole — a whole whose form (that of the sphere) is the most perfect and most inclusive of all" (*Works,* IV, 194).

11. On this point Poe may have derived something from the "Controversy of Life" which had been a topic of considerable interest in England throughout the 1820's and 1830's, had engaged the attention of some of the most distinguished medical minds, and would receive, in the very year *Eureka* was published, its fullest statement in Coleridge's *Hints toward the Formation of a More Comprehensive*

Theory of Life (Philadelphia, 1848). Every life, as with electricity itself, has a positive and negative principle. Magnetism and electricity, as well as physical sciences generally, are merely man's discoveries of the primal laws of God and the universe. "Life as Life," Coleridge wrote, "supposes a positive or universal principle in Nature, with a negative principle in every particular animal, the latter, or limitative power, constantly acting to individualize, and, as it were, *figure* the former. *Thus,* then, Life itself is not a *thing*—a self-subsistent *hypostasis*—but an *act* and *process. . . .*" (p. 94). Taking this line of thought, Coleridge posited that there is no death. Poe could not have known Coleridge's small book, but its ideas demonstrate how current were these principles concerning the spiritually organic nature of man and life.

12. Though *Eureka* does not examine the question, other statements of Poe suggest that, by this analogy of man's body-soul organism as a duplicate of the body-soul constitution of the universe, Poe for a time assumed the immortality of the individual soul: ". . . the only conclusive proof of man's alternate dissolution and rejuvenescence *ad infinitum*—is to be found in analogies deduced from the modern established theory of the nebular cosmogony" (*Works,* X, 159–160). In a letter to James Russell Lowell, in phrases which would be repeated in *Eureka:* "The unparticled matter, permeating & impelling, all things, is God. Its activity is the thought of God—which creates. Man, and other thinking beings, are individualizations of the unparticled matter. Man exists as a 'person,' by being clothed with matter (the particled matter) which individualizes him. Thus habited, his life is rudimental. What we call 'death' is the painful metamorphosis. . . . At death, the worm is the butterfly—still material, but of a matter unrecognized by our organs—recognized, occasionally, perhaps, by the sleep-walker, directly—without organs—through the mesmeric medium" (*Letters,* p. 257). The only reference in *Eureka* to this idea of man's immortality is contained in the passage on the cyclic process of creation and annihilation which Poe likens to the rhythmic throb of the "Heart Divine." For an interesting comment on this question, see B. R. McElderry, Jr., "Poe's Concept of the Soul," *N & Q,* new series, II (April 1955), 173–174.

13. *Pragmatism,* Lecture III: "Some Metaphysical Problems Pragmatically Considered."

14. *Works,* XVI, 311.

15. See A. N. Whitehead, *Process and Reality* (New York, 1929), Part I, chap. 1, and *Adventures of Ideas* (New York, 1933), p. 288.

16. See S. C. Pepper, *World Hypotheses,* chap. iii.

17. See *Pragmatism,* Lecture V: "Pragmatism and Common Sense."

18. This summary of the question is not in any way to suggest that nineteenth-century idealism or even later Pragmatism was not without flaw or that they were superior systems. Any other metaphysic or hypothesis must sedulously eschew the categories and criteria as proof for its own system which it has rejected as false in another. Data which disprove one form of cognition are not always capable of proving another: the chair I sit in may have the capacity to hold me; but, if I am not sitting in the chair, I should be wary of employing corroborative evidence to prove that the chair has the inherent power to hold me unless that evidence is in conformity with the known data of experience. I should not guess or "have a hunch" that the chair will sustain me — unless, of course, I have established a working hypothesis which will allow my "hunch" to be corroborated. Nineteenth-century idealism or organicism, especially the variety that poets like Poe and Whitman posited, started with the "hunch" and went on to infinity with hardly any concern for evidence except what was apparent to them in an animate universe. Emerson made the same mistake, except that his willingness to submit his ideas to the tests of sense data left his thought shot through with honest paradoxes. See Sherman Paul, *Emerson's Angle of Vision* (Harvard University Press, 1952), pp. 132–169, and Stephen Whicher, *Freedom and Fate: An Inner Life of R. W. Emerson* (University of Pennsylvania Press, 1953), pp. 109–122.

19. *Works,* XVI, 206.

20. Laplace stated: "Motion is a proper measure of time; for since a body cannot be in several places at the same time, . . . it must pass successively through all the intermediate points. If it is actuated by the same force at every point of the line, which it describes, its motion is uniform, and the several portions of this line will measure the time employed to describe them" (*System of the World,* I, 21).

21. David Hume, *Treatise of Human Nature,* Book I, Part III, Section II.

22. *Symbolism: Its Meaning and Effect* (New York, 1927), p. 32.

See also George Santayana, *Scepticism and Animal Faith* (New York, 1923), chap. 1.

23. See *System of the World,* II, 325. Whitehead, in a slightly different context, termed this fallacy "the presupposition that the sole way of examining experience is by acts of conscious introspective analysis. Such a doctrine . . . is already discredited in psychology" (*Adventures of Ideas,* p. 290). In Poe's time the most devastating assault launched against Laplace's "Calculation of Chances" was that of J. S. Mill, *A System of Logic, Ratiocinative and Inductive* (London, 1843), II, 70–85.

24. See André Malraux, *The Voices of Silence,* trans. Stuart Gilbert (New York, 1953), pp. 131–272.

25. See Samuel Johnson, *The History of Rasselas, Prince of Abyssinia; Works* (Oxford, 1825), I, 220–223, and "Life of Cowley," *ibid.,* VII, 14–17. For a detailed examination of Johnson's critical theory, see W. R. Keast, "The Theoretical Foundations of Johnson's Criticism," *Critics and Criticism,* ed. R. S. Crane (University of Chicago Press, 1952), pp. 389–407. See also Abrams, *The Mirror and the Lamp,* chap. 1, and David Perkins, "Johnson on Wit and Metaphysical Poetry," *ELH,* XX (September 1953), 200–217.

26. A summary inquiry into Romantic critical theory on these points is M. H. Abrams, *The Mirror and the Lamp,* pp. 47–69. This positivistic argument Poe sneeringly quoted and applied in "Mellonta Tauta"; see *Works,* VI, 204.

27. See Mill, *Logic,* Book I, chaps. v and vi.

28. *Works,* XVI, 196.

29. *Ibid.,* pp. 240–241.

30. *Ibid.,* p. 193.

31. In the popular mind, as opposed to the artistic mind, this matter had curious reflections. The popular argument against which Poe protested at frequent intervals went something like this: If art is autonomous and if the artist is a specially endowed being or craftsman, then he is an autonomous being whose every motion and thought is part or reflective of his artistry. What his art is, is the expression of his whole nature, not just the artistic or imaginative nature. Consequently, what the artist is as a man, as a citizen of society, is a necessary part of his art: The poem without the poet is inconceivable; and what the poet is, morally, socially, religiously, constitutes something that must be added to the poem for full under-

standing. Fenimore Cooper carried on a gallant fight against this fallacy by taking into the courts his conviction that the book, not the writer, is under review: the writer's private life is private and separate from the writing. Poe warred against the same situation in his repeated attacks not only on literary cliques and puffery but on the "didactic," a term which generally denoted a writer's special, individual meaning in a work of art. It would be the artist himself revealing himself, by the very nature of his being a *different* man speaking to men. Let his personality, his particular way of life be known, and the poem, the painting, the sonata would become immediately clear. Thus the vitriol that so many modern readers discover in the reviewing and criticism (the two terms are different) of the first half of the nineteenth century is not so much, as Poe pointed out, an attack on bad art as it was the unmasking of the bad artist before one can see why the art is itself bad. Whatever the man is the work of art will be; discover the man, and the work comes clear. See Abrams, "Literature as a Revelation of Personality," *The Mirror and the Lamp,* pp. 226–244.

Index